Delivered--
From Temptation

෬

From Temptation to Salvation

by
Genna Sapia-Ruffin

AuthorHouse™
1663 Liberty Drive
Bloomington, IN 47403
www.authorhouse.com
Phone: 1-800-839-8640

© 2010 Genna Sapia-Ruffin. All rights reserved.
©1993-2009 All rights reserved. No part of this book may be reproduced, stored in a retrieval system, or transmitted, in any form or by any means, electronic, mechanical, photocopying, recording, or otherwise, without the express prior written permission of Genna Sapia-Ruffin.

First published by AuthorHouse 5/3/2010

ISBN: 978-1-4490-6972-8 (e)
ISBN: 978-1-4490-6955-1 (sc)

This book is printed on acid-free paper.

TABLE OF CONTENTS

ACKNOWLEDGMENTS   vii

CH 01. "Mississippi Tears"   1
CH 02. "It All Started With My Mother"   7
CH 03. "Black or White? Black or White?"   23
CH 04. "The Way You Do the Things You Do"   43
CH 05. "That Darned Tammi Terrell"   71
CH 06. "Okay Kid, Me & You"   91
CH 07. "Far Out, Man!"   113
CH 08. "R_X Limousine"   133
CH 09. "Makings of a Man"   175
CH 10. "Wedded in the Twilight Zone"   203
CH 11. "Die, Bitch, Die"   223
CH 12. "I Am Woman"   237
CH 13. "The Valley of Death"   269
CH 14. "Tales From the Parkside"   293
CH 15. "Don't Bring That Half-Breed!"   321
CH 16. "Northern Arizona Times"   351
CH 17. "My So-Called Life--The Movie"   381
CH 18. "And in The End, The Love You Take
         is Equal to The Love You Make"   407
CH 19. "The Long Road to my Salvation"   415

DAVID'S DISCOGRAPHY   451
Epilogue For David   461

Acknowledgments

First of all, I must express relief that this project is finished and deepest gratitude and glory to The Holy Trinity. None of this--including me-- would have happened without You.

As always, I still need to thank both David Ruffin Senior, the natural Love of My Life, and our son David Junior. Everyone being both student and teacher, you two guys have given me a life-time filled with opportunities to learn many lessons that have been hard but fair. Now with the completion of this second book, it is my greatest hope that I will now be used mightily by my Father in the ministry for which He originally and Divinely created me. So thank you for your parts in that; couldn't have done it without you!

To my friends and support groups: visionaries are few and far between; thanks for your individual and unique contributions along the way. Thanks again for the invaluable assistance in compiling the discography, and thanks again to all the photographers, especially for going out of the way for me when I needed it.

Deepest special thanks and love to Kelly Jo for always "being there" for me. Thanks to my wonderful pastor and church family who has been more of a family to me than any blood family I ever had. Thanks for the much-needed hugs—and so much more!

And again, I want to say that I hope I haven't offended anyone in the Ruffin family, but please understand that I had to do this. It's only the truth. As I told you in the attorney's office in 1991, Lynette: "Forgive me. All I did was fall in love with your father." And love doesn't die.

Chapter One

"Mississippi Tears"

In "Mississippi Tears"--a book he wrote and published in 1999--Quincy B. Ruffin Senior (David's step-brother and oldest of the five Ruffin children: Quincy, Rosetta, Rita Mae, Jimmy and baby Davis) relates his experience as it applied to the Ruffin household in Mississippi. He clearly describes how his life, at five years old, took a drastic nosedive for the worse when his mother, Ophelia Davis, married his step-father, the violent and controlling Eli Ruffin. The family sharecropped, moving from one plantation to another to another. Quincy was eleven or twelve by the time Davis/David was born. Mother Ophelia, who hadn't been well anyway, got worse and died from lack of medical attention when David was less than a year old. David was sickly too. Big sister Rita Mae, at six years old, was able to help Quincy to care for him. Rosetta had died as an infant of one year and one day old. Jimmy played alone, living with doubt and fear--according to Quincy.

The main weapon that Eli used to wreak devastation and destruction was apparently an 8', rawhide leather whip--most likely just like the one he had seen used on the backs of the men who farmed and sharecropped, and/or was even used on his back as well. One wonders how a poor black man in Mississippi in the late '30's came to possess such a thing. Perhaps it came directly from a forgotten hook or nail in a dim barn back wall on the plantation. It had to have come from somewhere.

In any case, with it Eli whipped the chickens, the dogs and the hogs--as well as Quincy and Rita.

According to Quincy, Eli also hit Ophelia and controlled her completely. One can only draw their own conclusions as to whether or not Jimmy and David were whipped.

Quincy did say, however, that David "managed to outsmart Eli" from the time he

Delivered From Temptation

was a little bitty thing and avoid both the plow and the pain of the whip. But don't you guess he knew? Don't you guess he lived in doubt and fear as well as did Jimmy? He saw what his brothers and sister and stepmother went through. He felt the pain in his spirit, even if not on his little back. I'm sure it deeply affected both of them. And one would have to surmise that it was the singular motivational force behind David leaving home at a very early age--fourteen, from what I've heard. Maybe he was afraid his luck in avoiding Eli's whip would run out. So he ran out instead. His leaving to go on the road singing with a gospel group was much to the dismay and heartbreak of his dear step-mother, Earline from what she herself told me before she died. She raised him. She loved him dearly; he was her baby.

I have a purpose for saying all this. I never read Quincy's book until the fall of 2003, so at the time I first published my memoirs, I did not know exactly what it was that had terrified David and impacted his life in such a negative way, although I knew it was something dark. I did come to know, however, that there was an important part missing from my book. I didn't know what it was, but I came to realize that the book was one-sided and out of balance; there was no redemption for David--only what seemed like negative things.

After reading Quincy's book, I see now why David was used to living pillar to post and not really having a home. (Even our "home" on Parkside only lasted four years. After that, he never really had a home again, making do with living here and there, much as Quincy describes their childhood after their mother's death). I see now also how he learned--that is, failed to learn--to be a father. He had no model. Now I see how he learned--that is, failed to learn--how to treat women. He had no model. I see how he learned to beat our dogs and horses. I see how he learned to brutally whip our son with a leather strap. I'm just grateful he didn't have a whip. I see how being deprived the counsel of that good and sweet Christian mother left a hole in his spirit regarding women (and life in general, most likely).

And I saw that he didn't want much to do with God (except in his last years, so I'm told and hallelujah), since Eli Ruffin was a so-called preacher. Quincy never says that in his book, but David had always said so. In that case, David probably wanted to go as far away as possible from what his father represented to him--the Name of Jesus! And

Delivered From Temptation

that he did. I believe he was coming back to God near the end though; I believe he wanted to and that he had to and that he knew he had to. You can only run so long. He was a prodigal son returning to a Father who dearly loved him, even after he had squandered his inheritance and gifts.

Reading Quincy's book has entirely set me free from any bitterness, anger or resentment toward David and has filled me instead with compassion. Mind you, not with forgiveness (for that came long ago), but with true compassion----not only for him, but for all abusers. In talking with other abused people, I've found that this is not an easy gift to come by, and I thank God for it. This is the crucial, absolutely vital area in which society has inadvertently looked the other way and in the process, has dropped the ball. We, as a people, have wound up putting a bandage on the cancer of domestic violence, instead of addressing the issue--the healing of the spirits of the brokenhearted men who were meant to be the hub around which the strong, healthy family is built and thrives, but who have instead become just a tossed-away blight on society which has become a worldwide plague of biblical proportions. And that's what has become of the brokenhearted.

Genna Sapia-Ruffin

We must change this cycle starting now, if humanity—as we've known it--is to survive. Here is your servant, Lord. Take me.

If still available, you may be able to order "Mississippi Tears" by sending a money order for $10.00 + $2.00 postage payable to Quincy Ruffin at Q.B. Books, P.O. Box 682093, Orlando, FL 32868; or from Four-G Publishers, P.O. Box 2249, Winter Park FL 32790. ISBN 1-885066-57-0; PH: 407-679-3331.

Chapter Two

"It All Started With My Mother"

God! He and I were so much in love. We were in the kind of heart-breaking love that kept us up all night long some nights--talking, crying, making love both tenderly and frantically. We were in love so hard it hurt. That was back in the days when it was romantic and nobody's business if you did. Nowadays, they've dissected it, analyzed it, identified, and categorized it. They've changed the name from "love" or "romance" to the psychobabble "co-dependent" and "dysfunctional". Well, thanks a lot guys. You're right, of course, but was that something that I really wanted to know? I keep threatening to write a book entitled "Don't Call ME Co-dependent!" And it would take that to express my feelings on the subject. But first, I have another story to tell, a true story--a natural love story.

When I was born in Baltimore, Maryland back on September 28, 1943, the effects of World War II were still in place, and Grammom Ethel drove a streetcar. She brought it to a screeching halt dead on the track and left a car full of passengers sitting frustrated but helpless outside Johns Hopkins Hospital to run inside to see her newly-born only granddaughter. According to my mother, Dorothy, Grammom's initial reaction was, "Oh my God, it's a nigger!" There were two possible reasons for this, the way I figure--both based in ignorance. First of all, Mom's two oldest boys, Snookie who was ten and Jimbo who was nine, took after her Dad in coloring--light skin, and light hair and eyes. I, on the other hand, was born all dark and hairy, they said--darker skin and very dark hair and eyes. Mom said I had a headful of hair and more growing way down the middle of my back. Imagine!

Secondly, I'd always heard, growing up, that when I was born, Mom had been working in a "colored" bar on Bond Street in Baltimore. I can't imagine why this was, but it seems her husband/my so-called

Delivered From Temptation

father, Ralph, was on a ship in the Merchant Marines at the time. Maybe she simply needed the money. Now, she and Ralph surely were together when he was on shore leaves, but perhaps Mom and Grammom had some reason to wonder whether I belonged to him or to the son of someone at the bar. So Grammom wanted to see me for herself—badly! That's why she had to stop the streetcar. I guess I was cute and irresistible, for at some point she put all the questions on a back burner, and nicknamed me "Sweetie Pie." My birth name was Genevieve.

Most of the people at Motown Records during the '60's and '70's called me "Genni" or "Ginnie" or just plain "David's girl." As in David Ruffin, that is; as in "The Temptations."

"How did you meet him?" That's the first of four questions everyone asks me. But before I get into that, some background...

Every little thing in my life's particular set of circumstances was designed to bring me to the time, place and particular state of mind necessary for what was to become my life years later. As they say in the "B" movies, "It all started with my mother."

Genna Sapia-Ruffin

My maternal grandmother, Ethel, was Dutch. Her father, Tom, was Irish. Both were alcoholics and eventually died violently. Ethel died of a broken neck sustained in a car crash when Tom drove drunkenly into a big old apple tree. After spending the following year soused and in a stupor of guilt, Grampop had his buddy blow his brains out for him in a game of Russian roulette while they were both conveniently intoxicated. What a legacy.

In 1935 in Baltimore, Maryland, Dorothy met and married Ralph. She was sixteen and he was seventeen and Italian--Sicilian, to be exact. Ralph was one of nine kids in a huge family ruled with an iron fist by his mother, Jenny. His father Salvatore was there, but The Matriarch ruled. They had immigrated from Italy, and were lucky enough to scratch their way up through a series of successful restaurants in the Baltimore area. The last one was in an area called "Little Italy."

The restaurant was a big, narrow place with several floors and it was sometimes spooky. I still don't know whether my cousin was teasing me or confiding in me when he told me there was a body buried in the basement. This cousin also told me that, when my father and uncle were young, they

Delivered From Temptation

tied a black teenage boy onto a bicycle and dropped him permanently into the inlet of the Chesapeake Bay by the local morgue. It was insinuated that, if I in fact, did have a black father, as was sometimes hinted because of my looks, timing would suggest that this would've been him.

My parents divorced when I was four years old, and because of it, Mom fostered quite an ugly case of resentment towards me. After all, I was Daddy's adorable baby girl, which in her mind took her from that coveted position. My brothers looked like her side of the family, while I looked like my Daddy. In fact, I was the only dark-haired, dark-eyed, olive-skinned child in our world. There was a big gap between my brothers and me and as life would soon enough reveal, they weren't crazy about me either.

After the divorce, Mom moved us to Bean's Cove, Pennsylvania, with her parents. We lived in the rear of the bar they owned. If I remember correctly, she remarried in less than a year to Step-father Number One, let's call him "Bob," who was--guess what-- an alcoholic. The newlyweds took us along when they moved to that one-acre farm in Friend's Cove, Pennsylvania. We stayed there for seven years until I was eleven years old.

Genna Sapia-Ruffin

Mom and Bob had three babies (the first boy, then a set of twins--one of each gender--when he was one year old) in the first year. Still they spent what seemed to me like every night in some beer joint. Though most memories of the time period are kind of blurry and surreal, I do vaguely remember that at some point we got a TV. However, this didn't prevent those two darn older brothers of mine from acting like I was their play-toy there for their enjoyment and entertainment--to help them occupy all that unsupervised time. They began to play games--and I don't mean Checkers or Old Maid. Their games had a more sexual tone. Brother Snookie, at age sixteen, was removed from the little farm after he molested me. I was ten years old, and I was sleeping on the sofa. Suffice it to say, it's not cool to be awakened by a finger going into your vagina. Thanks to all of this dysfunction, anytime anyone has asked me if I'm an only child, I've learned to reply, "I'm an only child in a family of six." I looked different. I felt different. I was separate from my parents' oldest sons and from Mom's second set of kids. Needless to say, I was alone.

From the farm in Friends Cove, we moved to a duplex in the big city of Hagerstown,

Delivered From Temptation

Maryland when I was about eleven. This is where most of my physical abuse took place; the screaming, the name calling, the withholding of affection, the throwing of shoes and the beatings with belts and extension cords. The alcoholics were raging and I was often treated like the negative stereotype of the step-child. Surprisingly though, it wasn't done by Bob. Most of the time, he was okay. It was my mom. She seemed to take pleasure in abusing me emotionally, verbally, and physically. For the entire five years I was there, the abuse was ongoing. I felt like she hated me. There were no motherly touches, hugs, or kisses. In fact, the only time I remember her saying "I love you" was years later when I was about twenty-three years old. As a child, I remember being very much on edge emotionally and whenever I could get her to help me with my homework, I'd always wind up sobbing just from getting to sitting near her which, in turn, caused her to scream, "Quit'chur bawlin'!" Sometimes I'd ask her if she loved me and she'd snap, "I feed and clothe you, don't I?" Mom screamed a lot.

There were times when my brother, Jimbo, lived with us at the duplex during the five years that we were there. While I've blocked out a lot of my memory of him, I

Genna Sapia-Ruffin

do remember when my mother found him trying to hang himself in the basement. I also recall those endearing times when he used to smack the heck outta me, as well as all of those warm moments when he'd hatefully pick me up by my head and swing me around. I remember his DA and Mohawk haircuts, his black leather jacket and the crucifix he tattooed on his forehead, which was actually pretty scary and bizarre for the late '50's. I have very vivid memories of yelling at him often and saying, "I hate you! I wish you were dead!" So, when he finally put a double-barreled shotgun into his mouth and blew the top of his head off, hysteria took over and I secretly blamed myself. I was sixteen and he was twenty-one. It was three days after Christmas, 1959. In fact, as fate would have it, I was the one who answered the phone when his wife called with the news. She had just made the grisly discovery in their pantry. Even though she'd just been upstairs putting their two baby girls to bed, she somehow managed to call. The sounds she made were unintelligible and pure horror. I only heard guttural, animal-like sounds in my ear; screaming mixed with growling. In a very shrill pitch, she screamed an indecipherable *mantra* of two words again and again. I found out later what it was: "He's dead, he's dead!"

Shortly thereafter, Mom had somewhat of a mild nervous breakdown and was put into a rest home for three weeks. This chain of events forced me to reflect on the past in ways I had refused to do for the majority of my life. All my life I felt my mother never loved me. I was forty-something when I finally gave myself permission to stop trying to win her approval. In 1984, I was finally able to reveal my feelings to her. But it didn't happen easily. She was in one bedroom, while I was in another. We had to yell our feelings back and forth because we just couldn't do it face to face. She'd actually invited me there to try to work things out after seeing what an emotional mess I still was about our relationship. She said because she was getting old, she didn't want me to be left on Earth with all that baggage. "A-ha! A true mother was in there after all", I thought to myself. Better late than never, I guess. I traveled halfway across the country for that session. But it was certainly worth it. I finally understood. Although her ways had clearly affected me personally, it really wasn't personal. She herself had been a troubled woman in search of her own happiness. I think it was then, too, that she thanked me for raising her consciousness racially. Suddenly I realized that if all I had gone through had helped one soul to grow, then I was eternally grateful for that opportunity.

As Mom explained in later years, "non-demonstrative" was the only type of parental behavior she'd learned, since her parents had been that way as well. That's just "how it was" at their house. She shared with me that when she was breastfeeding me and I was eighteen months old, she was needed at the Merchant Marines Infirmary in Norfolk, Virginia. Daddy had gonorrhea. When she received the distressing news, naturally, she had to drop everything including me and go. She was, after all, in love. She was, at age twenty-four, living with her parents, with three kids. She told Grammom that she was worried about the fact that I was still breastfeeding. But Grammom told her, "Just leave her with me and go. I'll handle everything."

Mom said that she did call her mother when she arrived in Virginia to ask how I was. Grammom told her, "She's fine now. The first time I stuck a bottle in her mouth, she just knocked it on the floor. So, I stuck

Delivered From Temptation

in another one and smacked her ass. That shut her up." How endearing.

I understand, though. I can relate, I've come to terms with it all, and happily so I might add. I've long since forgiven her. I'm sure she did the best she could with what she had. Don't we all? Back at the duplex, she'd brought home another drunk by the name of, oh let's call him "Richard". After months--or years--of them sleeping on a sofa-bed in the living room while her second husband Bob and we four kids slept not-so soundly in our beds upstairs, she finally divorced the first one and married the second one, Richard (or Dick, as I called him). It was easy for her to make the transition. After all, the three of them had been drinking buddies, so what followed was no surprise.

My high school years were hell at home. Dick and I disliked each other intensely. He was more of what I later came to identify as a redneck than anyone I'd known up to that point. Come to think of it, I never knew of such a thing until then. Not only that, during high school was when I first met black (well, it was 1958, so I think most folks were still saying "colored") people. Shocking, I know--sorry. Gosh, I led a sheltered life up until then! That is how ignorance is often perpetuated, I've concluded--isolation breeds oblivion. Strange as it may sound, something pulled me naturally in that direction.

A boy Tyrone and a girl Beverly, who were both "colored", were in Biology 101 with me. We bonded instantly. In my innocence, I told my mother about my new-found friends. That was a mistake. This was also a very confusing time for me because here is where people began asking me if I were "mixed." (Huh?) Additionally, I was being ostracized by both students and teachers. In fact, it was a teacher who initiated it. I was warned to stay away from Bev and Tyrone. And, yes, Mom and Dick did hit the redneck roof.

But that wasn't the only reason I didn't like this Dick. True, he had a huge beer gut, was ugly as hell and looked as if he stunk-- and I hated his hillbilly drawl. But the main reason I couldn't stand him was because he beat my mother. Once, he broke her jaw and left her for dead. Well, actually the two of them more like brawled and he ended up getting the best of her. I was a senior in high school in the 4-h club. At 4:30 one dark morning, I got up to go to our bake

Delivered From Temptation

sale. I had to pass Dick on the staircase and couldn't help but notice that he had a paring knife protruding from his upper left back near the shoulder blade. The knife had a bloody tee shirt wrapped around the blade. He said my mother had stabbed him. When I asked where she was, he said, "She's dead." I looked over the railing across the room at the open sofa bed where they slept. She was lying there naked and stiff, with her back toward me. I approached her. Surprisingly, my eyes were dry. She was dead, all right-- dead drunk. I left her like that and went on to my bake sale, embarrassed, disgusted, and afraid. But what could I do? That was the nature of their relationship. That was how they showed love, I guess.....

Still as lovers do sometimes do, she and Dick often threatened to break up. Once I even came home from school to find her unconscious with her head in the oven; the windows closed. On the table was a note- -something about how she couldn't live without Dick. I remember feeling disgusted as I turned off the oven, pulled her back, and opened the windows. I did just what was necessary to save her and when I saw that she was breathing, I left. I was really pissed. I have no idea where I went, but I knew I had to get out of there. When I tried to talk to her about it later and tell her how much she'd scared me, she just pooh-poohed it. She said not to worry. She'd used the suicide threats on men since she was sixteen years old. "Ohh, okay. That's nice", I thought to myself.

All this craziness transpired while mom's second husband, Bob, and the kids they'd had together lived in the same house. Fortunately for them, they were too young to remember--I hope. By that time, I had truly had enough and just had to move out. I could not take any more. But where would I go? I was still six months from graduation and although I was an Honor Student, I was truly struggling to remain honorable. In order to do this, I moved to Baltimore to be shuffled around from one to another of my father's relatives, winding up back with the brother who had molested me and his wife. After waking up one night to find him trying to ease into bed with me (his wife sleeping in the other room), I had no choice but to go back to Hagerstown in the middle of my senior year of high school. My father apparently made the "arrangements" and until I finished school, I moved in with my best friend Sallie and her family a mile or so away from where my mother and her two husbands lived in the duplex.

Delivered From Temptation

    Back then, I was what I kindly refer to as a "nerdette" in high school—a bookworm and a teacher's pet with two similar new friends, Lorna Kay and Wilma Jean. Lorna was a little runt like me, yet she had breasts. Because I had none of my own, she graciously allowed curious me to touch hers one night at a sleepover. Wilma Jean was built like a grown woman and had what seemed to me like absolutely humongous ones. I, on the other hand--at 4'11" and 98 pounds--had no figure and was a "perfect 36"--12-12-12! Taking gym class only made me even more self-conscious. I finally talked my mother into getting me a starter bra. It was a size 30AAA. Frankly, I think it was just a white Ace-type bandage with a bow and straps! But I was the only little misfit who still wore undershirts in that gym class with those big girls. So emotionally it was absolutely mandatory. Not only that, I was already wearing size nine shoes. I looked like the letter "L". I wasn't in clubs or groups with the popular girls (blondes with boobs--some things never change), nor did I have any sense of belonging anywhere. Nevertheless, my school life was quite full between being on the honor roll, participating in 4-H, being an office helper, and a student teacher in English and

Spanish. Still I yearned for the popularity of some of the more-developed girls. But as the popular *cliché* says, "good things come to those who wait"! (Peggy, you never knew I felt that way, did you? Please forgive me; I guess I too was one of those who misjudged you. And thank you so much for contacting me after all these years and reminding me that I did have one great friend and *confidante* in you! And that I was a friend to you too. That changed my life. It gave me hope that maybe my childhood wasn't as entirely sad as I had remembered it after all. I miss hearing from you).

Chapter Three

"Black or White? Black or White?"

Mom and Dick had, by this time, moved to Baltimore, leaving ruin in their wake. She left the three little ones behind with their father. I doubt if those kids ever forgave her for that, and I'm sure she never forgave herself either. Matter of fact, she died 5/3/88 from a stomach aneurysm--just blew herself up; something which I believe was caused by all her pent-up negative emotions collected and internalized from a whole lifetime.

For the first year, I tried to live with Mom and Dick, but they wouldn't allow all my friends inside (only the white ones). So we often just hung out and/or rode around until after Dick went to work at dawn. Or, we passed out in the car--whichever came first. Many early mornings, I'd be coming in when they were in the kitchen throwing condiments at each other--salt and pepper shakers, sugar and creamers, bottles of milk, whatever.

It was at that apartment, she told me later, that mom had found Dick smelling my dirty underwear. So, I guess I got out of there in the nick of time. But not before I went through a year of torture, frustration, humiliation and drunken degradation regarding my having black friends. She'd go through my phone book and scream, "Black or white? Black or white?" as she ripped out pages and threw them on the floor like so much garbage. He and Mom went especially berserk with the idea that there was a chance (no, make that a given) that I might (God forbid) have a black boyfriend. They even sent me to a shrink. I refused to go after the first humiliating time. It was a joke. A disgustingly bad joke. He was a racist too. The first thing he did was ask me if I was pregnant, so I pooched my stomach out and sat as if I were. That shrink needed a shrink--far worse than I did!

The "pregnant" part was especially hurtful to me as I was still a virgin. In fact,

Delivered From Temptation

I had just gotten my period a few months before. I was so innocent that I couldn't quite figure out how to put in a tampon at eighteen--my mom had to help me. One night, a drunken Mom and Dick followed me to a jazz club--a spot frequented by athletes--where I worked as a waitress. She argued with Carter, the owner, she humiliated me in front of all my friends and co-workers, and, for an encore, she attacked me. She punched me in the stomach, ripped my necklace off me and threatened to rip the earrings out of my pierced ears when I reached to take them off in anticipation of same.

After much embarrassment and many threats, they finally staggered out. I was in shock. Next day the place blew up. Exploded. Kaboom. I've always thought that Ralph was responsible.

I'd heard he carried a sub-machine gun in the trunk of his car and he often shadowed my friends in an effort to find out where I was living (read hiding), and who I was seeing (read screwing). Once he tailed my girlfriend's car so tight that she had no choice but to jump out and ask him what the hell he wanted. A big confrontation ensued. He also ferreted out the house of an older male friend--good ol' "Willie Off the Pickle Boat" as he called himself, and threatened him. And when he finally did trace me, he just put a big plain scrap of torn white paper in my mailbox to terrify me. And, yes, it did work--very, very well. Shades of Little Italy--again.

He watched and waited, then appeared at my door just after I got home from my job at a wig shop. I was scared and too intimidated to not open it. Having finally come face-to-face, we had a huge argument. He wound up strangling me on my bed, screaming how I was a disgrace to the family name. A family which, by the way, did include such things as drug users, dealers, thieves, bookies and God-only-knows-what. But, hey, no nigger-lovers allowed. *Botta-boom, botta-bing!* Mom used to have two favorite sayings: "A wop ain't nothin' but a nigger turned inside out", and "Ain't nothin' worse than a nigger but a nigger-lover." I apologize for her. I don't like and I don't do racial slurring, thank you. The words just don't feel good in my mouth. But this is what I had to listen to as a young girl--I guess she did too.

Later Ralph informed me that he hadn't tried to kill me or I'd have been dead.

Delivered From Temptation

Whatever. And, yes, this is the same Ralph and Dorothy who, as newlyweds, were victims of bias themselves. As I was later informed by my hypocritical, two-faced, racist, sexist boy cousins whenever they screwed a black girl, "This is different." Indeed.

Ralph just happened to be going to trial at that time for illegally booking numbers, so I figured I'd better take advantage of this unique opportunity. Although I was terrified of it, I pressed assault charges in hopes that, together with the first charges, they would carry enough weight to get him jail time, in spite of his connections to the judge--A Nice Italian Boy from the Neighborhood.

Anyhow, he did get a sentence of six months in jail. The main thing I remember, besides fright, is trying to rush past him where he stood under guard by the back door of that courtroom. He had on the signature overcoat he always wore Little Italy style, but his hands were cuffed behind his back. Regardless, he still petrified me.

I must have gone into *slo-mo* as I passed him, because I remember his hissing that no matter where I went he'd find me. He listed several cities, including Detroit, so I'd think--

make that know--that he was one step ahead of me. And for years, I did look behind every tree and jump at every shadow. I figured that while he was in jail would be an auspicious time for me to get out of town--even though I knew he'd be in hot pursuit the moment he was released. At least I'd be a jump ahead, plus I had no choice.

Then, when I was twenty, I met my David. And he said he loved me. He didn't have a horse or shining armor, but he was my knight just the same. This was the savior my mother had always promised. But I don't really think she meant for him to be quite so tall, dark and handsome. Especially the dark part! This brings us back to the first question people always ask: How did we meet? Let me put it this way:

David Ruffin! Even the mention never failed to arouse emotion. If you'd ever seen him perform live, regardless of your gender, that name incited a riot in your heart. If you were among those who'd had the "honor" of actually meeting the man, you had a definite reaction to him. That was the effect he had. His charisma enchanted many--others hated him. Still others both loved and hated him. I was one of those. It wasn't always like that--at first he didn't elicit such strong emotions

Delivered From Temptation

as love or hate. At least, not from me. In fact, the first time he tried to attract my attention, he simply succeeded in attracting my indifference. Which, knowing him as I do now, may have been a large contributing factor toward his piqued interest in me. Anyhow, interested he was!

Let's see--where do I start? Where does one begin in order to make sense out of love? Yes, love. At first sight. At least, that's what he'd always claimed hit him that hot, sticky June 21 in l964 at Carr's Beach, Maryland. On the other hand, it took me at least four whole hours to fall in love with him! Ah, yes. Carr's Beach! I went there that day with my buddy, good ol' Willie Off the Pickle Boat, under vigorous and repeated protest. But it was stifling hot, and, what the hell, my roommate had gone off with her new boyfriend. Of all the idiotic nerve!

I really had wanted to stay in all day and sulk, but it was too hot. So I let Willie drag me to the beach. I think he really just wanted a "glamour girl," as he called my roommate and I, on his arm.

Oh yes--by the way! How did I get from "nerdette" to "glamour girl?" Forgot to mention that little miracle, huh? Well, first of all, I grew a body. Finally! After suffering without one for the entire four, long years of high school, wouldn't you know it, the summer after graduation, I grew a body! It was three inches taller, in fact. And it had curves! Encouraged by a girlfriend, I bought a hot-orange and chartreuse two-piece bathing suit--my first ever. Modest by today's standards, it was daring for me then. And I must say, I wore it well. Hell, I was stacked!

   I spent that summer working at the Ocean City, Maryland restaurant of my dear late Aunt Josie. She was the only relative I knew with enough *chutzpah* to continue, in spite of my father, to show love to not only me, but later on, to my "half-breed son" as well. There my two-piece and I were soon noticed by the lifeguard on Aunt Josie's section of beach. We had a summer love (no sex--I was to remain a virgin for three more years) during which I soon found out that he was a part-time singer in a local band--the first I'd met. He was fascinating--what they now call a funky white boy. It was my introduction into soul music. And that was it for me! I was home. I bought my first Ray Charles album because of that boy. Soon I had sixteen of them. The boy broke my heart, but it was a fair trade, as the next three years found me spending all my time

Delivered From Temptation

with music and musicians and their fans and friends.

Ah, the Entertainment World; it was my world. Everything there wasn't either black or white like it was everywhere else. We all hung out at dances, cabarets and so forth. Color lines were blurry--it was great. I'm sure there was discrimination going on behind the scenes, but for us, it was more about the music. We were all pretty innocent, looking back. It was sort of like the movie "Dirty Dancing", in fact--except that some of the summer help was black.

For me, it was a one-way trip. I liked belonging somewhere--at last. Someplace where the people spent less time on judgment and pre-judgment than on creativity and fun! So, at twenty years old, the Summer of 1964 found me once again a glamour girl in a bathing suit at another beach--Carr's in Annapolis.

As Willie and I arrived, I noticed a huge sign with a long list of singers who performing there that day. Chuck Jackson!? Whew, that got my attention! He was a major star at that time. I perked right up! A stage show at a beach? Never heard of such a thing. Well, not only that, Carr's had an amusement park, swimming, food and drink pavilions, not to mention a bar with a tropical decor. This was a wondrous thing, indeed, as I'd never seen anything like it. Once I'd seen Chuck Jackson's name, I barely noticed the other names under it--Little Stevie Wonder, Charlie & Inez Foxx, The Soul Sisters, Mittie Collier *et al*. And then there was the little-known group, The Temptations, barely perched on the threshold of success.

Those were the days of the processed hair-do, before the advent of black awareness and pride. And in my fairly small town of Baltimore, if ever you saw a 'do, you could bet a star was in town! So you can imagine my excitement when, as I sat at the open-air bar, not one but six of them traipsed through on the way to the dressing room. I'd never seen Chuck Jackson, but I figured that one of these guys was him. But who could the others be? I was thrilled. It was much later when I found that these were The Temptations and Cornelius Grant, their guitarist and musical conductor, aka "The Sixth Temptation."

Well! By this time, I had gotten way over pouting about my roommate, and was ready to have some fun! I gravitated toward the stage area, and tried to see who

Delivered From Temptation

or what was happening up there. Needless to mention, the place was jammed. In the course of my climbing up onto some wooden construction, and hopping up and down for a better vantage point, two rather husky guys must have seen me and taken pity on me, because they offered to hold me up on their shoulders. I jumped at the chance! Although I can't imagine it now, I believe I sat between them, with one *gluteus maximus* on each broad shoulder. And so the show proceeded. The acts came, the acts went. They were all equally okay, but we were all anxiously awaiting The Star.

As just another part of the blur, that group, The Temptations, had come and gone in a quick flash of white-on-white precision, and although I hadn't especially noticed David, evidently he had noticed me. (From the "If I'd Only Known Then What I Know Now" Department: The thing I most regret is that I cannot go back and rewind the tape to that fateful three minutes of "The Way You Do The Things You Do", because I didn't catch it that first time! And even though I must have subsequently seen the show a thousand times, I'd gladly pay anything to see "my" Temptations, David Ruffin, Eddie Kendrick, Melvin Franklin, Paul

Williams and Otis Williams, perform just once more).

Unbeknownst to me, the owner (who I knew, but didn't know he was the owner) saw me towering above the crowd. He motioned for me to join him backstage, which I happily did. Oh wow! Just how lucky could one girl get?! I was about to find out. From my precious spot, I watched in awe and amazement as Chuck Jackson sang song after song; I also watched in amazement as the girls screamed and trampled each other in an effort to merely touch the shoe of their idol. In "I Don't Wanna Cry", he began to shed his sweat-soaked clothes, much to the delight of his fans, and the more he stripped, the more hysterical the crowd became. At one point, he threw his shirt high into the air, where it landed in the rafters. Shrieking girls clamored on top of each other in a hopeless effort to retrieve it.

Elsewhere, whilst my eyes were fixed upon this madness, apparently someone else's (four) eyes were fixed upon me. In fact, David later told me that this wasn't the first time he'd seen me. Little did I know that he'd spotted me earlier eating fried chicken, obviously long before I became

Delivered From Temptation

vegetarian--or *"vegetareyton"*, as he called it years later, God bless his little pea-pickin' heart. At any rate, a voice sort of mumbled something somewhere near my ear, but not loud enough for me to know, or care, what was said. Having been ignored, the person at the other end of the voice made a second effort to get my attention. All he succeeded in getting was a very dirty glance. I was really trying to watch this, the best part of the show, and this guy was here just bothering me! And oh, he was so persistent—and yet polite. He waited until the show was over this time; I guess he'd gotten the message. Finally he succeeded in accomplishing his mission with his third try. I never knew exactly what line he was running--I bet it was priceless--but whatever it was, it struck me funny. He'd been so determined! (He told me years later that he knew he had to get to me before Chuck saw me--imagine). He'd meant to be so serious, but it just made me smile. Finally, he did get my attention. Ironically, he's had it ever since.

Then the show was over, and the atmosphere was a lot calmer and quieter when we began to actually talk. He said his name was David Ruffino--he'd probably just seen his first bottle of Ruffino wine. So, some of the first words out of his mouth to me were false. Years later, when I asked him about it, he justified it by saying it had been his intention to change his name to Ruffino. I eventually found that he often used that as a catch-all excuse for lying--"his intention." Whatever it was, it had been his intention. Nevertheless, I finally agreed to walk with him to find some place to buy cigarettes (interesting, since nicotine is an addictive substance,) and our first afternoon together began.

He was wearing a pair of khaki pants (sort of peg-legged,) a gray and white striped seer-sucker shirt open and tied at the waist (a style he wore well all his life,) a St. Christopher medal (dubious patron saint of the traveler,) a pair of his yet-to-be logo eyeglasses, slip-in sneakers (sockless, of course,) and to top it all off, a red "do-rag!" (For years he denied the do-rag). Obviously, he was in no way dressed in a fashion that would indicate that he was with the show, let alone was the first tenor, second tenor and soon-to-be lead for The Temptations! (Dressing down became one of his trademarks too. He wore his good clothes regally, of course, but he would wear anything anywhere, and dared 'em not to like it)

Delivered From Temptation

I must interject this priceless story here before we leave Carr's Beach: I've said what DR was wearing, and as fate would have it, I was wearing something similar--for a one-piece bathing suit, that is. The bottom was gray denim boy-cut shorts with white top-stitching, belted at the hip with a wide, white vinyl contour belt, and the top was a V-necked sleeveless chemise with gray top-stitching. It, too, was made of gray and white striped seersucker--60's *haute'couture*!

Well, in the course of our travels that day, we covered the entire park, and at one place there were some bleachers and patios and tables. We sat in the bleachers in the midst of a little bit of a crowd. Apparently it was a rather progressive crowd for l964, and all genders were interspersed. Just after we sat down, a voice yelled down from a few rows up behind us. "Hey you, in the stripes." As we both noticed a little lisp in the voice, we turned and looked at each other. It continued: Can I have your autograph?" Now, up until just then, we weren't real sure which one of us was being hit upon. After all, we were both wearing those stripes. David quickly retorted without turning around, "I don't have a pen!" And under his breath, as he elbowed me, he hissed at me,

Genna Sapia-Ruffin

"And don't you get one, either!" The voice sang back, "You can use mi-i-ne." And then, in a lower octave, a change of mind: "No, you'll never break the point on my eyebrow pencil, honey!" David was not amused.

For me, it wasn't his clothing or style or mannerisms that made me think that David was gay. I can't imagine it now, but when I first met him, I actually thought that. And in all innocence, I told him so. Well, he had hit on me! To which, I was like, "Whoa! Whaddya' mean!? I thought you were gay! I don't know what word we used in 1964--I doubt if I said "homosexual"; I'd probably never have said "faggot," that wasn't my style. And, of course, "gay" wasn't being used then--not for that! It was Marvin's last name, for Pete's sake! Maybe I said something like, "I didn't think you even liked girls," or...I don't know what. Yes, maybe it was just his beautiful face. He had no facial hair, perfect skin, high cheekbones--just classic beauty; but there most definitely were a few gay men checking him out.

So he dragged (no pun intended) me away. I think he'd had enough for the moment, thank you. It was kind of funny, but it seems as though he'd had that particular cross to bear for most of his life.

Delivered From Temptation

Po' thing. I mean, we joked, but obviously it ate him up inside.

Believe me, I didn't think for very long that he was gay. To me, he was just very much a gentleman. He was sweet and considerate and, most of all, he seemed to be sincere. We waded in the water--and talked, we rode on the rides--and talked, we ate waffles and ice cream--and talked. It seemed as if we were getting to know each other. Of course, we found out years later that two people never really get to know each other, no matter how hard they try. The simple reality is that people are kaleidoscopes--constantly changing. That's called growth. It's both automatic and necessary.

At that early and simpler time in life, love was easy and uncomplicated; we fell in love before the afternoon was gone. While we were riding the airplane swings, brazen hussy that I was that day, I reached over, pulled him by the chains close to me, and kissed his cheek. (That was my Red Do-rag--I denied it for years! I couldn't admit it. I guess I was afraid that since I'd done this shameless thing, it took something away from our storybook meeting. Or maybe I thought it meant that he just did not love me as much as I dreamed, and that I was responsible for every bad and hurtful thing that followed--like I had given him "license to ill." Call the shrink; I'm not sure. In any case, it embarrassed me, at the very least).

In years to come, he always did love amusement parks, and he'd literally get furious with me because I couldn't even ride a Ferris wheel without throwing up. But that afternoon in June of 1964, we spent just falling in love; and when along toward evening, he said he had to go back, I was utterly clueless. I had no idea what he meant.

The dialogue follows:

He: "Well, I have to go back now."

She: "What for?"

He: "I'm on the show."

She: (sincerely)"Oh. Whaddya' do--light man or somethin'?"

He: "No. D'ju see that group with the white on?"

She: "Yeah?"

He: "Well, I sing lead with them."

She: (surprised, but nonchalant) "Oh. Okay."

Delivered From Temptation

At that time, Eddie had sung lead, thus far. So, either David could see into the future, or he was using imagery to create a manifestation. If so, he was ahead of his time--and out of his mind! Probably he was just ego-maniacal--a Capricorn who saw the peak and was driven to conquer it, oblivious of those used for toeholds along the way. According to brother Jimmie, this was just David trying to outdo him, as usual.

At the end of the second show at the beach, David invited me to this alleged birthday party for a singer on the show, Mittie Collier. It was to be at the motel in D.C. later. By the end of the day, after having had a very long and heartfelt debate with myself regarding the pros and cons-- worried what he'd think, but wanting badly to go, I decided to just take my chances.

It wasn't because David had acquired a little celebrity that I wanted to go; I'd already been pursued by a few famous boyfriends in my one year this side of virginity, and even before, really. Some in music, some not. Why, I had just broken up with one in the NBA, and a while back, there was the one in the NFL. So it wasn't like that at all. It was somehow different this time. It seemed so, so--real. The rest was just "looking for love in all the wrong places."

By the time we left for the party, I was already getting attached to David, and I was already afraid of losing him! So, I bravely took the approach that I'd go to the motel with the idea that it was a one-night stand (it was only the 60's, kids, not the 90's,) and leave it at that. That way, I couldn't be hurt. I was already pulling back in anticipation of his rejecting me. I decided to just make the most of it, and not to hold a charge on it. Right!

Chapter Four

"The Way You Do the Things You Do"

Well, the "party" was a flop, and I began to wonder if I'd done the right thing. I was glad that good ol' Willie had at least been kind enough to give me bus fare, even though he was complaining the whole day that he should have learned to sing or play the horn.

The most vivid and important memory of the party, was the jukebox. It had "The Way You Do The Things You Do" on it, and David kept playing it over and over. I would have thought it would be vulgar to play your own song, but interestingly enough, he made me see it his way in a matter of seconds. The two of us spent most of the time standing in front of the juke-box. I was singing along, and David said, "Oh, I see you sing all the parts!"

(In the years to come, I'd come to find out that he often said one thing to mean another. In fact, you might say that he spoke in reasonable similes. I, on the other hand, would be inclined to say that they were more like <u>un</u>reasonable similes! They had a certain kind of cock-eyed logic to them that often rendered the listener as stunned as a deer in headlights. By the time you'd made any sense of it, he had hit and run, while all you could do was shake your head. He had accidentally made sense! Again! Damn! Most of the time, I don't think he even got it himself--as if it were coming out of his mouth, and he didn't even think of it! Yet, that was the freaky part--you could never take even that much for granted. If you knew him, you can relate).

So at the party, people began wandering into rooms. David was flitting about--probably trying to hook up a room. So, it was now down to just the two of us. We did go to a room, but we were far from alone. There were a few Temptations and/or affiliates in other beds. I have no idea who they were, but they all shared rooms in those days--they couldn't afford not to.

Delivered From Temptation

Besides that, they all traveled jammed up in one big Motown tour bus. David's seat partner was Little Stevie Wonder. He was supposedly about eleven at that time, I think. When we were still at Carr's, between shows DR took me onto the empty bus to talk--some more. He sat in his seat, and I sat beside him in Stevie's seat. Precocious Stevie came bounding onto the bus, and being blind, plopped right down into my lap. I used to wear an onyx ring on my right hand--it was some of my father's gambling plunder, and it had a tiny chip in the stone by one of the prongs. This made it rattle ever so slightly when I talked, since I talked with my hands! When Stevie sat on me, of course my hands went up--all of us were blabbing at once--but Stevie grabbed my right hand and shushed us so he could listen to the rattle. As of then, he identified me as "David's Girl", with that big grin on his face and his head weaving from side to side. Anytime in the months and years that followed, as long as I wore that ring, when he'd "see" me, he'd grin, "David's girl."

Back at the motel, the other fellas slept in the darkened room, snoring away peacefully. Soon, no one existed but David and Genna. Well, I was Genni then. And I never found out what a sentimental old fool he was until after he died. In going through some of his papers, we found out that he had a favorite aunt, Jennie Ruffin, who was about twenty years older than he. Matter of fact, she died right after he did. And I thought he was just being mule-headed when he alone was the only one in my world who refused to change with the times and call me by my new name when I changed it around 1979. Now I think he just wanted to keep things like they were when they were safe and sound. That's who I was when he met me, and, by damn, that's who I would always be! Capricorns are plodders--they don't like change. He had a certain old-fashioned idea about me. Matter of fact, he often called me "Genni Mae." I guess he wanted to keep that old-fashioned idea).

So David and Genni were alone. It's amazing how much conversation can take place in a span of seventeen or so hours, and how much can really be said; and yet how you can feel the need to further express feelings and to deepen communication even more. Somehow our words were just not enough; we made the indescribably beautiful love only those in love can make.

Later, as we lay locked tightly in our embrace, the phone rang. With as little movement as possible, David answered it; he later said it had been Dee Dee Sharp. I heard him tell her that he didn't want to see her anymore, and that he'd found someone new. He hung up, and I remember hearing that soulful whisper of his. It floated the six or so inches up to my ear: "It's so good to have someone to care about and someone who cares about you." Call me crazy, but I think he really meant that. It may have been the first time in his life, as it was in mine, that he actually felt loved. I remember lying beside him wrapped in his arms, as I would come to do so many countless times in the years ahead, and feeling the sun come up. I wondered what the heck I was doing there as I listened to his promises and plans for us--all the while knowing in my heart that it was just a beautiful dream and would never, could never, come true. I lay resenting him for what I saw as a con, and resenting myself for falling for it. Or had I really fallen for anything? Hadn't I done exactly what I wanted to do? Of course I had. After all, that was the agreement I'd made with myself, after all. So if I never heard from him again, ever...what did I expect? It was fun while it lasted, wasn't it? His plans were now going in one ear and out the other. I wasn't about to let myself in for the Big Letdown.

Genna Sapia-Ruffin

So when it was time for me to get on the Greyhound and go to work in Baltimore--who needed sleep at a time like this--I smiled bravely, just as if I didn't care if I never saw him again! He didn't want me to leave, conveniently, but we both knew I had to go. He made me promise to call him the moment I got there, which I happily did. The rest of the day was a fog--more like a cloud. I was in love, and I was sleepy! Big time!

It was three weeks (but who's counting) before he called. He explained that he'd "been trying to get over" me. I asked him if it had worked, and he said that it had not. With that commitment, we proceeded. Next I got a letter from Montgomery, Alabama. What a shock! He missed me, he loved me, he wanted me with him. A letter! He had already informed me flat out that he never wrote letters (at that time, it never occurred to me to wonder why,) and that was only one of only about three or four letters he ever wrote me in life. Telegrams, hour-long phone calls, yes. But, letters? Never! It was beautiful. God knows, I missed him too--desperately so. After a few days, I started receiving the phone calls. All hours of the day and night. From other far-away places and all full of love-talk and romance and *beautiful-ness*.

Delivered From Temptation

He asked me to go to New York for ten days in July, which was the following month! He'd asked me several times already. I was in a state of indecision again. Finally, (as I'd hoped I would,) I gave in. I packed my suitcase and my tapestry wig-box, took off work, and fairly floated on that Greyhound to The Big Apple. I was so happy! I was ecstatic, in fact. I got a cab to The Bronx where The Temptations were staying. It seemed so far from downtown to the hotel! I winced at every tick of the meter, but it turned out to be a lot less than I expected. And anyway, David paid for it! So there!

At that time in his life, to me he was simple and relatively square and unspoiled. He could've really been a brat considering he hadn't been expected to live past age nine as a result of the rheumatic fever he'd had as a child, which both he and his stepmother, Earline, told me about in years to come. So each day he lived was a miracle and a blessing. What I mean is, he seemed honest and gentle, and he just wanted to sing. And sing he could! (I so enjoyed Earline's tales of his winning all the little talent shows when he was just a tyke. He wore bib over-alls, no shoes, and a straw hat; he'd sit down on the edge of the stage at the "white churches" and sing "That Lucky

Ol' Sun." And I think she said he carried a fishin' pole).

The Temptations were performing that July of 1964 at "Freedomland", another outdoor park, but maybe ten times bigger than Carr's. I'd never seen anything like that, either. On this show with The Temptations were, among others, The Contours, Kim Weston, and the late Mary Wells. Ah, yes. Mary. My first encounter with the "other woman." I just caught the tail-end of it, but it seems that DR was seeing her at the time. He broke up with her there, but Mary didn't want to let go. She threw me a couple of sarcastic remarks and dirty looks at the show, but it never fazed me. He seemed to have control, and that was the end of it. He and I then spent the rest of our time being young and in love and finding out about each others lives. It seemed we had a lot in common. (I've since realized that two ill people do not equal one healthy one).

It was also during this time when I began to hear talk. The Grapevine had it that DR was married! And with two babies! I ignored it as malicious gossip as long as I possibly could. And besides, every time I asked him about it, he hotly denied it. He denied having any idea why "they" would

Delivered From Temptation

say such a thing, or how they'd gotten this idea. Just jealous, he'd say. I believed him. I honestly did. I was that gullible--so young and inexperienced with worldly, older men, which is just what David was to me. I figured whatever he said had to be correct. Don't get me wrong, David, at twenty-three and a half, was only two and three-quarters years older than I, chronologically, but his years in the street, and my lack thereof, made him seem much wiser to me. Eventually, he did admit to one baby, but no such wife, thank you.

He seemed both proud and relieved to show me a snapshot of his three-year old, Cheryl Lynette. Naturally, I gave him the third degree--I imagine he expected that. Even in the face of my interrogation, he continued to lie. He claimed that Lynette's mother, Sandra, was dead! He said she'd died of childbirth complications. (H-m-m-m. His own mother, Ophelia, had died of complications following his birth). When I asked him why in the world he hadn't married Sandra before she died, he casually replied, "She wasn't my type--a one night stand. I didn't love her." What a rotten thing to say! And to tell me of all people! It seemed odd to me, but I figured maybe that was the way things were out there in

The Big World. So I accepted it. After all, I had no reason to doubt him. In fact, I guess on some level I was flattered. It placed me above her, as he'd said that he did love me. Since he knew she was alive, if I ever came face to face with her, I'd have become his unsuspecting ally. I think that's what he was planning. I say this because he was a manipulator, but brother Jimmie would later say I give DR too much credit here, that he was neither that deep nor that intelligent. Maybe that he was just saying the first lie that came out of his mouth.

Before that gig was over, David produced a photo of yet another baby girl. He said that she was Lynette's little sister Nedra, but that he wasn't the father. "What? How can you say that!?" I exclaimed. "This little doll-baby? She looks exactly like you." She was cute as a button, she was one year old, and I finally began to suspect that David was not telling the truth, the whole truth, and nothing but the truth--about anything!

When I showed up in New York, David took a whole lot of ribbing from most of the fellas. People can be so cruel sometimes in their ignorance. At one point we walked past Melvin Franklin, the bass singer of the group, where he sat at a picnic table

Delivered From Temptation

with two girls. They were all talking and laughing. He jeered at me in his basso voice, "Hey! Are you black or white?" It was obvious that I was the source of their entertainment. I retorted sarcastically over my shoulder, "Whatever you got your money on!" I had heard that one before, I guess. David and I then walked around a corner where he stopped, took me by the shoulders, turned us so that we faced each other, and asked me, "Damn, baby, what are you?" Later, Paul Williams, the baritone, on the other hand, after one second of silent deliberation, off-handedly permanently dismissed the issue as far as he was concerned by affectionately issuing the pronouncement: "She's Geechie-- paper-sack brown." It never mattered to him; I loved that soulful man from that moment on. And, now that I think about it, none of them ever brought it up again.

It was also on this trip that David first told me I was different from any woman he'd ever known. When I asked him in what way he meant that, he said with a straight face, "Well, for one thing, you're taller." Duh! And he was serious.

We went from the obscurity of "Freedomland" to "mainstream" at the Brooklyn Fox for one of the famous "Murray the K" shows. There were nineteen name acts--Millie Small, The Ronettes, Shangrilas, Ad-libs, Contours, Tempts, and Marvin Gaye, to name a few. By the time Marvin closed the show, everyone was leaving. The audience was exhausted; besides, his show was pitifully lame. I was embarrassed for him.

Our first New York gig, in July, was suppposed to be for ten days. One of those days, while he was walking around in his briefs, I'd teased him how he had legs like a horse. With a laugh he said, "That's good--I thought they were more like a mosquito." But our holiday turned into only four days--we had our first argument on the fourth one.

I discovered that he was insanely jealous when I exchanged social greetings with a couple of guys in the hall. I was instantly taken back to how badly I'd seen my dear brother, "Snookie-Wookie," abuse his wife in the name of love. I packed my little luggage right back up and got on the Greyhound bus and went home! I figured I didn't have to take that kind of crap, and I wasn't about to. Sadly, that may have been one of the last times I stood up for my rights with David. I was in love with him, true, but I figured that I wasn't that far gone yet.

Delivered From Temptation

The Temptations had progressed from the Motown bus to their own new station wagon. It very slowly inched its way backward out of the driveway of the hotel toward Harlem, where they would drop me off at Greyhound. "Ruff," the guys called to him. "Are you coming, man?" He bounded down the stairs, two at a time. Of course he did, with those legs.

He was yelling for us to wait, and I was never more relieved in my life. We made up on the long drive to the city, which was when he told me what had to have been a big lie. What he said was that he hoped that I was pregnant!

I could not believe it. Nor did I know how to take it. How sweet; thanks, pal! I stood my grounds and went home anyway. Naturally, I didn't want to, but it had become a matter of principle, and if I'd given in then, he'd have figured I was just like all the other girls. I wasn't and I didn't want to be treated like them. So I left. I wasn't sure if I was right or wrong, but I knew I had to go. And fast, before I changed my mind. On the way, I asked him again about that nasty little rumor of a wife and two kids. Again he reassured me that it just wasn't true. Well if you say so, I figured. Who else can I believe but you?

The guys tried to warn me at the start--in the very beginning at "Freedomland". But we were all so young then--from twenty to twenty-three years old. What they said meant zip to me; I didn't even know them. I didn't want to hear it. So they backed off for the time being. David asked me to go with him to New York again in August. This time they were playing at the world-famous Apollo Theater! Well, I concluded, no harm there at least. Then when he showed up pounding on my apartment door in Baltimore unannounced and unexpectedly one night, I was floored. I was also thrilled beyond words.

Unbeknownst to me, he'd hatched a clever plan. He and Paul Williams, his partner-in-crime, had conned the girl Paul was seeing to drive her '64 T-bird to New York from Detroit where they lived via Baltimore! What a nut case! I was swept. He knocked madly. I opened the door. I gasped. I nearly fainted. I can see our mouths moving now, but I can't hear what were saying. Next thing I know, we're in the back seat of that little T-bird with the porthole windows!

Delivered From Temptation

I don't know what we had for audio technology in the olden days, but I know David had his tunes. He had a tiny little turntable with a tall spindle for lots of 45's. He sat behind the driver, and I sat behind the passenger. We crossed our feet to the opposite sides--like an "X". We had to--we both had long legs. The turntable was on the seat between us. He was the disc jockey, of course. Don't ask me how it was powered--obviously batteries, unless he had a real long extension cord. Not that I remember, but you can bet that he had with him "The Way You Do The Things You Do." It was the group's first and only hit at that time. David had just joined them six months before, around his twenty-third birthday, and he was very proud of the song.

By the time we got to New York to play The Apollo, I was even more in love. I think I lasted there the whole ten days this trip. We stayed at the President Hotel, or The Teresa--I forget which one--in either case, it was like The Ritz of Harlem at the time. During our stay, I happened to see the laundry stamp "DRUFF" in the back of David's uniform shirt collars, which was the normal procedure: PWILL, OWILL, MFRAN, EKEND, CGRAN and DRUFF. This would one day become his trademark. Ten years later when he formed

57

a company called "Druff Productions", I shared with him that I knew his secret. We both laughed.

While David and Paul were at The Apollo all day, Paul's girlfriend and I had to entertain ourselves. Some days we'd hang out with them at the theater, and some days we'd walk all over New York. One day we permed each others' hair, and every day we'd shop. Macys? Saks? Not even. We shopped for cheap edibles. We'd buy fruits, cheeses, bread, peanut butter, jelly and Vienna sausages for David. He pronounced it *"Vyeena"* all his life. He had his way, too, with the English language, God love him! But, none of us could afford those dollar hamburgers and fifty cent Cokes in the hotel coffee shop. The infamous Coffee Shop--that's where Marvin Gaye tried to hit on me one night. He just said real low, "Too bad you're with David." I looked at him, got my change, and hurried away. Boy, how different history could have been!

Another night, the four of us went to some swank hotel lounge--I have no idea where it was. Those two wanted to sing, and didn't give a crap about a Motown contract. I guess they figured they could get away with one song each, and it was

Delivered From Temptation

the first time I ever really heard David sing! Or Paul, for that matter. To my surprise, they chose standards and show tunes. Paul sang "September Song," David "My Funny Valentine." Talk about your shocked! And then talk about your captivated. The two of them sang like real songbirds--they had so much class; I was thrilled. I wish you could have heard them; I know I'm glad I did. I'll never forget it, thankfully. There were only a handful of lucky people in the audience--I hope they realized in later years how privileged they were that night. I still think my favorite albums are the ones with that type of song: "In A Mellow Mood," and "Live at The Copa." Or is it "Meet the Temptations!?" Yeah.

In that first magical week, my love asked me two or three times to move to Detroit with him. Basically, he was asking me to quit my good job, leave my own apartment and its contents, and become disowned forever by my so-called family to come and live with him--a man I hardly knew--pretty scary! Probably what cinched it was that, amazingly, he said he wanted to marry me. He'd said it a couple of time already, but it was beginning to sound like he meant it. The more practical and cautious side of me (three planets in Virgo and Libra sun) said no. I'd shake the far-away look out of my eyes and say to him, "N-o-o, I can't." I didn't even know why; it just sounded far-fetched! I shivered at the idea of leaving my friends and familiar surroundings to go to a distant, strange city and start an entirely new life with this stranger whom I loved! And, OMIGOD, a singer! Mothers must warn their daughters about stuff like this. Wow! This would take a lot of thinking--and a lot of guts. Not to mention a lot of faith in him. After all, I did not know a single soul there except for him and his friends. I wondered if I could count on him. My Libra scales were working overtime.

Motown! The Motor City! The name fairly sparkled in my mind. It did sound tantalizing, in spite of what I'd lose. By the seventh day, between David's instigation and that of Paul's girl, I decided to take the leap. I'd stay at her place until David and I found an apartment. At some point, I realized that I not only could, but wanted very much to be with David in Detroit.

Once I'd made up my mind and gave him the good news, though, he freaked. Apparently, he never thought I'd actually have the nerve to do it, because suddenly, he just shut up for three or four days. He'd lost that great, goofy smile, and hardly spoke to me in as many days and nights. That was highly unlike him. It seems he had been caught in his own trap. And just to add insult to injury, he had the nerve to have attitude. Great! Looking back, it's sort of comical--I must have really blown his mind. I never saw him speechless again after that.

The four of us had but two single beds. David and I'd slept in one, Paul and his girl in the other--very cozy! David was sleeping with me every night, although barely, but he wasn't saying a word. He'd get up and go to the gig all day, come back and not say a mumbling word. And he was so very good at that mumbling! This continued for three very tense days. As you can probably imagine, I was not only perplexed, I was also pissed. Here we go again, I thought, "What the hell is this shit this time? Well, I'm getting out of here and out of this lunatic's life before it's too late. I'm sure glad I found out now--just in the nick of time." You see, I figured he'd just gotten tired of me that fast, or met someone else, or--who knew? I had no idea what was really on his mind. And something big was definitely on his warped little mind. Meantime, the fellas were still trying to let me know, without really telling me, that he was married with children. I guess a couple of them, probably Otis and Melvin, finally convinced him to tell me, which he did do at the last possible moment. But not easily.

By now the last-minute frenzies had set in--packing, bill paying, *good-byeing* and so forth. In the interest of privacy, he spirited me off to what was to become his favorite room, the bath. We sat right down there on the floor where he confessed the confession of every married man who played around--he didn't love her, she didn't understand him, they'd been separated longer than they'd ever been together, he didn't live with her now, the second baby still wasn't his--and he loved only me. When I asked the apparently dumb question of why he didn't tell me before, he said that he'd been afraid that I'd have left him. I yelled at him that he would have been right. But that now it was too late for me. Somewhere in between our first and this second argument, I had slipped the invisible degree into hopeless, helpless love. (Make that "co-dependency"). No doubt, this was music to his ears, if for no other reason than it meant victory to him--I'd fallen for the trap. See, according to Jimmie, all David ever saw in me or any other woman were dollar signs. I personally never got or felt that from David. He never

Delivered From Temptation

even so much as asked me to lend him a quarter, so I don't think he was trying to pimp me. But whatever, Jim.

Once again, my love repeated his hope that I was pregnant with his child. Looking back, I guess this must have been a common line, but I'd never heard it. I'd lived a rather sheltered life, I guess. At 20, I'd never been on a plane. I'd never been outside 150 mile radius of Baltimore, and never seen marijuana until DR whipped out a joint (much to my horror) at the hotel that trip.

After all was said and done, I wound up in Detroit. And soon--I think it was January of 1965--we were in our little third-floor, walk-up, roach-infested, coal oil polluted love-nest at Thirty-Seven Forty-Seven Gladstone, Apartment Three-Oh-One! We paid the seventy-five dollars a month to our absentee slumlord, which was too much, and lived the happy, simple life that only the young and in-love can. (But I guess that was me; according to Jimmie, David was the young and the liar). Gigs were few and far between for the young Temptations, and when they did come, the guys worked for peanuts. But it was okay. Between times, they rehearsed constantly for the upcoming

Big Time. We weren't worried about those little nickel-dime gigs anyway. We were gonna be rich and famous someday. And, more importantly, we were gonna be "we!"

Sometimes David would literally scream the first thing of a morning even before he got out of bed. He was trying to make his voice gruff. He'd say, "Do I sound like Wilson Pickett yet?" (Maybe he should have changed his name to David Gruffin. Ba-rum-bump). Jimmie says, however, that "David and Wilson Pickett and all of 'em" were trying to sound like him.

But me? Rain, snow, sleet or heat, I'd ride the city bus to my little hairdressing job every day at seven o'clock in the morning (I had to have been in love,) which was just about the time DR was turning over to go back to sleep. After a few months, it became obvious that not only were we on conflicting schedules, but I decided we needed more money. So, through one of the girls at the salon, I got a cocktail waitress job in a new kind of club called "go-go," in addition to my day job. After six months of double shifts, I decided to quit the salon, and just work at the bar. That way, David and I could finally be on the same schedule. Go-go had slowly begun to emerge, in its purest form.

Delivered From Temptation

A couple of us waitresses spent so much time bopping around, that the owner decided we should be onstage. Thus began my dancing career. After all, the hours were less and the money was more. Much more--five bucks an hour! At inception, go-go dancers wore costumes--fringed dresses with rhinestone straps, or psychedelic leotards (full coverage, thank you)--all with vinyl go-go boots and matching mod caps! It was the first such club in town--"The Hello Dolly." There were phones on all the tables! The dancers who were "the regulars" was a young husband-and-wife team, believe it or not! Lucy and Red, I think their names were. They did routines which included The Pony, Mashed Potato, Swim, Frug, and so on. We became the dancers between the shows. Peg Bundy copied that girl's hairdo by the way.

Somewhere along the way, word spread to Motown of my new-found talent. (Three years prior, I'd missed even my Senior Prom because I couldn't dance). One Thursday the phone rang at home--we only had one; it was in the hallway. David answered. Surprisingly, it was a Mr. Harvey Fuqua calling to ask if I'd dance Saturday night on the Marvin Gaye show at a popular nightclub, The Twenty Grand. I looked at David with dismay. I told him that wasn't sure I could learn the steps that fast. He gave me his standard cock-eyed look as he spat in his own motivational, inspirational way, "You can if you want to." Cool! It wasn't to be just me, but a small troupe. We'd have choreography, costumes--the whole works. The Gordys would be front row center. Even though I'd never done anything like it before, I decided to go for it!

Over the four years in which I danced on Motown shows, we had two choreographers--the legendary Chollie Atkins, and Elaine Horn. I think Elaine did this first show. We ponied out on "Hitchhike" and, of course, danced our hitchhike routine. I was paralyzed with fear, but fortunately, the spotlights made it impossible for me to see any faces in the audience, let alone the Gordys. And once the count hit, I was gone! It was great!

I remember another call on Gladstone for David from Motown around that same time. We only had one phone--the aqua "Princess" in the hall. It was the infamous Berry Gordy on the line. David was saying, "You can tell me how to sing, but you can't tell me how to run my "H-O-M-E", literally spelling it out. Gordy had been warning David about an interracial relationship and the effect

Delivered From Temptation

it might have on his Motown empire--and David's singing career--but David wasn't having it. Plus, we found out later when I danced on the Chris Clark show that Gordy definitely did not practice what he preached. Chris, an obscure, white singer in the Motown stable who had only one hit ("The Duck") was also rumored to be Berry Gordy's girlfriend. In fact, if recall, the third ex-Mrs. Gordy was also white. As Otis Williams once said to me, "Time wounds all heels." Okay...

Regardless, the relationship between David and I wasn't about to go away easily. He told me that for a while, who knows how long, The Temptations actually fined him a thousand dollars every time he took me to a gig! Man, if we'd only known then what we know now! David and I could be living well today on the proceeds of that type of discrimination lawsuit. We transcended the racism outside of Motown easily compared to what we painfully faced right inside their door. Considering that the root of racism is ignorance, I can chalk it up to that--and greed. However, it sure didn't provide any warm fuzzies for David--or for me. Quite the contrary, actually--we felt quite unwelcome. But--love prevaileth! Was it for me or only for the cause that Sir David championed? Who careth?!

In those early days, I was almost as jealous of David as he was of me. I guess we both felt insecure about each other. I was envious of the wind that blew on his face. I was jealous of his looking at Playboy Magazine. As he reminded me many years later, my eyes were so green that I drew, with colored pencils, a self-portrait in a two-piece bathing suit for him to ogle instead of the girls in the magazine. He was so touched--and bewildered as well, I think. I was so *naive.*

One day he received in the mail a purple and black sweater. He was sick in bed with the flu, so he was my captive. I asked him when he was going to stop trying to pimp. He fidgeted as he said, "I don't call it pimpin'. They just give me stuff." Maybe Jimmie was right--maybe David was a pimp in Temptations' clothing!

As my love sweetly explained, it was those same women who bought my clothes and paid my rent. And that they'd be there as long as he had fans. Oh. That made sense to gullible me, and from then on, I hardly was jealous again--to his frustration in years to come.

I guess I was gullible enough to believe him, too, that time he gave me crabs and swore he got them from that nasty cot backstage at The Apollo. Hey! It could happen!

Until I met David, I had always worn black clothing--or black with touches of white or gray. One of the ways, I found out some twenty years later, that a child from a messed-up family learns to cope is to become "invisible." One day he came home from out-of-town (actually it was Philadelphia--as you'll see, the first in a series of Philadelphia connections) and tossed a shopping bag on the bed at me. He just said, "I'm tired of you wearing black." He had bought me something! For the first time! There were two suits in the bag. They were both three-piece, in a manner of speaking. One was a royal blue knit straight knee-length skirt with matching sweater/jacket. With it was a pastel blue sleeveless shell sweater. The jacket had piping to match. The second was even more weird. And harder to describe. Let's see--the straight skirt and the sweater/jacket were sort of a dark mustard color. But they had sort of a network of raised little squares all over--sort of like chicken wire. They --oh, never mind! They sound bizarre now, even for David; but in 1965, they were hot! And, more importantly, they were my first non-black articles of clothing. The transformation continued. Hello, Pygmalion.

So, DR and I went along at home that way, I merry in my innocence, and unaware of his discontent and frustration. Strange as it seems, looking back, we really didn't know each other well enough on Gladstone for him to tell me how he felt; nor could I read his feelings at that time. Matter of fact, now that I think about it, he never knew me at all. For instance, he could never have written a book about me--probably not even a pamphlet! He didn't know that much about me. He was too self-absorbed to. Boy! He missed a lot. Pity.

Chapter Five

"That Darned Tammi Terrell"

"Did David really kill Tammi Terrell?" That is the second question people invariably ask me. When DR first started messing around with her, everyone knew but me. Just before the Detroit Riot, the two of them had gone down to the Twenty Grand Club, made the club rounds, and then shacked up for the night at the tacky Algiers Motel. It was obliterated in the melee within the next few days. Before he got home the following day, no less than twelve people had called to tell me all about it. Before he went to sleep, of course he dumped the contents of his pockets on the dresser. Included was the motel key. As the sadistic misogynist intended, naturally I saw this key. When I inevitably asked him about it later, and told him about the phone calls, he said with a yawn that if we ever broke up, it would be because of me listening to other people talk! I think it was also around that time when he made the odd statement that should have been a warning, "Everybody always leaves me, I'm not the one who leaves them." (Whatever that really meant). Nowadays, Oprah will tell you: "If they tell you they're not good enough for you, believe them, girlfriend!" And, "If they tell you they're separated, they mean since breakfast." But Oprah wasn't there for me in 1965.

David had sayings too--I call them *Ruffinisms*. About TT and the motel key, his only offering was, "If you look for trouble, you're gonna find it." And, "Did you see it happen? 'Cause if you didn't see it happen, then it didn't! happen" Frankly, you could be looking right at a thing or a situation, and he'd find a way to make you believe you were not seeing what you knew you were seeing. If you knew him, you can relate!

It was really a blow when, at two months pregnant, I woke up early one morning to find David packing. Maybe we were moving. We had been talking about it, after all. I was afraid to ask for fear of the answer,

Delivered From Temptation

but I somehow had to find my tongue, because he wasn't about to volunteer that information. I finally asked him if I should be packing too. He was squatting down at the time, and he peered up and gave me that infamous cock-eyed look of his as he said sharply, "If you're going with me!" Whew! Relief! At least that's what I thought at the time. But wait--what had he really said? Nothing. I found as time went on, that he had this exquisite way of doing that-- saying nothing. At least nothing he could be held accountable for. He could, and did, always correctly state that he "didn't say that." It was excruciating.

In this case, he didn't even give me that much. I went to work merrily thinking that we'd be moving that evening into our new apartment. But when I got home, the place was deserted. He was gone--lock, stock and barrel. No note, nothing. The next time I saw him was only when I hunted him down at the airport as he left for his next gig. I certainly got nothing out of him there-- he made me run just to keep up with him as he gave me a lot of non-answers. Two groupies ran at his other side--I felt like dirt. Yes, he'd moved without me, and no, he was not going to give me a key to his door. I discovered later, though, that he did intend to keep my key--to my broken heart. Dammit!

Just once he returned to Gladstone--he'd forgotten something, I guess. I desperately tried to tell him how much I missed him. He just gave me this strange, blank look for the longest. I asked him what was wrong, and he said he was trying to figure out what I could possible miss about him. He was talking true; I should have been listening, but this, too, was before Oprah. Next he said, "If you had an orange rug over there by the door, and it was gone, you'd miss that too." A different type of *Ruffinism*.

So. My Capricorn hero had been swept off his size 11D feet by the dollar sign attached to that darned Tammi Terrell. Nothing meant more to him than fame and fortune, and he meant to get his, as did she. Now, Tammi was a Taurus, and she did know what she wanted. She wasn't quite as ditsy as she acted. She saw an opportunity, and she grabbed it. She was going for the Big Time--on David's coattails, if need be. Of course, I realize that she probably didn't have to twist his arm all that hard, considering his penchant for the green and wrinkled.

Delivered From Temptation

And, DR, in true Capricorn fashion, was naturally going for the cash. What cash? Oh! Well! TT had convinced him that she was going to receive a trust fund of one million dollars when she turned twenty-one. And, that if he played his cards right...

Motown was instantly smitten with her. It was said that--dropping her serviceman "fiancee" Stanley like a hot-potato--she quickly got involved not only with David, but with Marvin Gaye and Berry Gordy as well (so I heard), and that's just the names of the "well-known". She always played around, though. Berry, Marvin, whatever band that was in town--but it seemed as if David never wanted to know. She could do no wrong in his eyes, and everyone snickered behind his back. It was embarrassing. But then, maybe there was just nothing he could do about it, considering who he would have to go up against and what the cost would have been.

Once a guy I knew who was also a friend of David's went to see him. He told me that although David wasn't home, TT answered the door in a see-through nightie. As she sashayed toward the back, she sang out over her shoulder with a giggle, "Don't l-o-o-k!" Yeah, right. I think that those who wrote that she was a promiscuous alcoholic were too kind.

Believe it or not, I still wasn't really sure about David and Tammi living together. Oh sure, I felt it in my gut, but had no proof. Before long though, The Grapevine confirmed my suspicions. She was, indeed, the reason that I couldn't have a key to the flat where my man now lived--with her.

Their respective careers grew large, as did my abdomen. They moved from the flat on Montgomery, first to a little apartment, and then later to a huge one on Hazelwood Street. For two years, they lived the high life. They had their California-King bed, they had their black satin monogrammed sheets, they had their thirteen foot black leather sofa--you name it. Then there was the "Black Room"--kind of a psychedelic den complete with bar, bong pipe, lava lamp, and fishnet hanging from the ceiling. *Fancy-schmancy.*

As for me, I was still dancing special shows at Motown, and when I did my last Christmas Show at "The Fox Theater," I was two months pregnant. I was the dancer in the stage-right cage doing "The Swim". Yvonne Washington, Denise Gordy, and another girl were in the other three cages.

Delivered From Temptation

All of Motown was on that show, including The Temptations, of which David was still a part at the time, Diana Ross and her Supremes, plus the darling of Motown and Diana's would-be nemesis, the Tammi Terrell. It was, at best, a very trying situation. As you can imagine, the tension was so thick you could have cut it with a knife. People were whispering and walking on eggshells. It was as if there was a time-bomb ticking somewhere--a major explosion was inevitable. It was just a matter of who would go off first--David, Diana, Tammi or me--and where and when. That was only the first in a long series of potentially combustible circumstances.

At the same time, I was on the welfare. Naturally, I did initiate attempts to collect child support--more than once--but that was impossible under the circumstances. You have to try and understand the workings of the so-called legal system and its inter-relationship with the social/entertainment circle in Detroit in 1967. The (Black) Fellowship prevailed.

There was one particular incident in which DR and I were subpoenaed to meet at the courthouse. Shortly after our arrival, David and his lawyer, as well as my public defender (black men all) disappeared together into some back room--most likely a bathroom. Lo and behold, my entire file vanished from existence from that point forth. My girl, Debbie Rhone, David's last woman (and she was one) told me twenty years later that she had seen it in the stuff he'd stored in the barn at the horse ranch they shared in Michigan--after he'd died. Think about that.

During the pivotal years with TT, David began his long, winding and rocky road downhill--personally, that is. Professionally, he was The Shit. The Big Shit--string of gold records, European tours, The famous Copacabana in New York (THE club), "The Ed Sullivan Show", "Shindig", *et cetera, et cetera*. The Temptations were the hottest thing since The Beatles. Actually, they co-existed with The Beatles. It was January of '64 when "I Wanna Hold Your Hand" broke on "The Ed Sullivan Show", and it had to be within a very few months when "The Way You Do The Things You Do" broke the same way. I'd say they were same, only different. Furthermore, The Tempts, along with all the other Motown acts, literally changed musical-- not to mention racial--history.

Delivered From Temptation

It used to both irritate and tickle David at how I could find him anywhere, anytime. As always, it was The Grapevine which kept me much too-well informed of his every move--a dubious distinction, to be sure. So, when I heard how he and TT licked each others nostrils, I was furiously jealous--and totally uncomprehending. I didn't get it until many years later how coke addicts were about that white dust. At the time, I thought it meant that they were in some kind of love I had never shared with him and never even heard of. Now, it just makes me sick. Besides, he always de-fuzzed my navel with a cotton swab, and it didn't even have cocaine in it--so there.

Although I was too big with child to dance, I was still scrambling for income, so I took a part-time waitress job. It was there one night where some jerk vaguely recalled, "Hey, don't you go with The Temptations?" "No," I spat. "Only one of them." Then he patted my protruding tummy as I passed and teased, "What's that?" As I pulled away from him, I shot back over my shoulder, practically thumbing my nose, "It's 'What Love Has Joined Together', and 'It's Growing'." *Na na na na na*. The one thing that God gave me to get through this thing called My Life is a sense of humor--for which I'm grateful. (See, those were titles of Temptations' songs back then--well, I guess you had to be there).

While I was pregnant, even though David was living with TT, he and I still saw each other. In fact, he took me on the road fairly often. That was me backstage at the Howard Theater in Washington. I was one with the five pound bag of oranges under my arm and the imprint of David Junior under the bodice of my red maternity dress.

David's stage persona had absolutely exploded, more than filling the role of the sex-symbol into which he had apparently been cast. His voice enchanted millions worldwide. Just as with the fans of each Beatle, each Temptation had his own following as well. David's fans shrieked at the mention of his name; they trampled over each other trying literally to touch the hem of his garment. They begged for autographs, they tore at his clothes, they wept, overwhelmed at his very presence, I suppose. They ran alongside of, and sat on the hood of, his limousine. Women waited in line for a chance to be alone with him and maybe have some kind of perceived intimacy. Clearly indifferent to the many both before and after them, they

Delivered From Temptation

just wanted their precious moment--so much more personal than a silly autograph, don't you know. I always wondered if every Temptation had sex every single time they had a chance. David said he wouldn't have had the time or the energy--I wasn't so sure. Yes, it looked like good old David had finally made IT--whatever that means. But completely unlike The Beatles, he took it all, and himself, way too seriously. And that he did not know how to handle. In today's vernacular, he needed to "get over" himself. The Tempts were well on their way to becoming a household word, releasing hit after hit--most of them led by David to the top of the charts. Yet, success was leading him into personal disaster.

Meanwhile, he and Tammi, who was doing pretty well herself, wore matching minks and diamonds (?) and toothy smiles in public. They made me sick! She had promptly finagled a niche for herself in the company, and kept kissing all the right body parts. They released one song after another on her--some on her own and then with Marvin (Gaye, of course). She and DR traveled in opposite directions quite a bit, yet they seemed to make good use of the freedom. It was this arrangement that allowed them to present their facade for as long as they did. The music business in Detroit was like a small town--everyone talked about them. And, o-o-o, the things they said. It's true that their affair was based on the Million Dollar Lie of hers, but then, I bet David didn't break his neck telling her the truth about me and soon-to-be David Ruffin Junior either. In fact, the relationship seemed to thrive off the mutual deceit and dishonesty.

Phase II of her Million Dollar Lie unfolded the first time she turned twenty-one in April of that following year--1966, I believe. David Junior wasn't yet born. She held her party at the Twenty Grand during her gig there. She kept trying to get me barred, but the owner, Bill "BK" Kabush, and Scotty, and Henry, and Christine, and Claudreen, and Dottie--and all the gang for that matter--had been watching out for me since I was too young to get in. After all, David himself had placed me there under their watchful eyes-- he felt I was safe there. It was the only club I could go to when he was out-of-town and be comfortable. It was home. I was proud that her demands were not met.

So, there I'd sit, six months pregnant, claiming my rights. I never had to say a word, and I wore my usual innocent look on

Delivered From Temptation

my face. It really pissed her off. But it was good for me, as it allowed me to feel less powerless in a powerless situation. Not only that, it was the only way I could have any measure of revenge--not to mention control. Once, after I'd made sure her show was well under way and she was helpless to stop me, I left and dashed over to their apartment where I knew David would be--just in hopes of catching a few "crumbs off the table." Maybe he would talk to me. It was pathetic. And to make matters even worse, he just about had a fit when I showed up at the door. He was all freaking out and paranoid-- as in, "Get away from here, leave, go home, hurry up before she somehow finds out you're here." Man, I'd never seen him act that stupid before--it was embarrassing. I was trying to figure out what the heck possessed him. ("CHA-CHING"). I wasn't sure if I envied her mysterious powers, or just thought he was a wuss--it was weird.

Actually DR and TT were a perfect match--not to be confused, Otis, with "good for each other." The Sadist and The Masochist--and druggies both. I sincerely believe that's when he really got heavy into cocaine--because when he left me at two months pregnant to go live with her, he was not using it. If he were, I had never seen any signs--physically or emotionally. So it would never have even occurred to me. However, he was paranoid that night--big time. Needless to say, I left. Sh-e-e-e-sh, already. I scratched my head in bewilderment all the way back to the Twenty Grand.

Now, the second time she turned twenty-one the following month was in Baltimore. She certainly didn't expect to see me there, and was highly ticked when I busted her. I had retreated there in one of my early attempts to break away from David "for good", even though I was already pregnant. I don't remember who else was on the show (not him) or what exactly possessed me--maybe easy retaliation, since my opportunities were so rare. But this time, since David wasn't there, she had been running all over ranting and raving about how she was going to beat my ass and "kick that baby out" of me. Martha Reeves was there, and was concerned enough to come and warn me--gives you a little idea of what a manipulating, scheming, literally treacherous witch Tammi really was--in my experience and by my observation.

It's true, she did have David certifiably blinded. The word voodoo came up on the Grapevine, and I guess there were certain pieces of evidence which could have been used that way. If it weren't voodoo, some sort of magic was going on! Things that make you go, "H-m-m-m."

David remained oblivious. Or, maybe it was a mere pretense for which he had his own agenda. Throughout the pregnancy, he could not make up his mind whether he wanted to claim the baby as his or not. One day--which must have been right after he deserted me, since I was about two months pregnant--we sat parked in my car in front of Motown talking. Just to see what he'd say, I asked him if he wanted me to have an abortion. He stared out the front window for a nano-second, yet at almost the same time, his head snapped toward me. He gave me that crazy look of his, and said, "You ain't killin' my kid." With that, he leaped out of the car to go to rehearsal inside. A-ha! He had clearly acknowledged paternity. I thought that was so sweet! To me at that time, it was as good as his saying, "I do." Okay, then. My God was in His heaven, and all was right with my world.

Several months later found David with his ear to my bulging abdomen. The baby kicked, as babies do, and DR jumped back.

"That m----r f----r kicked me." So sensitive. So, um, "David".

But then, later when "Little David" (as everyone but his parents called him), was born, "Big David" still sometimes said he wasn't the father--not to me, but I heard about it. He probably told it to any and everyone who wanted to hear it--chiefly Sandra, his wife. Although, I doubt they believed him, as we'd already been living together for nineteen months before I could even get pregnant. It was something we'd both wanted, although in perfect 20/20 hindsight, I'm sure it was for all the wrong reasons. Most likely, he just wanted to see if he could even make a boy, as he'd only produced girls with Sandra. I probably had been harboring some sort of *naive* delusion that somehow a pregnancy would miraculously bring and keep him closer--a common misconception, as it unfortunately turns out. But, once again, we had no Oprah. Not only that, it never even crossed my mind that it might not be a boy. I never even picked out a name for a girl. That's how badly I had tunnel-vision; it just never occurred to me. On some level, I suppose I was afraid that there was literally no chance of him staying unless I produced a son. Sounds like a third-world country, but pitifully, it was probably true. Maybe.

His denying DERj, as I came to sometimes call him, didn't faze anyone. Other than skin-tone and eyeglasses, they looked exactly alike--even the same hairline. Besides, everyone knew that I was completely, totally and disgustingly devoted to the man. At that time, I had no other concept of a relationship for myself than one of consummate dedication and, of course, monogamy. I had it so bad that I was probably the laughing stock of Detroit-- and the whole world, it seems.

When I gave birth, which was hell in itself, David was nowhere around. To make matters worse, I'd heard he was in Philly with TT where they announced their fake engagement onstage with that huge so-called diamond ring which--he told me later--she'd bought for herself. They were both very aware that he was not only married with daughters, but had me--a pregnant common-law wife waiting in the wings as well.

Oh yes--the third daughter, Kim. I don't mean this to hurt her--probably he was only saying it to cover his own sorry tail-end, but he claimed that she wasn't his. He had to, pretty much, because she was conceived while David and I were in our first apartment on Gladstone Street. She was born within the year before David Junior was, and clearly, it definitely would not have been in his best interest for me to think he'd gone back and slept with what I believed to be his ex-wife. He did tell me he was going to get the rest of his stuff--apparently that wasn't all he got. I, of course, found out later from Sandra herself--and it was a very rude awakening on the front steps of Motown--that she was still his wife, and plainly very much alive--not dead as DR had originally told me; although that's how I'm sure she'd have like to have seen me. Not that I blame her, considering that I'm sure he was lying like a rug to her as well. I can't even imagine.

Still, he often said that Kim wasn't his. Me, I was in the dark--in no position to judge either way. In any case, it didn't affect my feelings about her. I figured that if she weren't his, she may as well have been. It's true she didn't look like him, but she did carry his name. Nor did I see anyone else rushing forward to claim paternity. I will say here in David's lame defense: I came to believe that the reason he denied (at one point or another) no less than the last three of his four children was most likely fear of financial ruin being visited upon him by the respective mothers. That is, as opposed to any other lame excuse he managed to conjure up at the time--most likely along with the instigation by some, if not all, of his group-mates. The Motown stable was kept ignorant in those days--both financially and legally. Since DR was both Capricorn and country, he just naturally traveled away from that type of situation out of not really knowing the right, or least best, way of handling it. In time, it became painfully clear that he'd really never learned right from wrong. Or worse yet, he knew (sociopath), and didn't care.

Chapter Six

"Okay Kid, Me & You"

I had my so-called pre-natal care on welfare at the Clinic From Hell. Even back then it was a creepy, old, and nasty place in the Detroit ghetto. I want to say more, but I'd be sued for true defamation of character.

In "Admissions," when the clerk asked the father's last name, I replied both bitterly and facetiously, "Mudd" With utter indifference and without a shred of caring-- or even the common courtesy of looking up at me--she asked, "One 'D' or two?" Thus set the tone of my experience at this so-called hospital.

The air-conditioner was broken at the Hospital From Hell on the fourth of July weekend in 1966. Temperatures were over one hundred degrees, and the staff was sparse. Apparently, they were also hot, tense, and preoccupied with leaving. They paid little or no attention to the needs of me or my newborn son. I was in labor for thirteen horrific hours. I want to elaborate here too, but again, I'd be sued. The labor was difficult, to put it mildly, and, like I said, so was the birth. I'll spare you the gory details; the point is: I was going through torture. And I was alone. I was being blatantly disregarded not only because I was on welfare, but when they found out the baby was "Afro-American", I became "white trash." In fact, I became a non-entity, altogether. After wheeling me back to "my room", which I shared with an "Afro-American" mother-to-be, they brought in my newborn son. Oh, they brought him, alright, but took him straight to her. And she was still nine months pregnant. I had to demand my baby. Hell-o-o!

After endless agonizing over all that had happened thus far, I had to face that David and I were probably not going to have a life together with our little baby. In fact, I remember looking into his crib when he was first born and saying to him, "Okay, kid; me and you." It took much soul-searching for me to make the very difficult, heartrending decision to give him my last name instead of his father's. This was extremely painful for me at that time, not because of DR's celebrity, but simply because I loved the man so much. It was so drastic--so final. Yet, I loved my son even more, and I felt I had no choice. In 1966, society wasn't about to embrace with open arms, a multi-racial child. I figured it was bad enough that I couldn't do anything about that; the least I could do was to not further separate him from his remaining parent by the two of us having different last names. I still wanted the baby to have as close a name as possible to his father's, and I definitely wanted him to have his first two initials, at least. Trouble was that in those days, I had absolutely no appreciation for David's middle name, Eli--his father's name. His mother's maiden name, Davis, had been passed on to him as a surname. Apparently this is a common practice in some Southern families--one I had not yet learned to respect, as I now do. So, I named him "David Eric Sapia"--D.E.S. instead of D.E.R. It was the best I could do.

At some point during the pregnancy, I'd rented a room on Atkinson Street, a block from Clairmont where Melvin Franklin's family lived. I was seldom able to rouse myself out of my stupor, during which I played Billie Holiday music incessantly. I was in the absolute depths of a bottomless pit of dark despair and depression. David and Melvin were said to be distant cousins, and in any case, Mama Rose had always been a mom to me from the first time DR took me there and introduced me to them. She sympathized with my frequent tragic tales of woe. I'd sob as if my heart was breaking, and she'd cry right along with me. I ate there when I was hungry, I slept there when I was tired. Melvin's brother and sisters accepted me as family, too. And when Little David was born, Audrey--the youngest girl--never let anyone else babysit. If it hadn't been for the Franklins bringing me food or coming to get me, I may not have even eaten while I was pregnant. I was that pathetic.

Mama Rose knew, maybe more than anyone, how much I loved David. She also knew how much he dogged me, but like a good Motown Mom, she kept it quiet. Even from me. I wouldn't have believed it anyway--which she probably knew. Melvin had long since accepted and embraced me as family, so I couldn't understand it when he started suddenly giving me the cold shoulder. Finally one day I cornered him

Delivered From Temptation

and asked him what was wrong. He said he simply couldn't stand the way I let David do me. As for me, I was blind. I could see nothing but DR--not even myself. Matter of fact, I didn't even have a connection with the baby growing inside me until the day he was born. That's how focused I was on DR. I guess nowadays they call it "obsessed", if not child abuse.

So that was my "love" for David Ruffin. Sick. I suppose in those not-so-golden days, that's what a lot of people thought to be in love meant--to be a fool. Sick.

I even considered jumping over the bridge onto Lodge Freeway late that New Year's Eve knowing that DR was with Tammi. Once again, the Franklins saved me, but things only got worse from there.

During all this time, Dennis Edwards, who was a yet a far cry from being a Temptation, was also looking out for me. He was playing helluva organ and singing in his own band, "Dennis Edwards and The Firebirds." David had taken me to that bar on Joy Road and proudly introduced us as soon as he could.

Now, Dennis had a new gold Cadillac which he let me use when I needed it. One day, I dropped him off at Benny's Flamingo Barber Shop for his 'do, and went to Mama Rose's. There was a treacherous fireplug inches from the driveway, plus you had to back into traffic to leave. Naturally, I cut right into it with Dennis' l-o-n-g car. Oh my God! I thought he'd freak, but he asked me if I was alright, and said that was all that mattered. Whew! What a relief! Of course, that was over thirty years ago, and he was still seeing things fairly clearly. His path took many a turn for the worse not too long afterward. In fact, I'd say for the worst.

The too-few minutes I spent with him and Eddie K. at David's funeral (read "sideshow"), left me disappointed and badly hurt--not to mention angry, offended and disgusted. He was way wired up. And then when my son, David, attended Eddie's funeral in Birmingham on behalf of both of us on October 10, 1992 since I had to work. According to him, Dennis was stoned there as well. But then, I saw him again three weeks later, and it seemed he'd made a complete turnaround. He was coherent, friendly and clear--yet, by the tears in his eyes when we talked, it was obvious that he was hurting from the deaths of his two best buddies. I understand that he's settled down some now and on the Road to Recovery. Not

Delivered From Temptation

only that, but he won the lawsuit against Otis, giving him the right to use the name "The Temptations" for the group he now has on tour. God bless ya', Dennis. I'm glad you heeded my warning outside just after David's funeral when I hit you in the chest and exclaimed tearfully, "And don't let it happen to you!" Remember? Well, no, you may not.

At any rate, Dennis was escorting me out from time to time while I was pregnant and even afterward--babysitting me, so to speak. I guess now you'd say we were just "kickin' it." DR was on the road, not to mention living with Tammi Terrell. True, David was still spending time with me on Atkinson, but he used the same mailing address as she did. Needless to say, I was pitiful. I guess Dennis, among others, felt bad for me. Just after the baby was born, I was so penniless. I think it was the same day I came home from the hospital, or soon afterward, when Dennis gave me five dollars--that's how broke I was. I promptly used it to buy a little tiny pair of blue and white shoes--well, not that little. Or tiny. The doctor had exclaimed, "Size two!" when he spied the baby's feet upon delivery. Of course, Dennis had no idea what I'd buy with the money; I probably didn't know myself. It was the thing the baby needed the most, I imagine. Aside from that point, under no circumstances did Dennis want to be known for buying David Junior's first pair of shoes. In no way, *no sir-ee*, no thank you! I didn't get it then, but I think he was afraid that people might think that he was saying something that he wasn't about his responsibility as the father--considering the mentality of the people around at that time and in that space. He could not just be a caring person. The whole idea, of course, was ridiculous, but he knew how crazy his friend David could be. I never told anyone about the five dollars until now, which, as you'll soon see, turned out to be a darned good thing!

Dennis was a good friend, and although we never slept together, we did get accused of it once in 1966--in a very diabolical scheme concocted by Tammi Terrell. Her monstrous plot almost cost me my life, and if not for Mama Rose, I might have lost custody of the baby as well.

As I said, David was bouncing back and forth between the two of us. He seemed truly uncomfortable with the situation--as if he really couldn't make up his mind. I

Delivered From Temptation

think he wanted us both, but for different reasons.

TT was an extremely dramatic and phony person, and every week or so, she'd fake a suicide attempt in order to get his attention away from me and back onto herself. David's pimp friend Chuck and one of his girls were kind of living with David and TT, apparently. So every time Tammi would go through one of her various acts, the girl would call me and give me the real lowdown. For instance, TT called my place in the middle of one night, waking David and I, to claim hysterically that she'd downed this handful of pills. She'd really thrown them out the window. Incredibly, David got up out of bed and went over there. I told him that he was playing right into her hands, and his reply was, "Yeah, but if anything ever really happened to her, Motown would kill me." A-ha! Was this a peek at the true nature of their relationship at this point? What could I say to that?!

Maybe two weeks after the birth, David finally found his way back to me and his son. I could not detect any signs of instant bonding or emotion on his part. I don't know what I was expecting, but nothing seemed to happen. No wait, I take that back;

as Big David held his only son for the first time on his right forearm, with his hand under the baby's head, the baby peed right at him. I guess Li'l David figured he'd take the initiative. And that his father had it coming. Amen! We had survived, no thanks to him, but largely due to the caring and efforts of David's friends and their families. No thanks to me either, I'm afraid. I had been such an emotional basket-case that I was no good to me or to my baby. There is something, however, about giving birth that wakes you up--in a hurry. Maybe that's the purpose of the screaming that comes with it.

There came a point when David and I began to plan seriously to buy a two-family flat --one to live in and one we'd rent out. Against all odds, we had begun to claw our way back into some semblance of closeness again--even though he still tenuously shared the address with TT. She seemed to be losing her grip on him, maybe because of David Junior or not, but in any case, she got wind that David wanted to come back to me, and the forces of Hades were visited upon me.

Naturally, I was the one assigned to look for the property, so I was calling David often

Delivered From Temptation

with information. I lived in a cement block studio hovel on Stoepel Street then, without a phone. I had a roommate, Debbie, and she and the baby and I all slept on mattresses on that cement floor. I'd have to get change and spend money, plus walk two blocks each way to the pay phone out on the main street every time I wanted to talk to him. One certain day, I said my usual "hello", but he just hung up. This happened four for five times. By then, I was in a panic. I can't remember *verbatim*, but in some cryptic way, he finally alluded sideways to what had happened. It was something about what he had just gotten in the morning mail. I, of course, had no clue what he was raging and rambling about. He was just screaming something about some unforgivable thing I had done to him and about some legal action I was supposedly taking against him, which I wasn't. I couldn't get a word in edgeways. I was both bewildered and dumbfounded. I could not even defend myself. Even in this state of panic, it became apparent to me quickly that this had to be some manifestation from the mind of TT. I tried to tell him this between sobs, but he wasn't having it. Just like always, she could do no wrong in his eyes. I remember how frustrated I felt when, no matter what I said, he utterly refused to listen or to believe that it was all a convenient and fiendish frame. I felt so helpless and defeated.

Looking back, I guess her plot had its evil start one night when Dennis and I went to the Twenty Grand to hang out with the crowd. DERj was about three months old, and it was my first time out--which I deserved by now, to say the least. Big David was out of town, but TT was there social-butterflying. Dennis and I started through a doorway, and as we did, she literally blocked it. She meowed to me, "I'm glad to see you've got a man of your own--maybe now you'll leave mine alone." She had the audacity to then invite Dennis and I to dinner at their new apartment when DR got home--a cozy double date. Dennis and I kind of elbowed each other, and stifled a snicker. We graciously refused her kind invitation to the lair. But I had hardly heard the last of her.

Evidently, she was afraid that David and I were going back together, and she was not about to lose her ticket to ride--no way! Desperation breeds maniacal behavior, I suppose. And so, she plotted her wicked plot. She used her mysterious, murky powers to connive from God-knew-where, a copy of the letterhead stationery used by Social Services. By putting it together with her having seen Dennis and I out, she had her weapon.

What David got in the mail that baffling and maddening day was what looked like a letter from Aid to Dependent Children, which in legalese, basically questioned the paternity of my son, and astonishingly, indicated Dennis as the possible father! Of course, now I know that makes no sense, but it was enough to upset David and it scared the be-Jesus out of me! I couldn't figure out how she made that happen. Later, my friend The Grapevine, solved the mystery for me. It said, with a sneer and a scoff, that she'd paid with twenty dollars and a blow job to have the letter printed. Some comfort that was. I just shook my head.

I anguished about it and wept over it the entire day. That night when Debbie went out to the Twenty Grand, I succumbed to my feelings of despair--I tried to kill myself. This was not ordinary behavior for me, but I felt totally and utterly crushed. I just couldn't bear to be here anymore.

Debbie had said that she would be home about two in the morning, but she came home at midnight. She found me slumped on a bar-stool in the bathroom, my head down, and my arms in a sink full of running, warm, red water. I had sliced my wrists with my hair-cutting razor. I remember not wanting to feel the pain, so I closed my eyes as I made the first gash on my left wrist. To my great surprise, it didn't hurt at all; my eyes popped open in disbelief. I proceeded to watch myself repeat the motion thirty-two times. I must have gotten tired or weak or bored by then, because I only put eighteen cuts on my right wrist. Then, just to be sure, I drank a bottle of Merthiolate and took all the aspirins in the cabinet. After rousing me and propping me on the floor against the bathtub, I guess Debbie realized that David Junior was still in the other room asleep on the mattress. Later she said that she didn't know at that point whether he was asleep or I had killed him before I went into the bathroom. After patching me up, she ran out to the phone booth and called Mama Rose. She told her what more to do for me, and to make sure the baby was okay, and not to call the police for fear I might somehow lose custody of David Junior. Last but not least, Debbie called my hero, David Senior. His response was, "What're you calling me for? Call the police."

Delivered From Temptation

Obviously, the cuts were not deep enough to cause me to bleed to death--psychologists would say I never intended to die. Personally, I'm still undecided about that. I do, however, believe that I did slip just through the thin veil which separates sanity from insanity. I saw it happen as I made those long gashes. And then I watched myself s-l-o-w-l-y inch my way back, over time. It was a long time--a very long time.

It hurt me so badly when I found out what David had said to Debbie. Especially since I knew how he jumped through hoops every time TT even faked a broken nail. Years later, he explained to me: He didn't want Debbie to waste time calling him when she should've been spending those precious moments getting help for me. Yeah, right. As if.

Clearly, I lived. However, even though it would be another five years before DR began the physical abuse, I was a beaten woman. Weary and dejected, I took the baby and left Detroit once again to go to Baltimore to stay "forever." Once again, I failed. I thus recognized that I was an addict myself--I had to have my (dr)ug.

Almost immediately, I began to call him. Before long, when the baby was six months old, David sent for us to meet him in Cleveland at the Versailles Hotel. Gratefully, I dropped everything and ran.

It was the dead of winter--January of 1967. Cleveland was covered with snow and it was bitter cold.

When we first arrived, everything seemed to be okay. David took us to his room, and I had high hopes of reconciliation. Mommy, Daddy and baby makes three.

He was in a good mood that day-- and silly. He tried on one of my dresses. Evidently I had planned to wear it only at the show, because it was a chemise of brightly colored abstract floral voile with a lovely handkerchief hemline. Weather-wise, it was a little optimistic for Cleveland in January, now that I think about it. Don't get me wrong, David was never a cross-dresser, to my knowledge. It was just that, for some reason, he felt like seeing how he'd look in my dress on that particular day. He put it on, I zipped it, and he looked in the mirror. His hair was in a short kind of "burr cut"-- not very glamorous. He had on, of course, no makeup and no accessories--unless you count his wood-frame Elton John eyeglasses.

Delivered From Temptation

He was perfectly flat-chested with no butt and those horsey legs. He looked quite dreadful, confidentially. He stared at his image in the mirror for a quick minute, and rightfully declared, "Damn! I'd be f---ked up if I was a woman." His 6'4", 150 pound frame definitely looked better with men's clothes hanging from it than that dress!

As the sky got darker, so did David's mood. I was sitting on the bed trying to reach Paul by phone, when "Mr. Hyde" charged into the room. He mumbled something or other and I said, "Just a second, I'm trying to call Paul." He threw money in front of me on the bed as he yelled that I'd better hurry up because I was leaving. Naturally, I was mystified. Which is obviously just what he wanted--to keep me always bewildered and off-guard. I literally never knew what really happened, but suddenly he was flying around in a rage, packing my luggage. Not very neatly, I might add! As usual, I was at his mercy. He sent for his head flunky of the day to come and drive the baby and I to the airport as well as ordered him to make sure we got on the plane back to Baltimore. What he failed to mention, however, was that there was no plane back to Baltimore scheduled any more that evening. And, this he knew.

Even his own yes-man didn't have the heart to leave the baby and I stranded at the airport in the cold without money. He drove us back to The Versailles, in spite of the guarantee of incurring the Wrath of Ruff. I don't remember how much longer it was before DR finally got us shipped out of there, but he avoided me for the duration. If we ran into each other even by accident, he'd grumble as he turned right in his tracks and headed in the opposite direction. This was one of the many times to come when my hero, Paul Williams, rescued us. Why all the madness? We all wondered--or maybe it was just me. I should've known that one of his women was there.

Ultimately, the scuttlebutt got around to me that one of his groupies had shown up unexpectedly (no surprise there,) but apparently she was going to, or did, throw herself into the indoor pool over him. There was also just the faintest murmur that it was possible she was pregnant. I never heard another word about it to this day, but wasn't that about the time he was "seeing" a girl supposedly Dean Martin's daughter? A-a-a-a! *Paisano!* Anyway, that would explain his behavior that day at The Versailles--if you knew David.

Delivered From Temptation

It was said on the music circuit that when Tammi--as the young Thomasina (Tommie) Montgomery--was working for James Brown, he'd beaten her frequently. According to public records and news reports in later years, this was a habit he carried into his subsequent marriage. After that first stint, apparently she began working for yet another "soul singer" with the same initials as the first. Around l965-66, she found her way to Motown and Berry dubbed her Tammi Terrell. It was when Tammi collapsed in Marvin Gaye's arms on stage that the reports of the brain tumor surfaced. As fate would have it, she was living with David at the time.

Allegedly, the brain tumor was caused initially by the beatings inflicted by the two singers she was with before coming to Motown. Theoretically, it was then activated by one of the many blows landed throughout their two-year plus relationship by her so-called love, David Ruffin. The old Grapevine never concluded whether the evil deed was done with a hammer, a Hennessey bottle, his motorcycle helmet, or that plaster cast he had on his wrist from some mysterious fall down a staircase. I had heard all of the above.

For David, their living arrangement at that precise time turned out to be terribly inauspicious, as it caused the finger of suspicion to point straight at him. Trouble is, it never was resolved as to whether or not he held any responsibility in her death. Incredibly, no investigation or proceedings ever took place. Everyone just acted like it never had happened. In fact, Motown kind of just swept the whole thing under The Rug with the rest of the dirt. Gordy didn't do it for David's sake, by the way. Surely everyone knew then and knows by now that DR was never one of his favorite people--maybe he was jealous? But clearly, someone was being protected. Of course, Mr. Gordy was married to Marguerite at the time, as well as rumored to have had serious relationships going on concurrently with two of his singers, Chris Clark and Diana Ross. I doubt if any of the three would have taken it well if, in fact, he was also having a sleazy, tawdry, little sex thing with the likes of Tammi Terrell.

Anyway, the tumor--along with the cocaine, I guess--killed her within a few short years, shrinking her to the ninety-some pounds she weighed just before her death in 1970. I don't think David ever really resolved it. Operating, of course,

Delivered From Temptation

on the premise that he had a conscience, he never truly knew if he was guilty of her murder. And no one ever quite figured out why he went to Florida instead of to her funeral, since he supposedly loved her so, but maybe he just couldn't take it. Right? (I know, Jimmie--he "wasn't that deep.")

Quite a few years later, Bobby Womack and I were discussing the situation. He and David were very close. They shared a lot of their innermost secrets. Many a dark and smoky night turned into daylight on those two. In fact, Bobby shared with me after David died that he believed that he was the one who (as a pal, of course), turned David on to cocaine in the first place. I still wonder whether he was bragging or complaining, but to that I think I can speak for the whole family when I say, basically, "F---k you very much."

When I asked Bobby what David told him about the Tammi business, all he could do was shrug his shoulders. He said that David wouldn't talk to him about it, and had told him "a lot of shit hadn't been settled." I don't remember *verbatim* what Bobby said, but David felt as if he had been muscled into accepting the role of scapegoat. We'll never know. We suspect, but we'll probably never know.

Tammi's family had moved her back to Philly, and I just knew, that now that he'd had his "fling" with her, David would be coming back to me and DERj--now two and a half years old. We'd been waiting faithfully, if not patiently. Big David and I still saw each other, of course. After all, we had the baby.

Every so often David did buy him clothes, even though he still hasn't paid any child support. I'd be totally broke and not able to buy undershirts or diapers, but do you think his father would provide the necessities? Not David! He did seem, although, to enjoy bringing him exotic velvets, leathers and cashmere collected from his far-flung travels. I adjusted--as usual. Eventually I learned; as people said, that's "just David."

Once Tammi had gone to Philly, David moved a beautiful young gold-digger by the name of Tonya into the same apartment. Just David, I guess.

Chapter Seven

"Far Out, Man!"

There was a time in 1968 when I had a friend who was the opening act on the Joe Tex Revue. He knew I was a dancer, so when Joe wanted "go-go," the friend telephoned me from Baton Rouge, Louisiana. I went down there to join the tour in progress.

Mr. Tex had a casting-couch idea of an audition, but in spite of his spurned, freakish half-assed advances, I got the gig. Maybe he figured he had plenty of time on the cross-country tour to get into my pants, but since I was stranded at that point, I took my chances.

There was another new dancer too-- name of Lolita. We made a great team, and coincidentally, we made a great appearance, if I do say so myself. She happened to be an extremely light-skinned young black woman. It was hard to tell what either of us was. I say that only because most of the entourage was Muslim, even though it was before Mr. Tex became Joe "X". So, it was a very interesting scene. We were all traveling on a bus across the South and the fellas were not real sure how to take either of us. Once the initial tension had dissipated, though, they did take a liking to us, and seemed to become quite protective.

I was somehow, at one point, riding in a limo with the driver, a bodyguard, and a manager named Pat instead of on the bus with the rest. I don't know what happened with Lolita, but these three were perfect gentlemen with me. Maybe they didn't hit on me because they knew Joe had his eye on me, but I heard nothing after that first strange encounter. Maybe I just wasn't his type--or theirs, for that matter. H-m-m-m; I began to wonder what they'd heard from or about DR.

It was February; 1969, I think. It was the middle of the night, and we were approaching Phoenix--we were about forty miles to the East of it. Patrick slept in the front passenger seat while the bodyguard slept in the back. The driver, deep in his own thoughts, cruised along in silence, while I knelt in the back looking out the rear window at the black, incredibly clear sky. I had never seen so many stars and planets and celestial bodies in my entire existence. A life-long, on-going enchantment with the Arizona skies began that night for me.

At one point, I realized that the particular light which I was watching was moving West at a very, very high rate of speed. I called to the driver: "Norman, what does a UFO look like?" The bodyguard stirred at the sound of my voice, and he and Norman got sort of tickled at my innocent inquiry. They were acting as if it were an everyday thing. As we were also moving due West, the speeding light seemed to be passing directly over the roof of our limo. About then, we saw an vast glow of light on the horizon to our right-- like a city; but there was no city. We pulled over to the shoulder, and I jumped out with no shoes. In case you're not aware, Arizona is cold on a February night--any year. The guys yelled at me about getting out of the car in my socks, but I was oblivious--to both the yelling and the cold. I had a one track mind just then. Patrick was up by now, and all of us were buggin'--especially me, as it was my first such encounter. Suddenly, I saw two more identical shapes join the first one-- one from the South and one from the North. The three had passed over the limo, and met in front of us with the fourth one, which had approached from the West. Upon the convergence, in a blink they literally zoomed off toward the Northwest with a "Z" motion. Whoa!

Moments later, bright lights approached us head-on over the crest in the road, and we all scrambled back into the limo and sped out of there as fast as we could!

Well! I'm sure I won't be able to express just how hyper I was. Suffice it to say that I was positively freaked. Yet the guys no longer seemed to share my enthusiasm, which mystified me. They seemed to settle right back down, business as usual. Still, they all wore Mona Lisa smiles on their faces. Meantime, I was jumping from one to the other: "What's the matter with you guys? Aren't you excited?" They casually informed me that this was a common occurrence around there for them. Happened all the time. Wow!

When we arrived at the California Club in Los Angeles, I was still flitting about: "Guess what!?" I tried to tell everyone, but got zero

Delivered From Temptation

support from my fellow witnesses. "Why? Why?!" I implored them. They just shrugged; "No one would believe us anyway." I was helpless. Case dismissed--but not forgotten.

Okay, so there we all were at the California Club. Ike and Tina Turner were there with the Ikettes, and, to my delight and surprise, The Temptations arrived shortly after we did. The show didn't actually begin until the next day, so we all had some time to just hang out--between rehearsals, I imagine.

At some point, Ike Turner cornered me and, two inches from my face, leered a proposition at me to be an Ikette. "You don't even know if I can dance or sing!" His response was a slimy, smarmy, "It don' matta." I guess! I didn't have the pleasure of meeting Ms. Tina, my s/hero--she was probably tied up in the back somewhere-- but I still hope to when the time is right.

Meanwhile, The Temptations had showed up. I wasn't aware that David was on the gig, and evidently he wasn't expecting me either. Later he told me how secretly excited he was when he noticed my tapestry wig-box sitting in the corner with all the luggage.

He recognized it as mine--so where it was, I was. And vice-versa, to be sure. Wide-eyed and curious, I asked first Paul and then David what they thought about Ike's proposal to me. They each admonished me separately, quite succinctly and in the same way: "Don't do it." Their warnings both were centered around something like, "If you're an Ikette, you have to have sex with both Ike and Tina." That was it for me, although I had known instantly that I definitely did not like the vibe that Ike put out. I didn't know one thing about him at that time; he just seemed sleazy. I see now that there is something to be said for first impressions and/or instinct, after all. Of course, knowing what I do now about Men Who Control, if it were true--what David and Paul said--I'm sure Tina had little to say about it.

The rest of the gig went smoothly--no drama that I recall. David and I probably had our little *rendezvous*, but afterward, I went back to Detroit, and The Tempts continued their tour. When it ended, David went back to the lovely Tonya.

There once was a saint named Genevieve, it's true, but I have never claimed to be her, so I guess this is where I tell about my pot-dabbling days--although I wasn't doing it

Delivered From Temptation

at the time I met Ike Turner. Actually, I had never touched the loco weed until David Junior was a little over three months old. I was already twenty-three. It was right after I had reached a point of emotional breakdown in the worst way--I had just survived The Suicide Attempt. Then, in addition to my existing pain, I'd been forced to take the baby and leave the man I loved. I very much resented him for that. I was extremely angry and frustrated. I was going to have to find a way to cope, or I was afraid I wasn't going to be able to even continue--let alone take care of my son. DR was literally driving me crazy. Or, to be more correct, I was allowing it. One day my mind railed on and on: "How do other single mothers get through this? I need help; how in the world do they cope? I can't be the only person in the whole world who ever felt this hopeless and helpless." Then it dawned on me: "Oh yeah; that's right--drugs and alcohol!" I didn't have a minute to spare--the demons were right at my heels.

I'd found out through repeated attempts that I couldn't drink, so with trusted friends in music, and specifically as an escape mechanism, I smoked pot. It was virtually medicinal for me. Unlike the infamous Bill Clinton, I did inhale--a little. (I don't do it now and as Ringo Starr said, I got "tired of wakin' up on the floor").

But, hell! Music never sounded like that before. And food never tasted more delicious --and dimensional. Believe me, I felt better--way better. My spirits were lifted. I felt wonderful; I felt, well, happy. It was the first time I could remember that I wasn't miserable and depressed. Relief!

We were at a hall where my friends were gigging, and, man did we dance and laugh and act crazy. I had fun! That was a luxury, and I liked it. I was just about to turn twenty-four, so I guess it was about four more years that I smoked pot off and on, even though I'd never smoked tobacco. Still don't--go figure, huh?

During those times, I had some real psychedelic trips with pot. I've always had a low tolerance for drugs, thank God--including those of caffeine and alcohol.

The first I ever drank was two screwdrivers. I passed out, regurgitated with my head in the trash can of a public ladies' room all night, and woke up (sort of) in the filth on said floor hours later, incapacitated. I careened clumsily outside and did not remember getting home. None of the above, however, before first having both a laughing fit and a weeping jag. Make that a sobbing jag. Fun, fun, fun Over the years, the scenario was always very close to the same script, even though the drink and the locations varied. Laugh, cry, vomit, pass out--all in a fairly short period of time. I did that funky little dance for a few years, but never did master the art of consuming more than one or two drinks--just not my idea of a good time. I guess alcohol was blessedly poison to me.

During the approximately four years in which I tried to smoke marijuana, I had more than several-- but less than many-- extreme and intense experiences. That is to say, I never had a "normal" high. Everything was a trip with me--both good and bad. Although "reefer" was not supposed to be a mind-expanding drug when used alone, I guess it depends on one's predisposition to natural psychedelia. So I was a cheap date, so to speak. A couple of hits and I was a goner. First I'd get tremendously amusing. I know that other people on drugs always think they're clever, but in my case, it was true--I was hysterical. All my friends loved it. They even taped it--I was the comedic entertainment at any given time. I guess a life full of pain and frustration had finally found an avenue for release--wry comedy. Even David, who also took his turns at being the subject of my jokes, used to think I was hilarious. True, sometimes I'd cry if he'd recently treated me badly, but at least I no longer threw up before I went to sleep. And yes, I did sleep well, and enjoyed lots of food, but eventually I got tired of being a tad out of control--aka "One Toke Over the Line." After all, I had responsibilities; even if no one else accepted theirs. In other words, somebody had to have his or her head on straight in order to take care of "Little David"--it certainly wasn't going to be his father. I figured the kid at least deserved that much. As he so frequently reminded me as he was growing up, "I didn't ask to be born." To which my response--to both of us--eventually became, "On some level."

I don't intend to relate all the stories here of my adventures in Wonderland, although they were often intriguing, comical, colorful, and, for the most part, fun. Well, maybe I would tell, but I don't think I quite remember!

The reason I started this confession in the first place was so I could talk about the Puerto Rico experience, which I could not do without telling about pot. David

Delivered From Temptation

had sent for me to join him at a gig in San Juan shortly after he left The Temptations. It was an incredible resort hotel. Our suite had two floors--more like a condo. And it was full of all kinds of people--looked a lot like a James Bond movie, in retrospect. We got the fanciest red carpet treatment. He hadn't started the violence yet with me, so we had a lot of fun and did a lot of partying that trip. When I arrived, everyone else was already there. By the time I got dressed, they were on the way to the casino or somewhere. We were on the eighth floor. David took me out on the balcony to smoke a joint with him. In fact, it was just a little "roach"; he had already smoked his share of it. Now, I don't know what they grew in Puerto Rico in 1969, or what they put in it, but, Holy Shit! I only took, like, two or three little hits!

We were in each others arms, standing on a balcony with a concrete floor a foot or more thick, but when David started to pull away to go inside, I freaked. "Wait! Wait! Don't let go of me! My legs are sinking through the cement." He looked at me in utter amazement. As he pulled away from me, he muttered in disbelief and/or disgust, and turned and bolted to catch the others. He jetted past as he left me moving in *slo-*

mo through the cavernous master bedroom. I never made it past sitting on the lower edge of the king-size bed. The trouble was, it faced the mirror.

I was wearing a long sheath dress, split up the sides to the thighs. Dancer's legs. The dress had spaghetti straps, a built-in bra and a flat self-bow at the center cleavage. It was a neon psychedelic print in hot pink with hot orange swirls--a really nice polyester. I had my hair up, topped off with one of my little curled wiglets. I had on major big false eyelashes--double tops and bottoms. I wore the perfect earrings and, last not least, I'd found a sort of high-heeled Puerto Rican thong sandal with a cluster of jazzy plastic dangles on the throat of the shoe. They were vinyl--make that patent leather--and the color matched my dress. And, oh yes, I sported blue octagon-shaped specs as well. I was so fine!

Now, the reason I described all that was to relate just how high I was--and how easily I'd gotten that way! As all you women know, the first thing you do to get comfortable is take off all things itchy--like eyelashes, wiglets, earrings, specs, not to mention sandals. But, no! The second I sat down on the foot of that bed, and my eyes locked onto their own reflection in the mirror, I just left--vacated the premises. Elvis had left the building! David had gone to the casino, and the room was so silent it buzzed. I was too alone.

Hours later, Jimmie came through our suite from the casino, and when he came in that bedroom, I snapped out of my trance. That's when I realized I was still sitting upright, had one leg crossed over the other, and was fully dressed and accessorized. He spoke to me--maybe asked me what I was doing--and suddenly I was normal. I wasn't high at all--it was weird. So that's the kind of doper I was--not very good at it. But like I said, I did have the dubious distinction of being a "cheap date."

For his show the next night, David had me escorted to a special table near the stage--roses, champagne, bodyguard, the works. Moments earlier, just as he and I were in the elevator going down to the gig, I looked down and realized that although what I was wearing was elegant, it was (omigod) a pantsuit. At the time, it was still illegal for women to wear pants, although David Junior doesn't believe that. I gasped and said, "I wonder if they'll let me in wearing pants!" David looked at me as if I'd taken leave of my senses and said as the elevator doors opened and he whooshed away, leaving me with the waiting bodyguard, "Tell them you're Mrs. David Ruffin and you can wear anything you wanna wear." Well, alright then!

After the gig, we went back to Detroit. Our relationship was still not quite what I wanted it to be--but then, was it ever? He did, however, come often to visit me in whatever club I was dancing at the moment. One afternoon in 1970, he came in and sat at the bar with his back toward the stage- his usual position. The club was deserted, for all intents and purposes. When I finished my set, I sat beside him on a bar stool. As I wiped sweat from my face with a towel, I just looked at him as he hung his head. Then he said a strange thing: "Your friend is dead", referring to Tammi Terrell. Not that I didn't feel for him--I did; and I wanted to comfort him. It's just that I thought he should come home with me now, where he belonged, and where I could take care of him. Yes, I did fully expect for him to come back at that time--after all, why wouldn't he? No more Tammi. Only photos and trade mags and newspaper clippings and posters and telegrams she'd sent whenever they were apart. Only letters, Valentines, other

Delivered From Temptation

holiday cards and souvenirs--all of which I found years later in a seldom-used drawer in our bedroom after we'd moved to One-Seven-Three-Eight-Five Parkside Street. To put it mildly, I was perturbed. I confronted him, find in hand. He dismissed both me and my findings with something like, "What're you worried about--she's dead." He spun and walked away--case closed.

She died in 1970, so he had left the group two years earlier. The guys couldn't cope anymore, after four years of his shenanigans. I'm sure it took a lot to ask him to leave. They were, after all, more than co-workers. They'd become like brothers, and some even loved him. Most likely, there was a lot of turmoil--and a lot of discussion about DR whenever he wasn't around--until finally they agreed he had to go. Chaos emerged. Those of us who still cared about him felt it was not a very brave or diplomatic way to do it, in fact, it was downright funky. The group broke the news to him at a gig--to a wave of surprise and a sweep of emotion. After that climactic night in 1968 at Cherry Hill, New Jersey, he begrudgingly surrendered. In the name of progress, he was "replaced"--as if he could have been. It was more like a substitution was made--nothing personal, Dennis.

Genna Sapia-Ruffin

They'd been secretly training poor Dennis Edwards and had stashed him in the wings that night. I say "poor" because no one could have had more mixed emotions. Who could've said "no" to joining The Temptations? If he did that, though, where was his loyalty to his old friend David? So the group had hired guards to keep Crazy David out of the theatre-in-the round. (It seemed to me that in the midst of the chaos, he came madly swinging in on a rope. I was most definitely not on drugs, but Cornelius tells me this is a glitch in the banks of my memory, a figment of my imagination--I guess it's a fertile one). In any case, the switch was made. David went down hurt and fighting, but down he went nonetheless, and his career with The Temptations drew to an screeching halt. At that point, I began referring to them as "The Imitations", and things only got more absurd from there. As of now, there's only one original member. (Sadly, I've had to revise that number one by one far too many times since I started writing this memoir).

And so, David Ruffin struck out on his own to be the Mega-Star he'd been psyched into thinking he was. Mostly, he just struck out. Between Christmas of '65 (coincidentally just when he moved in with

Delivered From Temptation

TT), and '68 when he left the group, he went downhill fast. "Something" (some white powdery thing) happened to him--to his mind and to his career. He missed gigs or showed up late, he was irritable and hard to get along with, he was drinking and doing cocaine heavily--and his famous voice, his movements, and his looks reflected it. He clearly didn't know how to act. As for me, I believe he thought that was how a superstar was supposed to be!

So no more Tammi, no more Temptations. Nothing more to stand between us. Yet it still took two more long, difficult, awkward and unhappy years for us to really get back together.

It was at that point that David slid the pretty young Tonya into the picture, and it became obvious that he still was not "coming home" to me and his son. At the time, a friend of his had become my "shoulder to cry on." And, you guessed it, I started going with him. It was the "next best thing to being there." I was both desperately hoping to get DR back by trying to make him jealous, and also "settling." Giving up. I figured, "What the hey."

When he moved Tonya in, I changed. No more Mr. Nice Guy for me. For the first

Genna Sapia-Ruffin

time ever, I allowed myself to "vent," ever-so-slightly, just the teensiest bit of the huge store of anger, bitterness, and frustration which I had accumulated over the years. I couldn't even help it, it seemed. Or, maybe I just didn't want to help it anymore. In either case, I was at his place one night, most likely trying to get him back. As usual, all I was getting was ticked off. On the way to my jalopy, I passed his shiny, black Corvette convertible in the alley, and something finally snapped. I pulled out my good old hair-cutting razor--which I always kept in my pocket at night--and I put just a tiny little slash in the nice, new white canvas top. I took care to not miss a step, in case anyone was watching. The next day he shared with me, "Somebody cut my top last night. And I'd just had the frame fixed." A-w-w-w. If he suspected me, he didn't let on--nor did I. The satisfaction I got was disappointing, though. What a gyp.

At Christmas of '68 or '69, David had taken the baby for the holidays to his and Tonya's apartment--the same one he had with Tammi. Until this time, I was still in denial about him beating women; he didn't start on me until a couple of years later. But when I went to visit, and Tonya cracked the chained door, my world was rocked. Not only was DR gone, and the baby with him, but he had locked her in! The chain had to be opened from outside with a key--to me, a terrifying prospect which, thank the Merciful Lord, I never had to endure. When Tonya peeked through the space of a few inches, I saw a face I didn't know. True, it was the first time I'd seen her without her long, flowing hair, but more importantly, she'd been beaten to a pulp. When she confessed to me what had happened, I was shocked, astonished and horrified. He'd been gone for days. She was alone; and I suspected that she had little food or money. In a small voice, she said to me with wonder, "Doesn't he ever beat you?" I answered a resounding "No!" Now it was her turn to be amazed: "Wow." she said weakly. "He must really love you." I just didn't know how to feel. Now I do--it makes me sick.

Chapter Eight

"R$_X$ Limousine"

There was a Dr. Bader a few doors down from Hitsville, USA, the Motown recording studio, and somehow he came to be Motown's doctor in the earliest of days. We went to him for everything. I guess DR already had a file started at his office, and later, he took me there and then David Junior. Boy, now Dr. Bader would be the guy to write a book. Thank God for patient confidentiality. I don't remember whether or not it was Dr. Bader who suggested that DR get that limousine--David may have been too "grown" for Doc Bader by then--but DR did tell me it was "doctor's orders." Few people knew that. His brother Jimmie says it's a lie, that this was just David trying to outdo him, as usual. But I want to say here in David's defense: That big ego which everyone thought was him, in my opinion, wasn't what it seemed. My own conversations and experiences with him would more likely seem to indicate an inferiority complex simply manifested as that superiority complex. This is why he hung out with losers all his life. It is also why he limited himself to amateurs for management. I think he felt safer there. After all, if he ever broke down and got good management, and still failed, then he'd have no one to blame but himself. Couldn't have that. Plus, he really didn't trust himself to do the right thing--he knew he was going to mess up and didn't want to deal with that responsibility. And I'm sure that's why he avoided Los Angeles, even though it would seem logical to go where the action is in your given field. I can't tell you how many times I sat beside him on the edge of our bed in the years yet to come and just watched helplessly as he smoked a cigarette and scratched his head. Sometimes he'd look over at me for reassurance and ask things like, "Can I still sing?" "Am I any good?" That is, "Does anyone still like me? Am I okay? Am I entitled to live?" He did not feel that he deserved to quite win, personally or professionally--that Fear of

Delivered From Temptation

Success syndrome. However, he could not let any one know this--not even himself. Especially himself. (Administer dulling narcotic here--repeat as needed throughout future until inevitable death occurs).

The other reason he hung out with lowlife was because it made it easy for him to feel better by comparison. It gave him the control; it put him in power and he felt he could maintain that position amongst them. The other side of that same coin was the very reason he avoided intelligent people who had their heads on straight. The old Fear of Rejection, and Not Good Enough syndromes, in which you alienate them before they do it to you. He had suffered a lot of emotions wounds in earlier years, plus suffered from his lack of education as well--he was sensitive to it. He resented my intelligence, yet he coveted it. He once told me angrily that I thought I was smart and used big words around him just because I knew he wouldn't understand, or something to that effect. After that, I downgraded my vocabulary when I was with him so he wouldn't feel uncomfortable. It's just one example of how I was constantly under pressure trying to be the woman he wanted me to be--the trouble was that his ideas kept changing from one day to the next. It wore me out just trying to keep track.

I can't think of a time when I heard him read out loud, but his writing, if you wanted to be benevolent and call it that, gave the distinct impression that he was barely literate. His friend, Reggie, says that David brought his contracts and so forth to him for translation.

All of this is also part of the reason he couldn't stand being with me, but neither could he bear to give me up. Believe me, if it hadn't have been destiny, there'd have been no way we could've been together. He had to end it, by causing me to leave him, thereby absolving himself, on a higher level, of the responsibility of harming himself further. He told me from the beginning that I was different from anyone he'd known and that he wasn't good enough for me. I didn't hear him. When we first moved together on Gladstone, he asked me for a list of reasons why I loved him. He was serious. In my innocence, I tried all day, but could only come up with things that I didn't like about him. When he came home that night, I teasingly told him of my dilemma. As far as I was concerned, it didn't matter to me

Delivered From Temptation

why I loved him--I just did. In 1965, that was supposed to be enough. It wasn't.

At some point in our second attempt at co-habitation, on Parkside Street, I had taken a job selling Avon to buy food and to heat the place. He sat and pouted for a couple of days, then he told me that I had "emasculated" him (a big word he had heard). Years later, when I complained to a friend and confidante about it, he scoffed, "Didn't take much, did it?" Good one--as David would have said.

Again though, according to Bro' Jimmie, I give far too much credit. He says that the David I knew and loved never existed. That he was a complete fabrication of David's (I guess it's called an alter ego), and that all he ever said to me was a scam and a lie. And that all that he ever did was a perpetration. I must be a dreamer--a romantic, I guess. Gosh, it all seemed so real to me!

Nevertheless, I think David's problems stemmed from the same illness that apparently affects too many other black men: low self-esteem. History wants to rear its very ugly head here, but I'll just say that help can be found in therapy (in my experience, I had better success with Christian counseling, as opposed to any other kind of therapist, psychologist, psychiatrist or counselor), if you seek sincerely and virtually prostrate yourself before it. It is extremely challenging, but if you can sublimate the ego long enough to begin to see a light, it's well worth the struggle. Especially if the alternative is death, or worse yet, a living death. Take your pick--they both stink.

Back to my point--for whatever reasons, that limo did upset folks. Maybe DR should have had "Rx" painted on it instead of his eyeglasses logo--that might have kept down the static. Then again, I don't think he cared a whit about keeping down static, maverick that he was.

God--when was it when he got so sick? Maybe '67. He was consuming an absurd amount of Hennessy in those days--more than cocaine, it seemed to me. True, it wasn't me living with him. But it seemed to me, as if he--with the Hennessy and Paul with the Tanqueray--had just thrown caution to the wind. Now that they could buy good liquor, they drank as if each day may be their last chance at it. Maybe they just weren't sure how long the dream could continue.

Delivered From Temptation

Regardless, DR had been riding in the group's station wagon along with all the others until then. And they were gigging a lot. There was the five of them and Cornelius Grant with his guitar, not to mention all of their luggage. Easy to see how all those legs and egos could get tangled. And David? He was a man who always wanted his way--and mostly succeeded in getting it. So it must have been tense, to say the least.

There was never time or a place to eat decent food, so they ate a lot of greasy fried stuff along the highways--whatever joint was open late at night after the gig.

Naturally, David, as well as everyone else, had to wait until the majority was ready to stop the car in order to eat. This, along with the drinking, partying, working too hard, and being "rest-broken," produced a major ulcer. In fact, he used to somewhat more than half-way joke that when he was on stage screaming his signature scream in that familiar pose with his left arm across his waist, people never knew that the real reason was pain, not passion.

We were at the Club Venus in Baltimore. From where my bodyguard and I waited for him on the parking lot, I could see him start to collapse at the top of the very long staircase out in back. His support group helped him down, and at some point, from somewhere an ambulance screeched in. With lights flashing and sirens wailing, the driver spirited him off to a hospital. In the whirlwind, I haven't any idea how I arrived there--don't think I rode in the EMS. I guess someone drove me. But who?

By the time I saw David again, he looked absolutely comatose there in the hospital bed. He was in a fetal position with his eyes rolled up in his head. Putting it mildly, I was distressed--so things are foggy here. Even so, in the blur of whatever length of time I was there, somebody brought in a priest for last rites and it seems like I vaguely remember the faces of Melvin and Otis.

Needless to say, he lived through that one, but while he was down, he promised he'd mend his ways. Come to think of it, he always made me that promise when he was down. As if I were God! And for a while, he did seem to try. Part of that trying was the limo. After all, the doctor had prescribed less stress, more regular eating and rest, and of course, less alcohol. In hindsight, though, I imagine he was doing a lot of cocaine at that point; I wasn't the one living

Delivered From Temptation

with him, so I hadn't seen it yet. He told me, though, that the doc had suggested he travel separately from the group out of concern for his health. I must have been a real sucker, because Jimmie says David never had ulcers. Let the record show...

So, one of his stooges, probably Royce, hatched up the idea of the limo. Maybe it was even DR himself--it certainly was his cup 'o tea. As in, "Yeah! A limo! That's the ticket!"

He had all his punks around him at the time encouraging The Big Head and the You-Oughta-Haves, so no telling. The last thing he needed was to have his negative aspects cultivated. Yet, the more important the wannabes told him he was, the more important they became by osmosis. As long as they could join in perpetuating that myth, they would do it. And perpetuate they did.

B-r-r-r! Royce Moore! Now there's a name that makes my blood run cold, my skin crawl, and my stomach turn. First of all, well, I'm not saying he was a pimp, as I never saw him pimping, but then how would I have known if I had? And according to *Ruffinism*, you know, if you didn't see it, it didn't happen. He was the kind of bum that my father would have called a punk. A slimeball. A dirt bag. A dirty rat-bastard. Not only that, Royce made me wonder if there was such a thing as a bisexual pimp. I guess if there are bisexual hookers, why not?

When I first came to know about Royce, he and his colleague Chuck were David's ace-boon-coon buddies. Royce had a girl named "Toy," and I forget the name of Chuck's main girl--Linda, I think. This was the mid-60's--maybe 1965. At least, it was before The Temptations first went to London.

I guess David figured that women thought Royce was fine, thereby increasing his own odds with them even more--*vice versa*, I'm sure! Royce was fairly tall. His dark hair was "feathered", his eyes were big, his lashes long, his skin light. He had a brush mustache, he dressed well and drove nice cars. But he had a little soft voice--something like Mike Tyson's--and a girly little giggle. Frankly, I don't see what women could have seen in him (other than to get to David). He was just smarmy to me!

There were several people more instrumental than others in assisting DR along his chosen path of self-destruction, and I believe Royce was one of the first. And it remained on-going. Ironically, I don't

Delivered From Temptation

recall seeing his face at David's funeral, come to think about it. Matter of fact, I've since heard that he was a grocery bag-boy in New Orleans at the time--just desserts, if you ask me. Maybe he just couldn't get off work at the Piggly-Wiggly Market that day, huh?

He pandered to every need DR had or imagined he had. And when those needs ran out, the two of them made up some new crap. This, by the way, is the mystery man whom Otis Williams for years has referred to anonymously (and in the NBC movie as "Flynn") as the guy who frequently called David "Papa" while he massaged not only his shoulders, but his ego as well. He was the very guy who, right in front of the rest of the Tempts, would tell DR that the crowd was only there to see him. He also made sure that David stayed geeked up into believing that he was The m----r f----r.(Capital "M", capital "F".) Whether Dude was "bi" or not, he was most certainly a punk.

He got David women, he got him whatever he wanted. Then, if I remember correctly, he really wimped out when David got fired from the group--he sided with them, believe it or not. Later, DR forgave him for that. He was so understanding when it came to his boys--queerly so.

For instance, here's one for the books which I remember all too well. David was going to London and, as was his way, he'd appointed one of his cronies to "babysit" me while he was away. Normally, it was Roosevelt "Bucky" Smith, the group's valet-- this time it was Royce. (H-m-m-m).

David and I were still in our first apartment on Gladstone at the time, and I worked at a bar called The Purple Onion. The designated sitter would drive me to and fro, check on me occasionally at home, *et cetera*. And, oh yes--report to DR, of course. Actually, I didn't mind; I was just a twenty-one year old Baltimore babe in the Detroit woods and I enjoyed the protection. In fact, I was flattered that he "cared" that much. But then, unbeknownst to me, Royce and Chuck, aka "Dim" and "Dimmer", had an chance brain wave that night. Royce picked me up at the bar at two-thirty A.M. after work. Claiming he had to make some kind of business run, he refused to take me home first. He drove me to Chuck's "pad", saying he'd be back soon, and that he'd take me home then. Of course, I was exhausted from work and wanted to sleep--in my own bed. The back-stabbing dirt-bags insisted repeatedly that I could just go and sleep "a while" in one of the extra bedrooms. Chuck stressed several times how far away his room was, and how safe I'd be. Since I really had no choice, I went along with it, but under duress.

I was a hairdresser by day then, and carried my trusty razor handy in my purse. With one eye open, I laid down on a bed, on top of the covers with my clothes on and my purse handy on the floor beside me. Almost immediately, I felt the bed move. Chuck was coming toward me asking me if I wanted to fight then, or afterward. I asked him to repeat his query while I did some quick thinking. At the same time, I was reaching coolly toward my purse. He noticed and retreated, asking with a nervous little laugh, "What're you gonna do--shoot me?!" As I whirled around, razor flashing, I yelled, "No, but I'm gonna cut the f---k out of your face, if you don't get away from me!!" He scrambled backwards off the bed and toward the door yelling as he hastily fled his apartment, "You're crazy! You're crazy! Just close the door when you leave!!"

Next time I saw Royce the Slimeball, I asked him just what the hell he'd thought he was doing that night. The rodent shrugged and sort of whined, "I thought maybe you'd rather be with Chuck." In other words, the pimps tried to "turn me out."

I told David when he returned from England and I think I was more offended for him than he was for himself. I guess he forgave Royce for that too--so kind. It seemed he had a natural tendency to embrace the philosophy that boys will be boys. (*Author's note! I can't believe this is possible, but a trusted friend of mine who was there, has informed me that the above-described event was one of DR's little tests. He'd set this all up before ever leaving for London in order to see if I'd sleep with Chuck or I'd be true to him. And then David "mentioned" it, that is, bragged about it, to my friend. Call me crazy, but this seems like an all-time low, even for David).

Mr. David also embraced the philosophy that the act of rape did not actually exist. He said that there "might be such a thing as getting tired of fighting", but that was no such thing as rape. Right. I tried to tell him that that's exactly what rape is, but he didn't want to hear it--probably for his own convenience. Come to think about it, I did hear via one of his road crew some vague references to him having raped some woman or women on the road--I didn't ask details; I couldn't possibly stand to know.

I never told David for fear he'd blame me, but yet another one of his pimp friends actually did succeed in raping me. And the worst of it was, that after DR and I had moved onto Parkside years later, the sleaze continued to come around, as did Chuck and Royce. It was this particular one who never stopped tormenting me. DR even had us double-dating occasionally. Of course, he didn't know about it at that point. Sadly, I'd been afraid to share it with him--and I needed to. The Sleaze would leer and lick his chops and mumble dumb pimp shit every time DR looked away. This went on for the entire four years we lived there.

And when I finally did tell David, at first he almost seemed appropriately offended-- and defensive. But then, just as abruptly, he seemed to dismiss it, mumbling something about how he'd "remember that shit." As far as I could see, not a thing changed in their relationship. I, personally, have been privileged to never have seen the scum again. I bet David forgave him too, though. What a pal! Too bad he wasn't as much of a pal to me as he was to his "boys". Or to his son, for that matter.

I'd heard that Eddie had threatened to leave the group at first if they kicked David out. For reasons only Eddie knew (money?), he did compromise his stand, and continued. Sadly, that beautiful twinkle faded from his eyes, and yes, Otis, he did seem to have a "perpetual attitude" from then on. Is it any wonder that he wore a scowl? And did he really stop his little foot-pat? Or was that just my imagination-- runnin' away with me?

Of course, I have no idea what really went on within the group at that time. All I know is that Eddie loved the hell out of David, and not like a punk as so many of his flunkies did. I never had to feel jealous of Eddie. I was glad David had him for a friend, and unlike most of his other "friends," I was always happy to see Eddie's face at the door--except for the time he caught me with two black eyes. Sure, Eddie had his faults too, but at least he wasn't an instigator or a perpetrator like most. It was more as if he and David were lone castaways in a sinking lifeboat. And when the stuff hit the fan, even Royce turned his back on David and stayed with the group.

Delivered From Temptation

Soon after Ed and I first met, it became obvious that he disliked me deeply. He made it a point to avoid DR if I were along. He didn't speak to me at all for the first six months. Why? I wasn't entirely sure. Was it was a "jealous buddy" thing, a race thing based in ignorance, or some other kind of jealousy? I never did get it.

But remember, it was 1964. Eddie was from Birmingham, Alabama, and he was young. I bet he never intended to be racist. I'm sure that over the years, his friends were certainly not exclusively black--John Oates and Daryl Hall, for two. Regardless, clearly he did not like me a bit in 1964. I guess he didn't trust me. He probably figured I meant his pal no good, even though DR himself had told him that first day at Carr's Beach, "That's who I'm gonna marry."

Over the years, we did have a few dear moments, Eddie and I, when he chose to share some personal issues with me. Yet for the most part, he remained closed--not only to me, but to most. We certainly never became what I'd describe as "friends", but he was David's friend, and I loved him for being that. David needed that from Eddie. At David's funeral, my heart hurt for Eddie. His brother told me and I do believe that he took the death of his good friend very, very, hard. We got separated in the chaos at the end of the funeral, even though he asked me to meet him at his hotel afterward. Something serious, or someone, had prevented that from happening. I tried in several ways to communicate my sentiments to him afterward, to no avail. I wanted him to know how much both David and I always appreciated him. Sadly, Eddie died before I got that chance.

Debbie told me that David had said long before Eddie died that he (Eddie) in fact knew he had lung cancer. So, looking back, it's no wonder Ed became even more morose and withdrawn than usual. It's no wonder he lost weight, which he could ill afford to do. It's no wonder he was more sullen and angry than ever, and when David died--well, that was the last straw for him. I think that's when he threw in the proverbial towel.

It's also no wonder that he didn't care a whit about being arrested for back child-support at David's funeral, though he knew in advance that it would happen.

Racist (capital "R") Louis Farrakhan and his boys crashed David's funeral, and he crassly exploited it as his own personal political forum. I do credit him for the one thing he said which was true: He admitted that he had never met and didn't know David. And even though he directly insulted me and David Junior with his racist remarks, and again the entire family by telling this long, convoluted, obviously just incredulous tale of how he was requested by David "in his will" to be there--there was no will, brother--I still appreciate that he had enough muscle with him to intervene in and defer Eddie's arrest until just after he exited the church. There he was arrested in front of reportedly ten thousand people. It was pathetic. That's a mother who wanted her child-support real bad. No wonder he and I never got together after the funeral--he was in jail.

Eddie's mom did tell me he had sworn off smoking since his first lung surgery, but I doubt he really had much fight left by then. Besides, Eddie had been smoking forever; he smoked anything. His manager told me a few months after his first surgery that they were worried about him because he "hadn't picked his weight back up." Next thing I knew, someone called me and said, "Eddie's dying." I jumped: "What!?" The next day he was gone. I shook my head--still do.

Soon afterward, I had a two-hour conversation with one of Eddie's family members who said that the thing that really hurt Eddie the most was that he didn't really know how David died. They also said that Eddie had become very religious during his illness, and had pushed and pushed until he got everyone in the family to promise to start going to church.

These may be some of the most intimate details ever revealed about an enigma that was Eddie J. Kendrick--no "S". His brother told me that he was "supposed" to have been named "Lawrence!" That might have changed the entire time/space continuum between then and now--and everyone and everything involved. Including you!

Then there was Paul. Paul Williams--a gentleman and a scholar, in his own special way. He was not only an extremely talented soulful singer with his own loyal fans--both male and female, he was also a sharp, creative choreographer for the group until Motown assigned that position to the legendary Cholly Atkins. Not only that, Paul was a riot, as well. One of the things he used to do in the early days was out-heckle the hecklers. Whenever any drunk in the audience started to get loud (or stoopid as

Delivered From Temptation

they say), Paul never failed to nip it in the bud if he was on center mike--and it seemed as if he invariably was at just that moment--almost like he waited for them!. He'd say, "Hey! I don't come on your job and tell you how to push your broom, do I?" The crowd would roar in support, and the pest would curl up and die. Once per heckler was all it ever took.

In spite of his sense of humor, his vibe always seemed kind of heavy. It was as if it were a struggle for him to be happy--he was sort of a sad clown, I guess. You got the feeling that he was a weary old soul who had traversed this path too many times before. Even his feet reflected that. If you ever wondered why he sort of sidled, it was because his old feet hurt!

His birthday was July 2nd, David Junior's is July 1st. The Moonchildren are very emotional, and now that DERj is a young man, it's obvious that he has certain qualities similar to some of Paul's. Probably most of the group never knew it, but he became David Junior's godfather. He knew David Ruffin well. And he was so good-hearted--I guess he figured that somebody had better do it.

Genna Sapia-Ruffin

I mentioned earlier that Paul rescued the baby and I at the Versailles Hotel in Cleveland when DR sent us packing to the airport one cold January night because one of his women had showed up. It wasn't the only time something similar happened, I'm embarrassed to admit. Whenever it happened, DR would suddenly lose sight of right and wrong--his attention would go directly to his own needs, wants and desires. Basically, he'd just kick me to the curb and leave me stranded. It happened both while I was pregnant and after the baby was born--it made no difference to David R, Superstar. Often I'd have no money for food or milk--not to mention airfare. Needless to say, I'd be frantic.

It was invariably Poopie (Paul) who saved me. He'd give me whatever was needed-- money, food, milk; he'd give me his room if he planned to spend the night elsewhere, which he seldom failed to do, by the way. (Beauty is only skin deep). Sometimes we'd share a room if things got that tough.

Once, we even shared a hotel bed. I was stranded and he was drunk. What a pair. Melvin Franklin's mother walked into the room in the morning, took one look at the two of us in the same bed, and without a word, turned and left. In a moment, both she and Melvin returned, looked at us and left, still without a word. It was weird--not to mention embarrassing. Although Paul and I never had sex, I'm sure Melvin and Mama Rose thought we did. Horrors! If they suspected as much, at least they kept it to themselves. I think. No one ever mentioned it to me and certainly not to David, who most definitely would have confronted me with it. Big time. For sure. No doubt.

He was crazy jealous about me, and over the years accused me of all sorts of people, but not Paul. Later on I was given the gift of enlightenment by a mutual friend of ours, that DR was perpetually at the mercy of an ongoing and chronic case of "*the guilties.*" This malady apparently caused this irrational jealous behavior. Yet and still, never Paul.

In fact, when Paul died, David very sweetly and with great compassion, sincerely empathized with me. He knew I'd loved Paul, as he did. He, too, was devastated. Of course we went to the services together. David tried to sing his "Impossible Dream" but broke down and could not finish. The rest of the Tempts came to his aide, but they couldn't do it either. Oh yeah, I just remembered--right after that, the big cardboard cutout of a gold record that was attached to the front of Paul's casket fell and rolled down the aisle. Paul, the jester still. At the time, no one laughed; they only gasped. Sitting back down with me, David put his arm around my shoulders as he said to me in comforting my deep wracking sobs, "Stop, hon. You'll make yourself sick."

He and I were the last two to leave the grave-site and when it came time for my final moments alone with Paul, we didn't need to discuss it. Without a word, David just walked several yards behind me, where he stood alone with his beautiful hands folded and waited silently for me. I can see him clearly even now. He'd bought a handsome new suit for his friend's funeral. It was gray with burgundy windowpane plaid--double-breasted. As did all of his clothes, it looked fabulous on him. Paul would have loved it.

I placed my special black orchid on the coffin, and bid my tearful fond farewells to my buddy. At some foggy point, my sweetheart came and put his hand on shoulder and led me away.

Delivered From Temptation

I'd never been in love with Paul, but I was fortunate enough to have, over the years, become personal friends with more than one woman who was. It was easy to see why he was so well-loved. Like any of us, he had his dark side, but for the most part, he was sweet and caring and lovable. Rest in peace, you old traveler, you.

Of course, whenever someone you love kills themselves, your ego demands that you wonder what it was that you could have done to change the Will of God. It was no different for me.

As to whether it was suicide or not remains a mystery to many, me included. I've talked to people with convincing theories for both possibilities.

The date was August 17, 1973. I can't recall who called us at home that day, or which of us answered the phone, but we saw a lot of Eddie in those days--it was he and David who rushed to Cole Funeral Home a few doors from Hitsville, USA.

When David came back, he said that Paul was found wearing only a bathing suit and had no identification. I've since been told by the most reliable of sources, a family member, that Paul had on a tropical print shorts set, and he did, in fact, have his wallet on him. Ironically, though, the medical examiner in the case of David's death told me that David himself did die eighteen years later in a tropical print shorts-type bathing suit without identification. H-m-m-m. Then again, David had told me also, and had always maintained, that there were two bullet holes in Paul's head--one too many for suicide. This, too, was flatly denied by my source, who was actually at the scene. This person had been with Paul both the previous day and night, as well as earlier that same day, and saw nothing in Paul's demeanor at any of those times which would have indicated that he felt like killing himself.

But then, David had a talent for creating his own reality. In other words, he was a pathological liar. If he wanted a thing to be true, in his mind it became true--and so it was.

Yet, what prompted him to create this scenario--why would he have wanted it thought that it was murder? I do know that he strongly suspected a deadly serious conspiracy between Motown and the Mob to control Eddie and him. So, it's my guess that he figured if people believed that Paul

Delivered From Temptation

was offed for political reasons, hopefully an investigation would ensue. That might get him some believers. Which, may, in turn, expose Motown, and save his (and other) careers--not to mention his life. Perhaps, he felt that then, Paul's death wouldn't have been so obscenely wasted in an act as pointless as suicide.

Or, maybe I'm just over-estimating DR big time. Maybe he just said it for the drama. I always did say that the word "drama" started with the letters "D" and "R" for a reason!

The third question people inevitably ask me: "Why did David leave The Temptations?" He'd left the group under protest in '68, like I said earlier, but a lot was left unsettled. He hadn't accepted the departure very graciously. He'd made a lot of ugly noises and probably some threats. Actually, it wasn't so long before, when he'd made it well known that he thought he deserved a bronze statue of himself popping a wheelie on his motorcycle on the lawn of Motown. Creative, wasn't he? He figured if Miss Thing (my words, not his) could have her name in front of "...and the Supremes", he deserved at least as much. I used to tell him the difference was that he wasn't sleeping with Berry.

I guess this is as good a place as any to mention this: I'm glad that she and Berry both finally came out and admitted that they have a grown child together. It was very difficult for me when I wrote this not to tell it, since it was true that all of Detroit knew it anyway--I don't know who they thought they were fooling. Although I was dying to tell, I left it out because it wasn't my place to expose it. It would have served no real purpose in my story, and could have hurt the girl. Lo and behold, they announced it just in time for my re-writes. How serendipitous!

Anyhow, the real bitch of that whole situation was that it was obvious that David was much more talented and a much stronger performer than she (another DR as in drama by the way). Not to mention that he'd already been in the position of lead vocalist with a group called The Voicemasters prior to his coming to The Temptations. So, this was a burr under his saddle as long as I knew him, and I saw his point. It frustrated him constantly. At any rate, he had been blacklisted into career limbo in 1973 when Paul died.

Delivered From Temptation

That was the limbo that David was in September of '73. It was the twenty-eighth--my birthday, and he really wanted to take me out. Believe it or not, there was no entertainment in town that night except for Bobby Vinton. It must have been a week-night--that's how Detroit was at the time. The show was at the old elegant "Michigan Palace Supper Club" and we had a front row table, of course. While we were crossing the lobby, someone ran up behind us and said to him, "Didn't you used to be David Ruffin?" M-a-n, I cringed--big time. I hurt for him, certainly, but it also was things like that which could a trigger for me getting my ass beat when we got home. Then, just to add insult to his injury, they thought I was Freda Payne, who was hot at the moment. We went to our table, and in the twinkling of an eye, DR had mysteriously disappeared. I was tuning up to get ticked, but I was pleasantly surprised to see that he came right back. Next thing I knew, Bobby was dedicating "Happy Birthday to Mrs. David Ruffin." Just when you were least expecting it, DR could always pull a charm or two out of his hat.

Cocaine: Personally, I've been blessed to have never been a user. As hard as it may be to believe, and to his credit, David never once tried to get me to do it. By this time, though, his own use had gradually escalated into abuse--and that's with a capital A. Although, it is hard for me to know clearly how much he was using, because he pretty much kept it from me. And, I suppose I was glad he did. I honestly didn't know it then, but in analyzing it later, it must have been true on a subconscious level that I didn't want my own world, such as it was, to fall apart, so I didn't look too closely at how much coke he was doing. I guess I was following the *Ruffinism* which states "if you look for trouble, you'll find it."

It's been my observation that, in this society, men are taught to identify and value themselves only by their work and how much money they make. This creates tragedies. David had no idea what was going to happen to his career--what was to become of him. He was scared. He was scared and he used cocaine--a dangerous combination. It made him past scared, it made him paranoid. And belligerent. As a matter of fact, we had two Doberman pinschers at the time named "Bonnie" and "Clyde." I always joked that we should change their names to "Paranoid" and "Belligerent"--after David. Of course, I did not say this to his face!

Delivered From Temptation

So, back to the point, David felt that the organization "doing business as" Motown had had Paul killed as an example of what could happen to him and Eddie if they didn't toe the line. They were both still under contract, but making lots of waves--rebels with a just cause. He said that this "new" Motown had picked Paul because he was more valuable as a lesson than anything else. They had used him all up, and he'd become pretty much expendable at that point.

He also confided in me that someone had attacked him and Eddie and Cornelius at Paul's wake. They'd knocked them down, yanked David's brown leather shoulder bag off him, and stole his phonebook with all his business connections in it. They snatched off his jewelry, then threw it back at him while sneering something like, "Here, you can keep this." David clearly said that they were standing on his hand at the time. The three of them had seen the black sedan waiting across the street when they went into the wake. Cornelius told me recently that he had thought it was some people David knew, but it was not. In actuality, David felt it was a terror-tactic to get even more control and that they really only wanted to take away all his power via his phone-book and terrorize him and Eddie into submission.

Sometimes, David kept certain things from me just for my own protection, so it was, at best, sketchy then, and even foggier now, but he was very concerned. He even talked to me about plans to get DERj and I out of town for a while, but then things cooled down--for the time being.

Was it only that cryptic, paranoid imagination of David's at work? I guess we will never know. Or was it some elaborate scheme to get me out of the way so one of his women could fly in? Did her plans change? N-a-a-h-h! This time, I don't think so.

"They" blackballed him, for all intents and purposes. He never did get out from under that thumb. Makes one wonder who--or what--that power really was. It's sickening, frankly. ("Toby, bring me that whip").

Me--aka Sweetie--about age 5

Sweetie about age 7

Honor Roll Graduate--1961

Manager Wig World--early 1964

Meet The Temptations--June 1964

David & I at 20 Grand--1969 ish

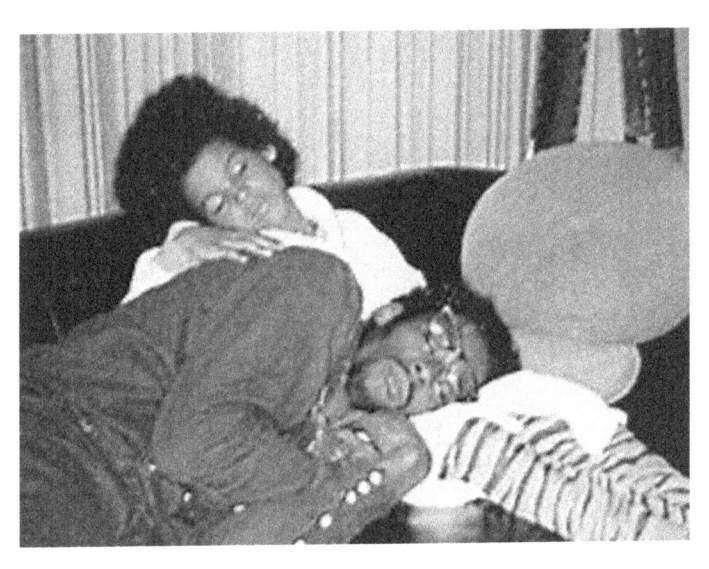

Davids Senior & Junior, Catching Z's--1971 ish

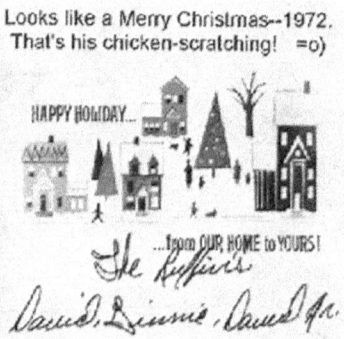

Looks like a Merry Christmas--1972.
That's his chicken-scratching! =o)

Our Merry Christmas 1972

A
Celebration
of the life
of
DAVID
ELI RUFFIN, SR.

January 18, 1941 - June 1, 1991

Monday, June 10, 1991
at 1:00 p.m.

New Bethel Baptist Church
8430 C. L. Franklin Blvd.
(formerly Linwood)
Detroit, Michigan 48206

Rev. Robert Smith, Jr., Pastor
Officiating

"... And now, the end is near and so I
face the final curtain. My friends, I'll say it clear,
I'll state my claim, of which I'm certain.
I've lived a life that's full,
I've traveled each and every highway
But more, much more than this, I did it my way..."

We Tragically Lose David--1991

Genna as in Jenna, not Gina as in Gina--2009!

Chapter Nine

"Makings of a Man"

Davis Eli Ruffin was born on January 18, 1941 in Whynot, Mississippi. (["In response to your inquiry] Whynot is the name used by a little community in the southeastern portion of Lauderdale County, Mississippi, on Highway 19 South between Meridian and the Alabama line. Mississippi state road maps show it. The Meridian & Bigbee Railroad, a local freight line that carries mostly wood products between producers and suppliers in east Mississippi and west Alabama, runs through it."...Buddy Bynum, Editor, The Meridian Star.)

According to him, his mother (Ophelia) had died some ten months after giving birth to him, the last of the Ruffin children.

She'd had heart trouble, he said, and complications had set in. God only knows what truly happened at that time and in that place. His father (Eli) then married Miss Earline, who had been a teacher there. Seemingly, they had known each other for a while already. From my knowledge of and conversations with "Mama" Earline, who seemed to me like a very sweet lady, the marriage was probably a blessing for the children, as I didn't get the idea from David that Eli was much of a father. David either inherited that trait or copied it, if the type of father that he became himself was any indication. Apparently Jimmie was actually more of a father to Davis. But who was Jimmie's model of how to be a father and a man?

"Mama" is now ninety-some years old, and still lived in Meridian until a few years ago. She now resides in a retirement home in a near-by town. I had kept in touch with her over all these years, until she went there and beyond my reach. Between her stories and David's, I've tried to piece together the puzzle that was his enigmatic past. (*Authors note: Earline Ruffin has since passed on).

There had also been vague insinuations about some kind of sexual abuse as a toddler--and older as well. I was not there--obviously I have no facts--but suffice it to say that I believe he had a traumatic childhood. I mean, who didn't, right? But he seemed to have never gotten over it. It had the potential of being the catalyst for a very emotionally wounded adult. That is, in fact, exactly what he became.

For years, I tried to find out more about his boyhood—find out why he was the way he was. What had he gone through? What had set him on a path of self-ruin? All we did know was that we knew nothing. Now thanks to Quincy, we do know more. For this I'm very thankful on so many levels.

Then there was the scuttlebutt about him going to jail at nineteen for writing bad checks. I'd hate to think what horror could have happened to the likes of him there-

-might explain a lot. I believe it was after he'd come to Detroit and begun to hang out with Eddie Kendrick.

There was another Eddie involved in David's life as well--a wannabe player from Chicago. He was a lot older than David. He talked and looked utterly "country"--homely, missing front teeth, and as was the case with Royce and so many others, he clung to DR in hopes of catching the overflow of women. It was he who really pointed David down the Road to Ruin, if you ask me. He made sure he had a good map and plenty of "supplies." He kept DR surrounded with plenty of his little girlies--he and his "main lady" both did. The two of them incredibly called themselves trying to "adopt" David when he was seventeen or eighteen years old. Probably what they were really trying to do was to exploit his talents--some might call it pimping.

In 1958, Vega Records made the first recording of what was supposed to be David's voice--it wasn't. It was called "You and I" w/"Believe Me" on the flip, under the

Delivered From Temptation

name "Little David Bush." I wasn't real sure what Earline meant when she told me she "put a stop to all that", but I noticed that no further recordings were made under that pseudonym.

While writing this memoir, I had the remarkable experience of listening repeatedly to those originals with the intent of identifying and verifying for the owner, a collector and former musician at Motown, if it was David Ruffin, in fact, singing. Unbelievably and without a shadow of a doubt, it was not. I know David's voice. I also know Eddie Bush's toothless voice. The man who recorded those songs was Eddie Bush, not David. God only knows why they allowed this fraud to continue all these years--God, Eddie Bush and Gwen Gordy. She was a co-writer and, surprise, Berry's sister. Wonder what that was all about? Perhaps it was an attempt to support the case that Eddie was trying to build, in order to create the illusion that David was his son--no doubt it had something to do with money. Or maybe David was shy! David Ruffin? Nah! I can't see that; not even back then. At least, not THAT shy! I just know what I know--it was neither David Bush nor David Ruffin. I wonder what they meant to do when it was time to go onstage? (*Author's note: Since first writing this book, I've heard that Eddie Bush denies that it was him and that, in fact, it was David. I could have sworn it was not David. But, now I don't know anymore. And I guess, for all intents and purposes, it doesn't matter at this point anyway---except to his children and grandchildren).

According to Earline, his father "did not support" David. She said that, although "it was Jimmie Lee who put the devilment in him" (whatever that means), "none of them wanted him." She told me that Eli "gave David to some singers in Texas" at the age of fourteen or fifteen. (This may have been when Jimmie started calling him "Permalube" for the way he was wearing his hair--most likely his first 'do).

Moreover, Earline said, "They took all his clothes and put him in a big coat and left him in Texas." Luckily, she had

Delivered From Temptation

taught him where he lived and how to get home. Somehow, he found his way onto a Greyhound. Somebody gave him cookies and an RC Cola, and he got as far as Memphis. He wrote her from there and she said she sent him money to get home. Both she and David had told me about the talent shows he had been in with the legendary Little Richard and with Elvis Presley. It seems like this might've been during the time that he was stuck there in Memphis.

There were both some profound parallels and differences between David and Elvis. What do I feel that David Ruffin could've possibly had in common with the "King of Rock 'n' Roll? H-m-m-m, let me see. We know they were both very talented singers and showmen from the South--both country and both Capricorn. But what else? Well, both suffered fatal drug overdoses, but one (the white one) died on his bathroom floor of prescription drugs (and palace or ghetto, it's still a bathroom floor). The black one, on the other hand, died of an overdose of non-prescription drugs on the sofa in a crack house. The first one (the white one), is revered, practically worshipped, and the other (the black one), is berated and scoffed at for the way he died. What is wrong with this picture? Think about it, America.

Another thing Earline told me was that David used to get teased about his looks as a child. He and his older sister, Rita Mae, looked alike and favored "Mr. Ruffin"--as Earline never failed to call him. They were dark, while Jimmie and half-brother Quincy (the oldest) were lighter. Not only that, but based on their looks as the grown men that they were when I met them, I imagine that the two older brothers were on the husky side. David, to the contrary, was "scrawny" even then. She said they taunted him, saying he wasn't part of the family and so on. I guess kids can say such stuff to each other. But it sounded like skin-tone bias to me.

According to David, his maternal grandfather, Levi Davis, was part Native American. Of course, I'd never seen the gentleman, but David used to describe him, although I don't think he ever knew him.

Delivered From Temptation

I've since gathered from Earline that Levi's legendary "long straight, black hair" was more a figment of David's imagination than anything else. Although it was true that Ophelia's hair did fit that description--at least in the single photo that David had of her. According to Quincy, though, it didn't "do her justice." Certainly, it showed that she did have very smooth beautiful skin and incredible cheekbones, so anything's possible. So after all, those chiseled features of David's surely could have been a reflection of that origin.

He did have fine and delicate features--and incredibly smooth skin. In the early days, he had no facial hair. At all! Couldn't grow any. He could never get sideburns to fill in, and he didn't shave, or need to. He had five or six tiny hairs on his chin, which he'd have me extricate with my trusty tweezers. He had those high cheekbones and an "Indian" nose. I always loved that nose.

According to David, he grew up relating to Earline as his mom, since Ophelia died while he was an infant. He was a very sickly, puny little runt of a boy, Earline said. They'd both told me that he'd had rheumatic fever when he was a baby. Evidently in those days, especially in the South, and maybe even more so under certain conditions, not a lot was done about it. She said that "Li'l Davis" used to sleep in the bed with her and "Mr. Ruffin." He whined a lot, and at night, he'd cry to her: "Mama, Mama! Turn over and hug me!" (Later, as a father himself, he'd had the audacity to get on David Junior's case about whining when he was little. At least until Earline told me that, and I busted him about it).

She talked about the times when, as a baby, she'd have to "lay po' Li'l Davis across my lap and pound him on his skinny little back" trying to keep him from choking on phlegm. She said she'd reach right down his throat with her finger and "pull out the strings of mucus" which often threatened to strangle the very breath out of his body.

Even though she was, of course, "only" his step-mother, she loved him dearly from a baby on up, and took very good and special care of him, probably more than anyone else.

Shamefully, as time and space (or was it fame and fortune?) intervened, David's contact with Earline waned greatly. To the best of my knowledge, it diminished to little or nothing. We had, one November in '71 or '72, sent first for my mother--who had acquiesced by that point--and then Earline, to come and spend two weeks respectively with us in Detroit. Evidently, it was one of the closest times David had with her since he'd left Mississippi. And, based on what I saw and heard, or rather didn't, it was more of a visit with me and David Junior than anything else. In fact, I'd confided in her how David had been beating me. Her instantaneous response was, "I'd a been waitin' behind the door for that sap-sucker!" I felt I had an ally. She was strong and wise and probably ahead of her time. I guessed she'd been quite a match for her old "Mr. Ruffin."

Between David and me, I was the one who made sure she got her greeting cards and gifts and pictures, and she'd often say to me, "Have you heard anything from that David? I haven't." She said that on the rare occasion--before he moved to Detroit--when he would send her a few dollars, the note would invariably read, "Buy yourself some Cokes, Porky Pig." Sometimes I still wrote that to her in a note. One day, while she was still living in her house, I called and called, but one answered the phone. I called fairly often, so this naturally concerned me. I did the only thing I could think to do from Detroit, I phoned the Meridian police and asked if they would go check on her. By then, she'd already been moved out and into the facility. I think first she was taken to a hospital, then to the home. The doctors described her condition to me as Organic Brain Syndrome. I asked for a definition, and it means that she just didn't comprehend anymore. Sometimes when I spoke with her on the phone, she knew me; other times she did not. I'm afraid it's a battle that old age always wins. After her "Li'l David" died in 1991, she just aged real fast. Judging from how she talked to me, that just broke her heart.

As for David, to me it's a hard-hearted man who'd just disregard--for the most part--even the woman who raised him as her own. Of course, I didn't find out about that facet of him until we were involved way deep--living together and with a son. So there hadn't been a time when I could have foretold the future by using that as a barometer. I'm not sure it would have made a difference anyway.

I don't know if David was in Meridian or Memphis when Eli died of heart trouble. He was fifteen and a half, Earline said. She was away, working as a teacher in "Newton County." When I asked her if Eli loved David, or "Davis" as she mostly called him, at first she said, "Huh?" I repeated myself, and her voice ominously dropped an octave as she growled, "Mr. Ruffin didn't love nobody!" (A while ago I asked Jimmie what Eli was like and he said, "According to Quincy, a lot like me." If by that he meant arrogant, self-centered, and obnoxious, I can understand why Earline said that).

Evidently, it was after Eli died that Jimmie took David to live with him. As Earline put it, "Jimmie was the cause of Davis leaving me." She said that he wanted David with him in order to manage his money, and that David was "bull-headed like Mr. Ruffin." (This I believe). Then, too, she said that David was "born gifted"; when I asked her if she meant gifted with his voice, she said, "with everything." She said he was gifted, too, when it came to money, but that he could "always be too liberal"--and "Jimmie Lee was always jealous of David", and "picked on him and fought him", and was "always mean and bullied him." (This, too, I believe). She said that once, when David was living with Jimmie, it got so bad that the police were called.

I don't know, all that could be the rambling of a mom with a favorite. Yet, I can appreciate it--I would've drawn the same conclusions myself based on personal experiences with the two of them later in life.

"Mama" Earline closed that particular conversation with me by saying "Davis was a sweet, good baby, and I miss him. Since he died, sometimes I just find myself just sittin' and cryin'."

David was a man who loved having women around--I'm sure now that he must have had five in every city and five in every town. Yet he didn't really like or respect them. Although, who knew then what a misogynist was? And how could a man who seemed so fun at first, be so demonic when the dark set in? Retrospectively, having raised my own son the hard way, I believe that David Senior was never taught that concept as a child. After all, how can a boy-child learn love with respect (as opposed to love without it) for his mother--in fact, for all or any women--if he doesn't see it lived in the home? Unhappily, this left David ill-prepared to be a Daddy, and/or a good example. Since his father didn't have the skills himself and David left home so young, a lot of what he should have learned by way of a foundation was missing. Seems as if he missed "Kindergarten", and was catapulted straight into the "College of Hard Knocks". If David Junior ever respects women at all, it's only by the Grace of God and his own determination; not because his father taught him to.

In regard to this convoluted issue of sexuality, as far as I personally have been able to deduce, DR was not gay. As far as I've been able to deduce, he wasn't even bi-sexual. But there have been occasions over lo these many years, when such men have approached me and, for a reason known only to them, felt compelled to try to convince me in detail of their various involvements with him. One even had a ring- -he related alleged times, dates and places. Another one--whom I somehow oddly never met, conversed with, or even heard of-- went so far as to write a so-called book a few years ago in which he'd like to have the reader believe that he knew all about Motown artists--especially David. Ever so

Delivered From Temptation

conveniently, David is dead, and thus cannot defend himself. Please allow me, to the best of my ability, to do so on his behalf. This person stated inaccurate and incomplete facts, and made oblique references--one of which was that he and David were something more than acquaintances.

What a laugh! Makes you wonder if this person really knew DR very well at all--or any celebrity, for that matter--which was his whole claim to fame. Just like all the rest, sweetie, you wish! Furthermore for the record, I never lived in Connecticut (of all places) in my life. Do some research, next time, pal. (*Author's note: since the release of said book, some friends--and some strangers--have expressed strenuous skepticism as to the validity and credibility of this guy. The general consensus seems to be, "Who the hell is he? I never saw him around either.")

Cornelius said, "I was around seventeen years and I never saw him!" Debbie Rhone said it was true that he had called her, but that he had "taken liberties" with what she'd said, taking everything out of context. She also recalls that David had actually told her that he had, in fact, taught the guy to drive--which astounded me, I must confess. I wonder if David had noticed that, by his own admission, the fourteen-year-old boy was gay. I do know though, contrary to what was claimed in the, *a-hem,* "book," that DR did not even have a car in 1966--let alone an emerald green El Dorado with a white interior. Someone has said that they thought it was Jimmie's. David Ruffin Junior said that he did recall the guy being on the road with him and his dad as they toured with Dennis and Eddie for the last couple of years before David died, but definitely remembers things differently than did the, *ahem,* "writer" did. Nedra Ruffin, probably the most misrepresented of all, says she only remembers one conversation with him--not the ten he inferred! And the limo was not lined with mink. I was there. He'd had scraps of an old mink coat re-fashioned into floor mats in the back.

Delivered From Temptation

Speaking of gay, there were plenty of times the subject came up. There were even times, more so in the end, when he'd talk to me as the old buddy I'd become and ask me why "faggots" were so attracted to him. I told him it was because he was so fine. But even years before, he used to ask me why people looked at us so. I told him it was because we looked so good. Mr. Insecurity.

In any case, he had issues about gays. And he was so fierce about it. He'd rant, "I'll kill a m----r f---ing faggot." It was his *mantra*, his call. But oddly enough, he wasn't actually as homophobic as he let on. He liked for people, me included, to believe that he was, but I watched him over many years--and to quote one of his earliest songs, "Action Speaks Louder Than Words." I had questions.

Around the end of 1971 or the beginning of '72, my friends and I arranged a *rendezvous* between David and Rod Stewart, who idolized him. You could (still can) see it in every move, every step--with every skyward toss of the mike and every growl that escaped his throat. It was so obvious, in fact, that my friends, in shock and disbelief, had come rushing to get me and dragged me back to the Princess Theatre in Royal Oak, Michigan where he was first gigging solo. This was before he was known, except to Small Faces fans. They say imitation is the most sincere form of flattery--in that case, I guess Michael Bolton admired David too. But anyway...

Rod's middle name is David, and they are both country Capricorns. So, all things considered, it seemed logical that we facilitate a meeting between them. Rod had a huge success at the time with David's smash," (I Know) I'm Losing You." David had been banished from The Tempts just after that release, and had been pretty morose lately. We just didn't want to see his thunder stolen away that cheaply.

So, we dressed him up and took him out. We had to drag him down to "Cobo Hall" in Detroit, which, by the way, is the greatest rock 'n' roll venue in the States! When we got there, Rod was already into "Losing You."

We *bogarted*--David's word for "pushed"--our way in, as was customary, maybe even a little heavier on the elbow action than usual. We were running up ramp after ramp like blind screaming banshees, trying to find the backstage entrance. (Whose heel was it that broke off their shoe? Mine, I think!) It was chaos. We crashed our way to the edge of the stage from the wings--we were frantic to get there before Rod finished that song! We practically threw David on the stage. Okay, now he was geeked! He had worn an off-white rib-knit turtleneck, a black leather vest, black boot-cut leather pants, and black boots. Rod was barefooted in a pink satin bell-bottom suit. The perfect foil; a tasty contrast of colors and textures--we could not have planned it better. Someone shoved a mike into DR's hand as he leapt onstage into his rightful spotlight.

If I told you that the crowd went berserk, would that describe the scene which followed? I think not--this was Detroit! They went totally ballistic. They moved *en masse* to the edge of that stage, and stayed there screaming, yelling, and throbbing as one in ecstasy for the entire forty-five minutes that David and Rod jammed that tune. They truly raised roof on the sucker that memorable night. Check out the photo and copy elsewhere in this book from a 1972 issue of *Creem Magazine*--history in the making!

Now, mind you, there had been rumors that Rod was gay too. Evidently it was the vogue in some rock and roll circles--mainly British--to start and perpetuate these sexual innuendos to keep the mystery and interest abounding, I assume. This they did to sell records and just because they loved playing with peoples' heads and had that power! It was a game--definitely a rock 'n' roll fantasy. If Rod were gay, I must say that he was the most successful gay man I'd ever heard of at having beautiful women and making babies.

But at the time, the game was still in play--people just weren't sure. Naturally, it came up in the car on the way to the after-party, and when David heard it, he hit the proverbial roof. He didn't want to go anywhere near Rod, as if he could "catch

Delivered From Temptation

it". He wouldn't even go in the party--we had to leave. He was chanting his *mantra* loud and long. This time I think it was more of a professional protectiveness. He really didn't want to get too close to the funky white rockers who admired his style just a little too much. He didn't want them to rip him off any more than they already had; he didn't trust any of them. At least that's what Jimmie told me. Can't say as I blame DR for that.

I don't think he really came to grips with the sexual issue. He did have certain feminine qualities, which I admired, but he hated them--even denied them. There were things besides his physical beauty, and besides the Libra moon in his zodiac chart. I used to say that in time he became Capricorn with Libran influence and I became Libra with Capricorn influence-- *Libracorns* both.

Take the time we were going to decorate around the big tree in our front yard. Of course, I wanted to plant beautiful flowers, but he wanted to insert plastic replicas.

Genna Sapia-Ruffin

Cost less, last longer--typical Cap, right? It only took a minute for him to realize that it'd be alright, after all, to have real flowers. He went and bought them right then, and merrily we planted my (live) flowers.

When his birthday came around in '73, he happened to be gigging at the good old Twenty Grand. I took a whole day and decorated the club by myself for the occasion and for the show that night. It looked fantastic.

Now, I always had a lot of wigs, and in all different styles. Straight, curly, black, blonde, red, shag-cut, Afro, you name it. To me, growing up in the hair and wig business, they've always just been fashion accessories to me. I had about twenty at that time. The last one I bought--a long curly black wig--was just too dark for me. This wig looked about like a Jheri curl was trying to look when that came out years later--only it was dry. David's hair had started falling out pretty badly by then, and he was curious about alternatives. Just for the hell of it one day, he asked me if he could try that wig on

Delivered From Temptation

to see how he actually could look with that style of hair. I said emphatically, "Of course", and I put it on him. He'd finally grown some long sideburns, and he looked good in it, to me. After all, it was the 70's! He kept it on for a while. He got kind of attached to it, and started wearing it around the house for longer and longer spells. One day he asked me if he could wear it to the store. I told him he could wear it any place he wanted to. I didn't go with him, but I guess that little excursion went without incident (who would've told the Emperor if he was wearing no clothes, anyway?) So, by the time his birthday gig came around, he was ready to wear it onstage that night.

And apparently, he wore it on at least one TV appearance on Soul Train after I'd left him. I say "after", because I knew nothing about this until fans sent me the magazine article with that infamous picture! (I was shocked, in fact, but now I have it framed on my "family wall").

He had a tailor, but David and I had done the larger portion of the designs for several new pieces of stage-wear for him, and they were rather *avant garde*--or to put it another way, "far out." And so was the tailor. But DR was in the mood for it all; so was I. One light yellow satin bell-bottomed jumpsuit--these styles are hot again, in some circles--had a floor-length full cape of hunter green velvet. It had a big dramatic Dracula-type collar, and a lining to match the suit. Another stunner was the "pink 'n' mink." It, too, was a jumpsuit with bells (polyester, I imagine. A-r-r-g-g-h!), and he had the tailor put some old scraps of white mink from glory days gone by onto the pockets, cuffs and collar for trim. He'd had peau de soie shoes dyed to match each outfit. With his build, he could wear anything, and wear it well. He looked great, and we both (dysfunction as a bond--how sweet) had always gotten a rush from shocking people. (Favorite bumper-sticker: "Being weird is not enough.")

Well, he was tearing the joint down. Everyone was on their feet, screaming--including me. One lady standing next to me yelled over the noise, "And you let him out of the house like that?!" "Let him?" I yelled proudly over the din, "I helped him!"

I've always been the kind of person to promote at least self-awareness, if not self-realization. Since all humans have both male and female factors, to one degree or another, I encouraged David to at least acknowledge his feminine side--maybe in hopes of dealing with it and dispensing with some anger. As far as I know, it didn't help him. When I left him in '74, he was still dealing with it. Of course, it was probably one of the main factors behind the violence. He'd denied that part of himself so ferociously, he'd swung to the other side of the scale. He'd just played it too damned macho for his own good. (I wish I'd known then what I know now about how to help people; my ideas weren't that wise back then. But, hey, I was lost too. I'm lost no more, praise God).

Chapter Ten

"Wedded in the Twilight Zone"

Sometime around October of '70, I met a man who wanted a wife and a kid. David had been evicted from the apartment on Hazelwood while he was on the road, and Tonya had taken advantage of the opportunity to high-tail it to Los Angeles to become a star. A friend of his arranged for the big, beautiful English Tudor house on Parkside Drive for him without his even seeing it. He was in a jam; his stuff was being put out on the sidewalk, so he didn't have a choice. He was probably happy just to get anything, and especially to have someone else deal with his mess. When he came in off the road, he was taken to his new address--his first house. All his stuff had already been put in place there for him. He was ego-tripping pretty hard during that phase--it was during his "I'm really the m----r f----r now" stage. That's capital "M", capital "F"! And most of his "friends" made sure he kept that delusion going. After all, it was great for their business. Never mind that they were killing "the goose that laid the golden egg."

Emotionally, I had hit a new all-time low. In the fall of 1970, I had reduced myself to things like parking in his driveway all night trying to get him to let me in, or to just look out the window.

That's the vulnerable state I was in when my "spiritual advisor" came into view. He was the *guru* in an East Indian "religion". (They prefer to call it a "philosophy", but I now prefer to call it a "cult"). Soon after, I met the man I married. Little David was four years and four months. He needed a daddy. It was clear that DR had no intention of settling down and taking on his parental duties, and I accepted that he was never going to come back to me. Oh, we still saw each other, but I wanted more--much more. ("You gotta watch what you wish for, you may get it.") I was just tired of waiting on Big David.

Delivered From Temptation

I needed a full-time partner, and the baby needed a male role model. Now, this guy knew that I was in love with David, but he still wanted to marry me. We would have an arrangement. I'd cook and clean, and he'd pay the bills. We'd have separate bedrooms, unless I fell in love with him and decided otherwise.

It just so happened that DR had started to pay a lot of attention to me once he thought I might be getting married. (He swore that's why I did it. That's not true, but if it worked that way, hey). Reg, David's friend and later mine, said that DR was really jealous because the guy was younger than he was, which he definitely was not--to the tune of thirteen years not. I guess David wasn't seeing clearly, with all that jealousy clouding his vision.

Then I did it--I married the guy, although I still can't believe it. It must have been around October of '70, and it was obviously strictly fate. I felt as if I were in a foggy segment of The Twilight Zone, trust me. My long-time girlfriend, Angel, gave me a stunning, bias-cut, black velvet antique dress with long beaded sleeves, which I wore at the ceremony. The "marriage" only lasted about two months--the moment he started trying to make me sleep with him, it was over.

When I told him so, he said he'd never divorce me. I told him, pointedly, that he could consider himself divorced as far as I was concerned and to go back to wherever it was he'd been before we met. He did move out of the house he'd rented for us in Highland Park (part of Detroit), and Little David and I stayed on there. My girlfriend Jeannie took her two boys and left her husband about then, and I moved them in with me. It was a fairly big old house, and when my girlfriend Brenda needed a place to stay, I moved her in too.

Needless to say, there was a lot of hustle and bustle going on there, and it must have looked a lot more attractive to DR that winter than sitting up all alone without heat in that big old huge Dark Shadows-looking mansion of his. He knew he always had an excuse to come over in Little David. He liked my friends, who labeled him "Big David", and they liked him. He felt quite at home there. He liked Jeannie's little boys, and he also got to spend his days with his son, not to mention his nights with me. My "husband" had long since moved out, and David must have found himself being pulled as if by a magnet, for he wound up practically living there. He just thought it was because he couldn't afford to buy oil for his furnace--surprise to him. It was Destiny rearing its ugly head.

He brought clothes over. He spent the Christmas holidays with us--and I pulled off a big surprise party for him there for his thirtieth birthday, soon after New Year's of '71. We were all having a ball, and I guess he was falling in love with me again. Or, the love he already felt was growing again.

One evening, he took David Junior and I to a movie, and when it was over, he just drove us to his house. That was it, really. That's how we moved into the house--we just sort of did. I remember him holding me in his lap in a big, white, round leather chair by the picture windows on that romantic night--nothing but moonlight illuminated the room (oh that's right, his electricity was shut off!) In fact, it was there that he said he thought I'd gotten married just to make him jealous. Oh sure, a few days later he must have taken us back for clothes and furniture and stuff--but, really, we didn't have to talk about it much at all. It was just time--and we both knew it.

It was one more chance--a new life. A seven year-old rocky-road love affair was finally settling down--David and me, and Little David. God was in His heaven. I guess both David and I had grown up somewhat since our first go at living together. We felt we were adults now, the baby was four, and we had a wonderful, big new house, and a car (not the limo, long since repossessed). No, David brought the black 'Vette. At that time, it had a Playboy emblem on the driver's door, but we *Libracorns* decided to paint it out. That, however, wasn't enough to convert it into the family car that we needed. DERj could hardly fit into the back window anymore, and when it was time, David Senior merrily traded it. (Not before I had my fun with it, though. He used to teasingly say he knew I was sneaking down to the corner, and then peeling out, but I wasn't--at least not consciously).

Of course, he hadn't had sense enough to invest money, so we started out broke again--just on a higher level. Our house note was more than six times what we paid on Gladstone just five years before, but it was still due the first of each month. Gigs were few and far between, again, but at least the pay was better. The music business is tough. It can chew you up and spit you out--especially if you're on their Shit List, which he was. David seemed happy to shed his old image and life and to clutch at a more substantial success--peace of mind. Evidently, he'd begun to wonder if that didn't lie in being a family man. Jimmie says David had always wanted to be a "good family man" like him. "Gettin' old", David called it. "Gettin' mellow", I said. Genevieve and Eli--the old marrieds--were born.

He seemed to love this new life. He tried really hard. He was so conscientious, so domesticated! He cleaned, he baked, he was the official gravy master. He shampooed carpet, he even hand-crafted and inlaid a big "R" monogram in the carpet inside the walk-in closet off the master bedroom. He vacuumed, he dusted, he landscaped; it was really very sweet. And what a feather-in-the-cap it was for us with the neighbors when we got the latest high-tech in garbage cans. Sears first came out with the one on wheels. And we were proud as peacocks to have our own. We were family, by gosh!

And, he was so fastidious about his personal hygiene. (He'd always been, really--that's why I was so dismayed years later when I saw him living like the addict that he'd become. It had gotten so he didn't care how or where he slept, or how he kept himself. It was both heart-breaking and disgusting. He could be all dressed up in a tuxedo for a gig, but his hair would have not been cut--as if the gig were just a chore to go and do, get paid and go right back and get high. He might be sleeping on a mattress in the midst of garbage the very next time he closed his eyes; that was the way he was living).

Early on one real cold, snowy January morning in 1971, I left David in bed on Parkside pretending to be asleep, while I went to meet my girlfriend Jeannie at the courthouse. I was going for my divorce, and I might need a witness. The minute I started to explain to the judge that we'd had an arrangement, he yelled, "Arrangement!? Divorce granted! Pay the clerk one dollar! That was it. I went home and crawled back into bed where my David still lay curled up sleeping. It was suddenly a very good morning to stay there too.

Then one day shortly thereafter, David slapped me. It both shocked and scared hell out of me. It was a powerful open-handed slap which knocked me from our vestibule to the opposite corner of that huge living room, where I landed in that big, round, white leather chair. I saw stars. I was both stunned and horrified. And, oh yes, humiliated--two of his worthless flunkies had stood by silently and watched. Although David broke my ear-drum, I didn't know it until I washed my hair that night and tasted shampoo. The reason he did it? Cocaine. Plain and simple. He was coming from a road trip, came in wired, found something he didn't like there (like his old girlfriend, Mary), and twisted everything to blame me!

In retrospect, I remember him once telling me on Gladstone, probably '65, that the only reason he didn't beat me was because I bruised so easily. I didn't take him seriously--there'd been no need to. He changed it all in that one pivotal moment in January of '71. By then his logic was overridden by a madness induced by his substance abuse. And my confidence was replaced by terror. He hated that. He used to beg me, "I don't want you to be afraid of me"--as if I had control of it. He really hated the change the fear caused in me--in us. And, God knows, even more so did I. And I would have not felt it, if that were possible. I tried to will it to be, just like I tried to will myself not to bleed, which I would've done for him if I could've, but it was too late. It was like a snowball rolling down the side of a snow-covered hill. Dammit--I hated him for making me afraid of him--he robbed me. That was the actual turning point--the beginning of the end for us.

A lot of nights between '71 and '74, I only had to hear the 'Vette in the drive, or his voice on the phone, or even just have a thought of the impending doom, and I'd get so sick to my stomach that I'd have to use the bathroom.

It wasn't until many years later--when I learned about energy *chakras* of the body--that the phrase "scared shitless" came to have new meaning for me. (The lowest *chakra* theoretically relates to lower emotions or nervous system and bowels--it's the fear center).

Then in September '71, he threw me a champagne birthday party and invited all my friends. He gave me a dozen long-stemmed red roses--and, oh yes, a Blackgama mink coat to match his. The only trouble was, he'd beaten me up just before that. At least the bruises were gone by the time of the party. I told him later that I didn't want him to buy me expensive gifts like that--only because I knew they were "guilty-gifts." He said, "But it's my (Capricorn) way of showing you that I love you." I replied, "If you wanna show me you love me, just stop beating me up"

Things only got worse from there. In November, he broke my nose for the first time. I was so pitifully needy and alone that I immediately attached myself to my kindly doctor. He was the first person who'd shown concern and sympathy since the beginning of my nightmare. Although, as was the custom in those golden days, he did not report it to the police to my knowledge. Having been anesthetized, I fuzzily remember mumbling to him, "I love you, Dr. Rollins", while being wheeled into the operating room. Good thing DR didn't hear--he'd have beat my ass again.

I knew I had to really leave David. Like a good little abusive, yet loving spouse, he never missed visiting hours twice a day, so I had to go straight from the hospital bed at six in the morning to avoid him. Taking with me only my life's savings of six dollars, I left him a note on the pillow in the place where he usually found me. Things were so critical that I had painfully swallowed what was left of my pride and called my father, of all people. He spoke to me for the first time in ten years (based strictly on the my leaving

David,) and agreed to prepay a one-way ticket to Baltimore.

The first words out of my "father's" racist/sexist mouth after all those years of his telling people I was dead and forbidding my name to be spoken, "What did you do to make him do it?" But still, he was my only escape--his sole condition was that I "leave the half-breed kid." I was so deadly serious about breaking all ties, not to mention desperate, afraid for my life, exasperated, weary and confused, that I did just that. Daddy convinced me it was for the best. He could be very persuasive when necessary.

I left my son at home with his father, *naively* thinking that I could make a clean break and start a new life. It was right before Christmas, and I knew as soon as I got to Baltimore that it wasn't a good time for this. I knew it was a big mistake. No way could I live without my little baby boy. I sobbed and wept and petitioned the Lord for three weeks. I stayed away as long as I could, then I went home--to my own little family, such as it was.

David and I had been in constant touch, in any case, and he had made every promise on the face of the earth, and then he wrote some new ones: He'd get help, he'd get off drugs, we'd see a marriage counselor--why, we'd get married! What a concept! He'd never hit me again, of course. The baby needed me. We belonged together. Call me crazy--I couldn't stay away.

Weeks later, at Christmas, he gave me a lovely white-gold wedding ring set. The bands were fashioned after intertwining vines. The diamond wasn't huge, but it looked perfect to me. He hid the box in his robe pocket and waited until everything else was opened to surprise me with it. It was an utter and breathtaking shock.

The following spring, I had to leave him again for the same reason. I went to Baltimore of course, but this time I took my kid with me. I still couldn't make it past three weeks. Again, I returned to him.

Watergate Complex, Washington D.C., October, 1972: David had a gig at a D.C. club, so we took the 'Vette and flew down there--talk about being "on the road!" At the very same time at which The Break-In was taking place, we were just down the hall making mad, passionate love. We had joked repeatedly before we left about my being out of birth-control pills--I think we both sort of wanted another baby, but neither of us really wanted to take responsibility for allowing it to happen. We had our wishful thinking--yet our life was so chaotic, I'm sure both of us were equally skeptical.

That was one minute. The next minute, David started going mad at the end of the night in the club. Needless to say, I was in a state of utter and complete dread. For another one of his imaginary reasons--perhaps something someone said or did--he beat me really badly. It was the first time he'd done it outside the house. In the confinement of the inside of that Corvette, he mentally and verbally terrorized me all the way to Detroit and into the house. (He was going further and further with each beating--maybe he was right and I should've known what to do to stop him. Obviously, that's what he wanted me to do. But short of shooting him in his sleep, I did not know what to do, and why should I have had to know what to do to stop him?) Later we talked about how the worse he beat me, the angrier he was at me for "letting" him do it and so, the worse he beat me. Actually, he was angry at himself, but since he couldn't literally beat himself, (he utilized the cocaine for that little trick,) he beat me--an extension of himself. It was complex, and he was out-of-control. Amazingly, he looked to me to end the insane cycle. This could only mean killing him, which I could not do. Maybe Jimmie was right in saying that his brother wasn't that deep--maybe his brother was just crazy.

When he was out at night without me, as he often was, of course he'd be getting high--very high. Then he'd get paranoid and belligerent, as usual. He'd come in on a b-a-a-d trip. He'd feel the television and, whether it was warm or not, he'd accuse me of quick turning it off and feigning sleep when I'd hear the Corvette coming down the street. Sometimes this would be followed by a beating, sometimes not. Either way, I would be equally terrorized.

Other times, he'd come in accusing me of having been on the phone while he was out! He'd swear he'd been trying to call all night, and the line was busy. This was obviously before "Call Waiting." Of course, I was not on the phone; I was afraid to use the damned phone for fear he'd actually try to call. So, not only was I cut off from my friends, I was too intimidated to even enjoy the phone while he was out of the house.

Once he threw his big shoe at me from across the room and hit me in the back--left an imprint. I staggered around backward into the dresser, and my hand touched his big statue of Buddha behind me, for a mega-second it crossed my mind to grab it and knock David's fried piece of a brain out, but I couldn't. Later, I did call a shrink and tearfully ask him why I didn't use that sculpture to kill David. He said that it was because I simply wasn't a murderer. I guess that's always nice to know about yourself! Believe it or not, I felt absolved, as if there must have been something wrong with me because I had never defended myself.

So, once again, did David really kill Tammi Terrell? I was probably the last person in the world who wanted to believe that David ever did anything wrong--least of all kill TT. And I never did believe it. Not until the first time he nearly knocked me unconscious at the house in December of 1972. He said he didn't hit her? In my opinion, emphatically yes, he did hit her. But kill her? I couldn't see it--not until that day.

My hair was long, and as he was hitting me and throwing me all over the room, it must have been impossible for him to see where face, neck and hair began or ended. I don't think it mattered to him. He pummeled and punched until he landed a blow on my temple with one of his fast, skinny, long, mean, sharp fists, and it

Delivered From Temptation

almost killed me. Literally. Only my own distant, small voice repeating over and over, "Wait a minute, wait a minute, wait a minute" kept me conscious as my knees buckled and blackness swirled around me. In a flash, I saw, and later told David, how easily he could have snuffed out my life, just like that. This was the moment, too, that I had the very sobering realization that he could kill--accidentally or otherwise. Death was possible at the hands of this very man. This was also the precise moment when I no longer had the luxury of wondering whether he could have killed Tammi Terrell.

He was desperately sorry, as always, but I told him that the next time, he could be sorry as he wanted to, but I could be dead. Once that awareness manifested in me, it could do nothing but grow. As I told him, accidents do happen.

That was also the same profound moment in which I had the heartbreaking realization that I couldn't continue the pregnancy which did result from our night at the Watergate. What a sorrowful and earth-shattering moment that was.

As it happened, my mother was in Johns Hopkins Hospital (ironically, where I was born), for back surgery. I'd called her earlier and told her I was pregnant--right after I'd told David. She knew what hell I'd been going through, and she and my father got together and quickly agreed that I'd have an abortion. I strongly support choice, but for myself, I did not want an abortion. I was spiritually opposed. I felt it was murder. I didn't see it as cells, I saw it as my baby--our baby. And as David Junior's beautiful little brother or sister--something he'd wanted his whole little life. I never found a way to tell him (or anyone) until now. Sadly for both of us, it took him decades to forgive me--at least I hope he has.

Truth was, I felt as if David had backed me into a corner and robbed me of my choice. I shut myself down. I left my body. It was like, "You didn't see it--it didn't happen" all over again. Hopkins--a fine institution--had one of the only two legal abortion clinics in the entire country at that time. My parents just took over. They arranged everything, and I let them. It was a relief, for a change, to have someone else make the hard decisions.

As did my so-called wedding, *"The Procedure"*--as Hopkins so antiseptically and conveniently referred to it as-- felt strictly surreal. I was *slo-mo* in a fog--as if I weren't

Delivered From Temptation

really there at all. It was as if Mom walked me in, and Daddy waited at the other end--like an assembly line. I don't remember details--don't ask me to.

At some point, I went back to Parkside--I guess for about three months, during which time I found myself again having to petition the Lord frequently with each new beating. "If you only let me escape just one more time, Lord, I swear..." Mom had given me this tidbit for keeping my sanity: "He would have beaten it (the baby) out of you anyway. Just take it like that." When I tried to share the experience with DR, he simply declared that I wasn't really pregnant in the first place, and with that, he closed the case. Like the proverbial ostrich, he stuck his head in the sand: "Don't bother me, I can't cope." Or was it, "I didn't see it, so..."

After that tragedy, I realized that the only way I could ever have another child, especially with David, was if I were stable both financially and emotionally. This was certainly not the case at that particular time. In fact, that time never came.

Chapter Eleven

"Die, Bitch, Die"

It must have been about this time when I reached the point in my pain and feelings of helplessness that I began to consider one last desperate measure--getting a contract hit put on DR. At whatever time it was, I was dancing in a go-go bar (I was desperately broke, obviously). It was a sort of white biker type of place, and I figured that if there was ever going to be even a slim possibility of a hit happening, it would be from there. I wasn't sure how easy it would be to get "The Mayor of Detroit" bumped off in his own town, unless I ran into someone who didn't care about who he was. Or, ran into someone with empathy for a battered woman--an unlikely scenario since you don't usually expect a biker hitman to be a sensitive kinda guy. There's some serious bigotry in Detroit--more than I personally have ever encountered in all my moving around--so I thought that if this thing were going to happen, I'd have to hire a racist who was unimpressed by celebrity. Plus, I didn't have much money. (Where was Ralph when you needed him)?!

Even though I had to face the terrifying but very real possibility that somehow David would be informed of my activities, things were so critical that I did risk one half-hearted inquiry. I took his photo to work with me one night, and asked a certain guy if he would do it, but even he just looked at me as if I were from another planet. He mumbled something as he handed me the photo and walked away. I was too scared to ask anyone else, and I was kind of relieved to drop the whole idea. I felt lucky to have not been found out.

Mind you, now, if I could go to jail for my thoughts, I'd still be there. But that's all it ever really was--just a fantasy of self-defense dreamed by helpless abused women and children all over the world. Under it all, I still loved him--I just wanted it all to stop.

Delivered From Temptation

In the following spring, I took the baby and left again for five months, after yet another very serious beating. Paul Williams died that August, which was by far the worst of these three tragedies. David and I reunited just in time to pull together for Paul's funeral. Somehow I felt that he and I had somehow failed even Paul. Where were we when he needed friends? Caught up "Inside Parkside."

David was seven now. He and I had waltzed back into the house unannounced after the five-month separation, and David welcomed us with open arms.

All the while, he swore that the girl in the back room was with his flunky-buddy, "Flip", who was freeloading there. I did find out differently later, but I let it go. After all, I had been gone for five months. And my return was unexpected. It was kind of "cute" they way they all scurried around. She called me a few days later in a tizzy, declaring how she'd never have done it if she'd have known he was married. I felt powerful. Sick, I know.

We took a pivotal trip to Florida and Freeport in The Bahamas the following June, in 1974--the scene of the second beating away from the house--the first having been the Watergate Incident. It'd been still another hellacious year back at that house--it had long since began to look more and more like a dungeon to me. Bad times outweighed the good, by then. When we got home from Florida, he broke my nose again--this was the second and last time. Four years had passed between the two incidents.

It was the week before David Junior's birthday party was scheduled to take place. DERj was turning eight on July 1, 1974--we had that big party planned for the next weekend. But around three o'clock on the morning of June 30th, DR went nuts and beat me up badly one last time. I had no explanation then, nor do I now--the usual, I guess. The party was held, for the sake of the baby, but I was conspicuous by my absence.

Jimmie's ex-wife, Shirley, was an unwelcome intruder into our bedroom where I was hiding out alone. The door was closed, but not locked, and I guess she figured she was going to find out what the hell was going on. She called me and pushed the door. I was pushing from the other side, as I didn't want her to see me. But she was stronger. The door came open ever so slightly--just enough for my mangled face to show. She was wearing

Delivered From Temptation

her usual "cat-that-swallowed-the-canary" look and barely blinked when she caught sight of me. (After all, DR was her boy). She muttered something banal as she retreated. We've never spoken of it. Usually, I was well sequestered during such a time--oh, those closed doors--and he respected me enough to never hit me in public. Oh wait, that's not respect, that's fear of being seen and going to prison again.

Well that's right. He did hit me just that once in Freeport. And that little bit at Watergate, if you want to count that. In fact, I believe that no one ever saw me. Well, except for Shirley, Eddie Kendrick, and Reggie--but only once each. And well, the doctors and the police. And, oh yes, my girlfriend Angel saw me in the hospital that time. And her mom saw me when she took me in one violent night. And then those two flunkies who silently watched him break my eardrum that very first time--practically no one. And, yes, of course, now I'm being facetious.

But there was David Junior, of course. When he saw me that particular morning of his birthday, he said, "I thought Daddy promised he wasn't going to do that anymore, Mommy." I told him that was true, but that he'd lost his temper. Weak, I know--but what else could I say?

I took my son and left on the day after, for the last and final time. Really. I left Detroit on Friday, July 5, 1974--Independence Day for me--and on Monday, July 8, I was in therapy back in Baltimore. My past three failed attempts at escaping the dangerous situation I'd lived in, had taught me well that I couldn't break that addiction alone. I recognized that I needed help, thank God, and this time I ran straight to it. I was there for thirteen blessed months. It was the best thing I ever did for myself, other than to leave my David, of course.

The first time I dragged myself into that therapist's office, I had already been seen by a medical doctor. I had a broken nose, two "cauliflower" ears, two broken ear drums complete with a collapsed Eustachian tube, slits for eyes, bruises of every color graduating in concentric circles from under my eyes all the way down to my jawline on both sides, a gash across my nose from the diamond ring he had borrowed from Kenny (his favorite pusher-man), and a bruised right forearm--beat up from blocking blows. In fact, during one of those blocks, the diamond in the beautiful white-gold wedding set he had bought me our first Christmas at the house put a tiny nick in his poor fist. Then he got mad! He pulled the rings off my finger in a rage. I never saw them again. (No doubt some dealer did, though). He was yelling, "Gimme these!" At that point, I was exhausted. I just didn't care. I said, "Fine! I won't be needing them any more!" It had been an all-nighter. The worst ever. At the end of it, he pinned me down on the bed by straddling me and repeatedly punched me in the face. Good old Kenny's diamond ring smashed across the bridge of my nose, breaking it. Blood was gushing down my throat with an alarming velocity, and I was choking. I begged, "David, I'm drowning!" He screamed, "I don't care --die, bitch, die." I knew it was the last time for me--one way or another.

Several hours later when I finally sneaked a peek into the mirror with those painful eyes, I absolutely gasped. I did not recognize the swollen, mutilated face before me. It looked to me like a police photo of a bloated body that had been dragged up out of the Detroit River after having been in there a week. Or, the unrecognizable face of the losing boxer brutalized in a fight.

In the aftermath, King David had gone out on his Harley with the eighteen-inch extension. (In keeping with everything in his world, it was extreme and probably dangerous). I, in the comforting arms of darkness, finally sneaked out on our porch to sit in the warm July night air. I wept as I sat there alone in the silence. Soon I found myself fantasizing about what would happen if he got killed that night on his bike. I mentally looked through the house to see if there would be anything I wanted for myself before calling the girls and their mother. I wondered what I'd wear to his funeral--or if I'd even go. I'd long since quit contemplating suicide--I'd figured out that he wasn't worth it. Nor was he worth doing time for--not to mention that'd I'd have a real hard time explaining to David Junior why I'd murdered his father. That's when the cold, hard fact hit me that it was down to me and my son, or him.

It really was the absolute hardest thing I've ever had to do--leaving him. The first three times, I'd followed my good old instinct and sneaked out while he was out-of-town. I could only stay away three weeks, three weeks, and five months respectively. This time I figured the jig was up, or if it wasn't, it just oughta be.

It was business as usual the next morning with David, like always. Normally, while he was acting like nothing had happened, I'd be planning my escape for sometime within the next few days. By now, I could actually pack mentally. I'd even "pack" inside the dresser drawers--rearranging them so I could grab what I wanted and run whenever I got a chance. Once he even asked me, while feigning nonchalance, what I was doing. I just played it cool--"spring cleaning", I said. He just shrugged, "Oh." Maybe he was suspicious, but just didn't want to know.

On that day I gulped and bit the bullet. I guess I figured I had nothing left to lose. Besides, I was just bone-tired of it all. I said calmly and quietly, "Well, I'm sure you must know that I'm going to leave you--there's no use pretending that I'm not." Somehow, it took five long, heart-breaking days to actually get out of there.

Sunday he blocked my VW Superbeetle in by parking the limo across the drive. Monday he took the baby with him as he was supposedly going to the bank to get me traveling money. He was gone all day. Tuesday, after I managed to at least pack, I asked him to help me with the bags. He said that he wasn't about to help me leave him. I kind of snorted and told him he'd been "helping me leave along", as I slid/threw the bags down the stairs.

Wednesday, and so far, we were both suffering a tremendous amount of pain. David Junior, now eight, wisely seemed to make himself invisible, but I'm sure he suffered greatly as well. In fact, once when he was about five, DR called me from the hallway to tell me that the baby had been kicking the cat. We went to him on the basement landing. I stooped down and took him by the arm and asked him,"Why are you kicking the kitty, honey? You love the kitty." He just squirmed and shrugged like little kids do, and said, "I dunno." Brought tears to my eyes. Then I realized why he kicked the kitty--because I took out my frustrations from his father's abusing the both of us on him. And he, in turn, took it out on the kitty. It was the only place in the pecking order where he had any power. Pathetic.

Thursday. Big David and I had been taking turns crying. It was tragic. And what made it really heartrending was that we still loved each other. That's when I found out that sometimes love is not enough. It wasn't as if there were another man or another woman. It would have been so much easier if that were only true. But then, I guess that's why they call it "girl"--it becomes your woman. The last thing that happened--before I finally swooped DERj off the front porch, and slowly backed the VW out--was the worst of all. David Senior and I stood outside the vestibule in the living room body-locked in each others arms. I was sobbing and pounding him on his back and screaming, "I hate you for making me leave you!" He was saying softly into one of my swollen ears, "You don't have to go. Just put the bags down. Just come on upstairs." He took me by the hand, and for a split mega-second, I almost took that step--sometimes I still I wish I could have. But then something inside me grabbed my gut and twisted hard. I think if I'd looked in his eyes at that moment, I'd have seen yellow irises with vertical slits, I swear. I turned and, with hot tears on my face and anguish in my heart, I literally ran outside while I still had the strength.

He followed and stood on the porch like the statue of the fool he had become as he grimly watched us leave. He later told me he was just hoping against hope that I'd only go around the block and then change my mind. He wasn't that far off. I just had to get out of that driveway--I was shaking and sobbing. I didn't really want to leave, although I knew I couldn't stay, so I found myself driving to the nearby Twelfth Police Precinct. They knew me, and let us just hang out there for a while until I sort of got myself together. They never said a thing-- they didn't even extend an offer of help.

From there, I called my father "collect." I called my mother "collect." They were both invaluable as motivators and sources of strength--even if it was for all the wrong reasons. Actually, they were claiming their victories, but I didn't care. I knew that I couldn't make it without them pulling me from the other end. That's how defeated I was. They knew I was coming and had helped me plan my escape route to Baltimore. My mother, in her Dorothy-Regina-Leary-Sapia-O'Neal-Kelly kind of way, said, "Just keep bringing that Bug on down the road." I cried all the way. Frequently, I had to stop and call one or the other for the willpower to go on. You see, I still wanted to turn around. On the way, eight-year-old David turned to me and said, "Mommy, did Daddy ever love you?" All I could say right then was that that was something I'd often asked myself. And that, evidently, he didn't love me quite enough to marry me.

Delivered From Temptation

In retrospect, of course, I like to think that he loved me enough to not marry me. We developed a practice when David was just a tot. Whichever one of us he was with would buy a card to the other and stick it in the baby's hand, and say, "Here, let's send this to mommy/daddy." Or we'd dial the phone number of the other, and say, "Here, talk to Mommy/Daddy." In later years, it became, "Call your father/mother"--just any means to make sure he always stayed in touch with the other parent. I'd always loved that deal unspoken between us--we just automatically stuck together in that way. Of course, it was good for DERj too. It was a habit of staying connected and of saying "I do love you."

After his father's death, David Junior told me that when they were last on the road together, his dad would still often say to him, "Call your mother." David Junior was fairly grown by then, and would say, "Call her yourself. You know you're the one who wants to talk to her." I asked him what was his dad's response to that: "Sometimes he'd say 'You know better than that'. Sometimes he'd say, 'Yeah, maybe I ought to'." DERj said that it was at those times that he could feel his father's sadness.

Then, in the blink of an eye, reality would set in and he'd think better of it. That's why I say he loved me enough to leave me alone. And I love him for that. (I can practically hear Jimmie laughing in disbelief and see him shaking his head). So now I guess I'm in love with a ghost.

It was many, many years before I forgave David for making me leave him, and I believe he turned it around in his head to where he never could forgive me for leaving him. Up until the day he died, I still considered myself a recovering addict and/or masochist, always counting how long I'd been able to stay away "this time": fifteen, sixteen, seventeen...

(*Author's note: After being born again in 2004, that addiction [a craving for love, as all addictions are on one level or another] is gradually being replaced with the love of God filling my spirit. Praise Him for His Mercy and Grace).

Chapter Twelve

"I Am Woman"

My mother handled getting the upstairs flat for David Junior and I on Annapolis Road in Baltimore near her aunt and uncle. We were both a mess emotionally, and for me, it was physical as well. But I was driven to kick it this time. I knew it was my last chance. People were willing to help me now who were never available before and wouldn't be again. I knew I had no choice but to take advantage of this window of opportunity. As early as two or so years before, some little voice deep inside of me had begun to warn me that something was not right and that I was going to eventually have to choose to save either David Senior or myself and child. It must have been around the time Helen

Reddy put out "I Am Woman"--David Junior says I sang it around the house all the time.

My father handled taking me to South Baltimore General for a complete physical on August 14, 1974. Everything from top to bottom was x-rayed. My eyes, teeth and ears were examined. My eyes were expected to heal completely, but the bite of my teeth was changed permanently, and that left Eustachian tube was collapsed--still is. Surgery may or may not have stopped the constant clicking in my ear.

And, oh yes, this time it was the bridge of my nose which broke when DR hit me with that borrowed diamond ring on his hand, and it had already healed badly. The doctor had to re-break it with a hammer and chisel in order to set it right. Happily, I was under anesthesia at the time. The bone in my right forearm was only badly bruised, not broken, and the varied contusions and abrasions would heal--a hell of a lot faster than my heart would. Not to mention my mind.

Being indigent, I was able to get the therapy as well as the medical help I needed through a free clinic. It was in the course of filling out their many forms, answering their many inquiries, and going

Delivered From Temptation

through their battery of tests that it was accidentally found that I carry a Sickle Cell trait. Suddenly, I was elated. I was so happy to definitively find out my heritage at last. Unfortunately, my elation was very short-lived when I discovered that things were not that cut-and-dried, and that Mediterranean peoples carried the trait as well as Africans. So I was back to being either Italian or black. Either/or would have been fine, but I was just back to not knowing again.

(Since I'd been with David, I had reached the conclusion that it didn't matter what I was. I was human and I was loved). Of course, I immediately became concerned for my son. He tested negatively, however, as did my mother. My father refused to test, and I wasn't speaking to David at the moment. Besides, as long as DERj was alright, it didn't really matter if Senior had it or not, since he and I were not going to have any more kids.

So, I was looking for all the help I could get--medical, emotional, financial--plus, I enrolled in school again in an attempt to break my usual pattern of going right back to David and to buy myself some time. It was a fashion institute. There were eighteen subjects--illustration, copy, architecture, history, furnishings, design, display *et al.* I worked my butt off, and in a year, about a month before I finished with my therapist, I graduated as valedictorian.

On the other hand, David Senior was not helping. He wasn't willing to let go graciously. I understand completely--I was acting the same way. Anytime one of us had the idea that the other might be getting over it, the one in panic mode would rattle the other one's bars. It was a case of my not wanting him any more, but not wanting to let someone else have him either--*vice versa* for him. It's really a terrible illness.

Thus, he flew to Baltimore repeatedly throughout that year. He begged until my heart almost broke. He gave me money. He called every Saturday at noon. He wanted me to marry him. We were still hooked. It was insufferable.

The shrink had asked me why I'd come. I wailed that I had come because I was sick; that I had to be sick, because, "Look at me! Yet, I still love him and I want to go back to him." She protested, "You're not sick, you're just in love!" She was not joking, but it really sounds so corny now, not to mention dated, and I see top-hats, canes and white gloves moving pertly in unison to a show-tune

Delivered From Temptation

when I think of it. I'm embarrassed for her--for the women of the times in general. I'm sure we're all wiser by now. The important thing is that it helped me feel okay about myself at that crucial moment.

You see, there were three specific things that I gradually realized I had gone there in search of: My self-esteem, my confidence as a woman, and an identity. David, typical of an abuser, had stripped me of all three. Or, now that I have since had to learn the hard-but-fair lesson that there are "no such things as victims, only volunteers", I should say that I allowed him to do it. Yet, it's not that simple while it's going on. As is typical, he kept me and the baby both financially and emotionally dependent. I had become what I now have to refer to as an "emotional cripple." He kept me isolated from friends, and had long ago alienated me from any family who even might have come to my rescue, had they ever an inclination, which they did not. He inculcated me with the brain-washing that convinced me that I was the scum of the earth, thereby deserving such treatment. Maybe he wanted me down there with him.

Hence, I was in therapy big time--three times a week (although I did not yet trust the system which had played me off so many times before. I mean, I'd "gotten" it back in Detroit when I was prenatal and went to Legal Aid where their only concerns were whether or not DR killed TT, and why he had left The Temptations--not my child support. I didn't even confide in the therapist for the first three weeks just who this lover of mine was--and then with trepidation and caveats. By then she knew me well enough to show the proper reaction--none). I was such a mess that she had to give me her home number, which she had never done before, because my crises tended to hit mostly nocturnally, after her office hours. Naturally, David did not want me to get over him and leave him alone in the madness. At least, not until he got over me first.

I was, of course, nursing the delusion that it was possible we might reconcile if he agreed to all my stipulations. However, he had to actually change. Going for therapy was the most obvious thing. I was also more skeptical than I'd ever been before. In the process of investigating all angles of the options, I decided to find out once and for all if he was still married.

Sounds stupid, I know, but I still didn't know for sure. He was, after all, a master of deception.

As a matter of fact, the only way I came face-to-face with the reality of just how married he really was happened on the steps of Motown after I arrived in Detroit with him. It was probably my first day in town--I was just bubbling. I was sitting/leaning against the rail on the porch, facing the big picture window. Cornelius Grant was beside me, and there were a few others hanging out at the side rail. He and I were talking and laughing. People began coming outside. I have no idea how many, because I only saw the first one. She stopped in front of me and said, "Is your name Genni?" I was still smiling as I turned and said it was. With a furtive glance in all directions to be sure that David wasn't around, she said to me as she swept by, "I'm Mrs. David Ruffin." So much for bubbling!

I think Cornelius practically had to grab for me to keep me from pitching backward off the rail, just like in the cartoons! I was utterly stupefied.

And, then too, all throughout the following years, David would tell me whenever it was that I asked him, that his divorce was now final. Why, when we moved onto Parkside (was it the first or second year?), he actually initiated our wedding plans for the approaching June. We registered, we ordered invitations--we had my girlfriend across the street handling the whole shebang. I was already wearing my wedding ring set he'd given me the previous Christmas. Well, June came closer and closer. Unfortunately, he had been administering those periodic beatings, and my confidence in marrying him had greatly waned. So, when June finally did sneak in, we both held our breaths and neither said a word. At the end of the month, we just sort of looked at each other out of the corners of our eyes and let out a sigh of relief. We each had different reasons, of course. Mine is obvious. He, deft poker player that he was, knew all along that he was still married. Even so, he chose not to tell me.

Even though they had been separated maybe seven years, I was always kept in the dark about the final divorce. Maybe he was just too afraid of the financial destruction it could bring. Or maybe it was just because he could get away with it.

We lived as married, we said we were married--it's no wonder people came to take

Delivered From Temptation

us as married. Even Eddie Kendrick said, after we'd split, that he'd thought we "were legal."

So, on October 23, 1974, three months after I'd left him for the last time, I decided to call long-distance to the Bureau of Vital Statistics in Detroit to determine his final divorce date. A two dollar money-order told me they found nothing. This was my second vain request for the same information. But this time, I called him about it. He convinced me that there was some kind of record-keeping error. Honest! Immediately following his death, my son and I went there physically, and there is to this day, no record of a final judgment, so for once in his life he could've been telling the truth. Either he truly believed he was divorced, or he knowingly committed bigamy.

Then he met Miss Joy, the next "Size 10" Mrs. Ruffin. It happened just the month before I made the above-referred phone calls--only two and a half months after I split, and probably around my birthday. (He never was one to sit around too long alone--he couldn't take the voices in the silence. Jimmie laughed facetiously and assured me that his brother wasn't that deep when I told him DR did coke because he couldn't stand the voices).

As usual, David had made his twelve-o'clock-noon Saturday loving phone call to me in Baltimore from what used to be our house, but this time I needed to clarify something or other. I called right back, and when this British female voice lilted, "Hull-oo", naturally I hung up. I just knew that I'd dialed London or something by mistake. I re-dialed, and again she answered. I think she said, "Ruffin Residence." I asked who in the hell she was and she said condescendingly, "This is Joy, who is this?" I couldn't believe my ears and repeated myself. (I'm sure I didn't phrase it quite that way, but I sure felt that way--steam was coming out of my ears!) When I said I was Genevieve--the name I used whenever I needed to mark my territory--she was quite taken aback. We started right in having a conversation of sorts. (She always had this constant tone of superiority in her voice-- she was this princess, after all!) It was more like a mutual interrogation, actually. She wanted to know if we were still married and when we had gotten divorced. Still the enabler, I told her smugly to ask David. She wanted to know why I left him (you can see that she'd had experience with this type of thing before--months later when I asked her how many times she'd been married, she'd replied, "Four or five.") When I told her it was because he was so jealous that I left, she said that he had told her that I was the one who was jealous. And, that judging by the photo of me he still kept on top of the television, she could see why he'd be jealous. This was something a little different for me. I didn't quite know how to take this one.

Needless to say, I was in agonizing pain in the months to come; I had to tell my friends to treat me like the junkie I was and tie my hands if they had to--anything to keep me from calling David. I had to break my patterns. I was that serious.

My therapist was working her butt off with me, but when Christmas of '74 came and DR wanted to take Little David to spend the holidays with him and Miss Joy in the Detroit homestead, I bugged out. My shrink somehow convinced me that I had to do it, had to let go, and promised to help me through it. Under major protest, I did allow him to go, but kept a tearful vigil by my phone the whole time. I deprived myself of all possible holiday happiness (Genna of Arc) in case David called. (I don't remember that he did). I really was a basket-case then. Those were the longest two weeks of my life.

After my thirteen months with the therapist, I took DERj and moved from Annapolis Road to L.A. in pursuit of that elusive butterfly of (self)love. It was 1975- -City of the Angels. Life there made me wonder where those old angels had gone- -they sure weren't in Los Angeles! I shifted us back and forth about once a year for four years. Looking for myself. Stalling for time. Getting chewed up--and spit out. Seeking answers. Hunting for the Gateway to Recovery, basically. It was there I began the next phase of my struggle to recover from being an emotional cripple. I had a few very good and wise friends who had moved there from Detroit who proved to be absolutely invaluable to my very sanity.

David, too, was curiously running back and forth to Los Angeles a lot all of a sudden, and it was all I could do to keep my center of sanity. It seemed like every time I'd start to get my head on straight, he'd blow in. Of course, he always contacted me, although once I unexpectedly heard him on a live record store promo on the radio, and it took all I had not to lose it. It was that which prompted me to more drastic measures. I took to envisioning myself seated, holding onto my chair. I began to think of him as a hurricane. Yup, Hurricane David. I figured, "He blows in, he'll blow out. Just hold on. They're only emotions--they'll pass. Hold on tight. And pray!" And they would pass. It wasn't easy at first, but it did help a little. And then a little more. I was beginning to utilize any and everything that was shown to me inside as a way to help myself recover. I needed it all--I was an emotional disaster area. This was when the second, or practical, phase of therapy began. Healing is ongoing, I've come to find out.

On one of these many trips, he wanted to take David Junior home with him (and to Joy)--again. When I had left him for that last time, I was only able to stuff a very limited number of things into the VW--and my electric blanket wasn't one of them. (I had left all my furnishings and furniture on Parkside--at some point, you just want to live). Los Angeles was chilly in winter without a furnace, so I asked David Junior to bring my blanket.

It didn't fit on DR's California-king bed; he wasn't even using it. Yet, DR wouldn't give it to him for me. When Little David arrived back in L.A., the blanket had been smuggled into his bag by Miss Joy. I had a secret ally!

She had a boy of her own (whose middle name was David), just two years older than my son. Her boy was in London at boarding school most of the time, but she was very concerned about children. Anybody's--but, in this case, especially David Ruffin Junior. No, really--it was wonderful. She could not even fathom the way DR treated him, and was highly offended, as any decent human being should be. She immediately took him under her wing and protected him. She didn't try to "steal" him from me, and I came to trust her. She took better care of him than his father did, and I respected her for that.

When I left David, I had yelled that he'd better get a young girl or a European subservient woman, because no one else was going to put up with his shit. So when I found out about Joy, I chided, "I'm glad to see that you took my advice." "It's not like that", he sneered back. In fact, he told me that, once he had accepted that his son and I were not coming back after two and a half months, and he'd met Joy, he decided he might as well "go with that"--said she reminded him of me, and she conveniently had that son near Little David's age. Evidently, that meant something to DR. He had, he confided, even called her by my name in bed. (All bull, no doubt). He also said, at some point in my whining, that I'd probably like her if I got to know her. He'd never have said that if he had thought for a second that it may actually encourage me to do so. Not surprisingly, I was utterly green with envy throughout their entire relationship. I guess at that point I figured, "if you can't beat 'em, join 'em!"

Like I said, she was this "princess", and had charmed David with her clever tales of furs and houses and gems, all collected from her many divorces from royalty--both real royalty and imagined royalty. She, of course, suffered the same delusion about him--that he had money. Why yes, it was a limo he'd met her in, but rented. Oh, the story about the little mansion in Detroit was true enough, but he neglected to mention that he couldn't afford heat most of the time. And, although she didn't want him to know it, her baubles weren't all they were cracked up to be, either.

I must say, I did admire how she had him jumping through hoops--there was no harm in it. For instance, she made him buy her a huge pear-shaped marquis diamond engagement ring. She'd told him haughtily and with genuine disbelief that it was simply how it was done where she came from. That was good for him! (I bet the Capricorn sneaked in a Cubic Zirconia). He did need somebody to whip him into shape--and Miss Joy was just the one to do it. She swore she'd leave him unless he made her an honest princess, and I believe she would have--at that point. She issued her last ultimatum, and he indeed married her on April 9, 1976. It was an occasion of which I was not informed, until I painfully stumbled across it (and how sickeningly "beautiful" she felt), in Jet magazine--after the fact. She said she'd wanted to tell me "in a civilized manner", but David said no! Then, I believe that in spite of themselves, David and Joy saw their separate ulterior motives actually fade into hopeless love--or what they individually perceived as love. You see, it's not that I believe that David couldn't love--it was just that his interpretation of the very concept of love, as well as of respect, were just--well, different from everyone else's.

Delivered From Temptation

He had told me how much he had learned from me, meaning at my expense, and was trying to put it all to good use in the new marriage. Thank you very much! He took her everywhere; he bought her everything. He even bought her driver's license--which is why I suspected that he just might have purchased the marriage license as well. It was back to the Bureau of Vital Statistics for me. The license was real. At least it was a real piece of paper. On it, as witness, was that name which again made my skin crawl: Royce Moore. That punk again!

So! I ultimately found out that it was not until he wanted to marry Miss Joy that he actually got divorced from his first wife-- if, in fact, he ever did! Should I have been hurt? I was truly devastated, but only briefly. After all, I still say he did me a favor my not marrying me. After I finally "got" him, I began to wonder just what it was I had gotten and why I wanted him. I figured his first wife was laughing at me. And Joy had to pay his attorney ten thousand dollars he owed just to get out of the marriage. It wasn't how she had planned it, to be sure.

He carried on his association with me and David Junior throughout the marriage to Joy, as he continued to travel between

Detroit and Los Angeles. And Joy and I continued to converse by telephone--a situation he'd dreaded as long as I'd known him. Two of his women were comparing notes--that could get dangerously close to the truth and blow his control all to hell. (I imagined his world as a place with an all-encompassing bubble over it--"*Ruffinland.*") He had, in fact, at one earlier point, slyly hinted to me that he'd like to have all three of us living in one house! H-m-m-m-m, why did that sound vaguely familiar?

Then one day he slapped Joy for the first time. She packed and split for London at once. They had made up long distance, and this was her Grand Return. He flew all the way to La Guardia Airport to meet her just 'cause she had too much designer luggage. W-a-a-a-h! That really made me want to throw up. But secretly I wished I had that type of power over him.

At the time, I'd briefly lost my mind and moved from L.A. back to Detroit. DR had rigged things so that Joy and I would both wind up at the same time at Druff Productions the day she came back. We'd not yet become acquainted and neither of us knew of his plan. It was quite a scheme, and a few of his closest flunkies were

Delivered From Temptation

conveniently in place to observe the master at work while they moved silently about as props. He was good, damn him. He played it so nonchalantly and casually, as if it were one big coincidence.

Whether it was intended to or not, this particular con made me feel especially uneasy and small--and probably Ms. Joy as well. In fact, I was feeling so defeated, I just figured what the hey, I might as well make one last desperate stab. I was sitting down at this point, and I think the room was empty except for David Junior. I said, fairly under my breath as Joy passed by, "You have everything; why don't you let me have him?" She stopped, looked down at me and said rather pointedly, "Yes, once when I was thirteen, I saw someone who had shoes, and I decided I would have everything." I had a new perspective--and a new respect.

Still trying to be a pimp, David then made the stupid mistake of sending us both back to the house to pack a bag for him, as he was suddenly, and strangely, going to Los Angeles. (He may have had a plan, but I think it backfired). As I drove her there, I was feeling very desperate. I decided to see how she would re-act to this fantasy DR had mentioned to me--the idea he had gotten from a pimp friend of his who did live with two women. After all, I reasoned, I'd rather be in his life in this limited, demeaning way, than to be shut out completely. I just couldn't handle that. In fact, I started to imagine that it might even be easier on me--having a sister for support. And, I guessed, she'd probably thank me for it too!

Well, I did carefully approach her with the idea, and she was, of course, properly and highly insulted. At first. But as she snatched clothes out of the drawers and fairly threw them into the suitcase, her attitude began to change. By the time we were ready to leave an hour later, she had warmed up to the idea rather well. We began to see how it could work to our advantage, and started to get quite a giggle out of it. We'd take him on alternate nights (no threesomes), and we'd both handle him when the sun came up. We figured he'd never know what hit him. We reasoned that, after all, since no one woman could deal with him, maybe what was needed was two at once! We could protect each other; and, as her first husband, who was British, had put it so civilly when we told him, we'd "have someone to chat over the cabbage with." Oh, it started to sound like a great plan--for us.

Delivered From Temptation

Joy and David were on their way to Los Angeles directly from Druff Productions, and although he had leased matching yellow his 'n' hers Gucci Cadillacs (they got repossessed, but she got to keep the matching luggage), Joy was utterly preoccupied. She later said that he kept trying to impress her with the cars, but she couldn't get interested. (That was something else we had in common--any old car will do when you're in love). Knowing DR, I'm sure this tweaked his ego. Once they boarded the plane, she decided it was safe to see what he thought of "our" plan. She later told me that he hotly denied ever having said such a thing to me, and forbade her to talk to me again, dismissing the whole sordid affair simply with, "She's crazy!"

Oh, yeah--that is right. I do recall his telling people nationwide after we'd split up that I was crazy. I heard that I'd shot into the house from outside, that he had awakened with me standing over him with a knife, and that I had stolen from him-- jewelry, I think. (As a matter of fact, it was he who took my high school ring when we first met, and I haven't seen it since). All of these things were complete and utter fantasies. In fact, he knew I should have been doing them. Maybe he even wished I would have done them. And for a second, I was crushed thinking about being misrepresented all across the country. But when I thought about it, I realized that those same people he'd told knew both of us. And, as well as they knew I was devoted to him, they also knew him as a liar and an addict--if not a batterer. So, who were they going to believe? I quickly flicked that feeling away like the irritating little insect that it was.

That was also about the time that My Friend Reggie showed me several casual snapshots of David and various other women--not fans--taken while we were living on Parkside. Nothing explicit, but still it hurt. I had lowered my standards so that I'd accepted that he'd never be true to me on the road, although he continually claimed he was. My conditions were that he not bring home any diseases, not get anybody pregnant, and, most importantly, that he did not fall in love. I don't know if he ever believed me when I'd say that, but what else could I do. For the most part, he did keep it out of my face and out of my house. Maybe that's even too gullible, but I guess that was our lame agreement. In actuality, I was not that sophisticated, but I didn't have super-powers either, so I tried to learn to play the hip role.

Delivered From Temptation

I learned something very valuable from one of those women that David had met when the baby was four or five. She was trying to virtually take over as Little David's mother or something. Outside the house, or behind my back--any place she thought she could. However, I had finally begun to really feel secure about all of that, and about all the other women who wanted to take that away from me. I figured that they could have been fake moms, substitute moms, pseudo-moms, wannabe moms all day long, but that there was only one David Ruffin Junior, and that there was only one David Ruffin Junior's mom, by damn! And wish as they may or might, no one could change that! I must admit though, that there was yet to be many a day on which I wished that I'd somehow been able to make a wiser choice as the father of my only child, which is ridiculous, of course. All in all, Destiny is as Destiny does. There are some schools of thought which teach that the very soul of the unborn child chooses, on some level, the parents it needs in order to best balance the karmic scales and to learn those lessons for which it came. Well, that's my consolation.

At some point, Joy realized that David and I were never legally married, and naturally she asked him why not. He claimed it was because I was "a woman's libber" and didn't want to marry him. (Well, at least the last part was true, and at least he did not say I had died in childbirth). And when, by phone, she asked me again why we split up, I assured her it was not because I was insanely jealous, as he had told her, but because he was abusive. Naturally, she was unwilling to believe me. I knew she was probably in the bedroom, so I told her to look up at the ceiling, which was very high, on my side of the bed. "You see that? That's my blood splattered up there, from the last time he broke my nose." "He told me that was Ragu", she offered weakly. I assured her it was not spaghetti sauce. She seemed certain, of course, that it would never happen to her. She'd been in abusive situations before, however--one from which, according to legend, DR himself supposedly rescued her right in the lobby of a fancy hotel in Los Angeles, all the while cursing such a man who would lay even a finger on a woman. That man was Joy's Egyptian husband *du'jour,* and David hatched some elaborate scheme for her to be able to sneak away from him and meet him in Vegas, which she did do.

I can't remember after which beating that he gave her it was, when she called me in

L.A. to warn me that he was on his way to seek comfort from me. She was divorcing him.

The state of wedded bliss had lasted two years. But it took Joy at least two more years to regain any use of her heart and soul. She was an old hand at marriages and divorces, and she usually bounced back real fast. But this time, she was cold-busted.

She was a lady of mystery at first, but that old 'Vine informed me that her main occupation prior to meeting DR was that of call-girl. Not a cheap streetwalker, mind you, but a very expensive lady who catered only to the very wealthy--mostly princes, sheiks and the like. That is, of course, until she lost her mind and got mixed up with the likes of David. Although she'd been born in Melbourne, Australia, she had lived most of her life in London. She was extremely charming and intelligent in a way, even though her formal education had been scant. She'd had her son when she was fifteen, subsequently sliding straight into the first in a long series of relationships and/or marriages that followed. I believe DR was the only American--the good, the bad and the ugly.

So, she had no real training for a career, but she managed to glean enough about interior decorating from the ether to call that her profession. At least it worked in that part of the world. She only took as her clients people who would "dump everything out of their palaces and redecorate every year", she told me. They paid her very well, she traveled all over the world with their credit cards in hand, and they usually bestowed upon her a lovely gratuity--such as a dining room suite or a fur coat.

At a specific point in the disintegration of their marriage, David Junior and I went to Detroit. He must've been almost twelve. I thought David Senior needed my support--a delusion which was put to rest for once and for all first thing the following morning. One of his flunkies set a big heap of cocaine on the table in front of him; that's when I realized he did not only not need me, he needed no one.

By that time, David and I had somehow gotten into an on-going pattern of putting each other up at our respective abodes whenever one had and the other needed. In 1979, I stayed in his guestroom at the house on Parkside for three weeks while I tried to figure out what to do next. Joy was

Delivered From Temptation

long gone, and some expectant girl was living in the house somewhere as well. I never knew who she was pregnant by, or whose woman she was, and I never heard from her--or about her--after she left.

It was also during the time that, somehow, it had come to be that Jimmie and his next wife and son were living there too--helping with expenses, according to Jimmie. I heard there did come a time when there was gunfire, or some kind of brawl between them one night, but I really don't know the details, as I was elsewhere in the house. Jimmie informed me recently that it never happened. I don't think the police were even called to the alleged shoot-out that time--I don't remember seeing them. I was so upset with Jimmie that night anyway, that I'd run out of the house into the night hysterically sobbing. It was one of those times, like he did after David's funeral, when he felt like pummeling me with his old "David never loved you" routine. He could be extremely cruel at times--although several months ago, he reminded me that it was because of something messed up that I said to his son just then. I can't remember what I could've said to my nephew. Nedra 'n' nem would probably know what happened--some of them were there, I think. In fact, Nedra lived with us quite a while there. Ever since the beginning, she was more accepting of me than the others. So, naturally we were closer. As a grown-up, she has said to me, "One thing I can always say about you--you loved my Daddy!!" She was also the one who accepted David Junior more than the others did. In fact, she alone has sincerely embraced him as her brother. She always cared about him; more notably, she still does--even after their daddy died. As a result, the two of them were closer. So, it was natural for her to come and live with us. She and I sewed, we baked, we shopped, we did hair. It was fun while it lasted. But then, *tsk tsk*, she grew up--and away. We've been in touch a few times, and I know that she still loves me, as I do her.

After the three weeks, I took DERj and went back to Los Angeles. Joy became an ongoing part of my life there. I was, after all, the only person on the face of the earth who really knew exactly how she felt and what hell she was suffering. She wrote and called me constantly and we talked long. I had then, in turn, become the therapist. Somehow, she'd lost the control and fallen hopelessly in love with David. He was, indeed, a powerful being. Exactly what the charm was, no one could ever discern. Joy

Delivered From Temptation

was devastated. My own strength grew in the face of her weakness. She needed my help, and I was glad to give it. She'd never done anything to me, after all. In fact, she'd done all she safely could to stick up for me and my son. I guess by then it'd become obvious to us both that it was neither my fault or hers.

Miss Joy fancied me royalty like she was, and had dubbed me Lady Genna--all my correspondence came addressed that way. I imagine she felt I deserved at least that title, if not one of "Queen!" She wrote that, although she had married for money before, her experience with David had cured her of it. From now on, she'd settle for nothing less than that which she called love. (It was sad that this had been her first real exposure to "love"--I'm sure she was messed-up in the head for good unless she was uniquely lucky).

At the same time, I was fighting for my own emotional recovery. It took me eight years of turmoil before I reached my first landmark. That was in 1981 when I first allowed a man anywhere near my heart. Although I'd left David in '74, it was the first time I had managed to trust anyone. He turned out to be both married and another big liar; however, at least the painful, messy experience did introduce me to the unfamiliar concept that I was at least lovable. I had come to believe that I could never love again. Nor be loved. I was also suffering from not being able to trust, and I believed that of which David, Mom and life itself had convinced me: I was not lovable, and/or even worthy of love.

Joy and I came to develop a mutual admiration society. I admired her for qualities I lacked, and she admired me for qualities which I had and she didn't. It was good to be recognized, appreciated and feel that I was worth something. We had birthdays less than a month apart, and late one August, she flew to L.A. so we could celebrate together. I think it was 1981. She must have been on a buying trip as well, because she was loaded with plastic. She bought me an expensive leather briefcase for school, and bought us matching gorgeous leather suits as well--size ten! We looked fabulous! She continued to use the last name "Ruffin", as she was "between marriages." So whenever we did paperwork, she got a big kick out of confusing the inquisitive salespeople or whoever it was. I must say, I got quite the giggle out of it myself. Just for fun, we would only insinuate my association with the name, and people would ask if we were sisters. We'd laugh and say that we were more than sisters. After half a beat, but in time to wipe that stunned look off their faces, we'd quickly say, "But less than lovers"! We didn't even know what we were to each other. Finally we settled on "wife-in-laws", an old Detroit street phrase that seemed to describe us best. Sooner or later, she returned to London to live. I heard she had a couple more marriages, eventually.

Ten years later, though, I couldn't help but notice that, oddly, Joy didn't make it to David's funeral. She was quite obvious in her absence--at least to a few of us. People kept asking me why she wasn't there. I tried to be magnanimous in my reply: "I don't know. Maybe she couldn't take the pain", remembering that David did not go to Tammi's funeral. Someone scoffed, "So?! None of us could take the pain." Amen.

Chapter Thirteen

"The Valley of Death"

In November of 1978, David again came to see the baby and I at our place in Los Angeles. By then, "the baby" was twelve and a half. His dad wanted to take him back to Detroit with him again--for the holidays. He and Joy, of course, had split; he was alone for the moment. Naturally, David wanted to go with his Dad. So we all agreed, and they departed. They called me when they got home, and DERj and I kept close touch. At first, Big David did too. But then, communications began to deteriorate--a bad sign, to be sure.

Thanksgiving, Christmas and New Year's had come and gone, and it was time for David Junior to go back to school. The two

of them decided he'd go to school there--
and that was fine with me. I just wanted the
boy to have his daddy.

Soon, I'd begun to feel all alone in Los
Angeles. After all, the only family members I
had were both in Detroit. So, I figured I may
as well move back too. Again.

By now, David Junior had taken to
secretly calling me. I'm afraid Mr. Hyde had
crept back into the house while Dr. Jekyll
wasn't looking. DR had begun to mistreat
his son again--verbally, emotionally, and
physically. It had gotten so bad, that David
Junior was calling me every couple of days,
begging me to get him out of there. I was
moving as fast as I could, but my lack of
funds was a severe handicap.

I arranged to stay with a friend in Detroit
while I looked for an apartment. My gut
instinct told me not call his father--that he
would not relinquish him of his own free
will. The minute I arrived, I called David
Junior at school and arranged a meeting.
I began going to the school every day
and taking David Junior to lunch. In the
meantime, I looked for a place for the two
of us to live. After about five days, the
principal got paranoid. He said he didn't
know what was going on, but didn't want to

Delivered From Temptation

get in the middle of a custody dispute. To appease him, I agreed to come only every other day instead.

The very next day David Junior called me from school. He was in a panic. He asked me why I wasn't coming and I told him what the principal had told me. "Mommy," my child implored, "you have to come today. I have to show you something." I knew by the way he said it that it was serious. I flew to his side. I brought him out to the car (it was Valentine's Day by now--very cold). He was wearing a big blue down car-coat, but he pulled that, along with his shirt and undershirt, up to show me his bare back. He was covered with crusted belt welts and bruises from the top of his neck as far down as I could see--it turned out to be to the tops of his heels. Needless to say, I was horrified--and nauseous. My head was spinning. I was blind with rage--I knew I had to do something, but I wasn't sure what. I couldn't decide to press charges or not (after all, his father would kill me), but I did decide to file a report and have the cops take photos "just in case."

With that decided, I drove him directly to the police station: good old Twelfth Precinct. The moment I walked inside, control was (blessedly) removed from my hands. Once they got a gander at his back, it was all over but the shoutin'. The police accompanied David Junior to the house to get some clothing and then to bring him back to the station. They wanted me to wait there--and they didn't have to twist my arm. I was terrified of David Senior by then. (David's phone had been shut off, but I had a few things to say to him, plus he still didn't know I was in town, so I sent a note with the police. It said something like, "Do not expect David Junior home from school today. He's in protective custody. You'll never hit me or my son again." Unfortunately, that turned out to be wishful thinking. I didn't know then how to set a boundary and keep it; I was too afraid and too "in love").

I don't think that any one ever said "no" to David Ruffin Senior. That's why he was such a brat. Well, I felt I owed it to him to break that pattern. Mind you, I was long since safely "Outside Parkside", or I would never have had the nerve. When he'd beat David Junior, he'd lock the door of the room they were in. That was terrifying to me--and intimidating.

Why did David beat him so that day? None of us could understand it. He said that David didn't make his bed fast enough. The baby said that he was up in the attic making a Valentine for his daddy--he was distracted. So, maybe it was even longer than a few minutes, David. Whatever. There's no justification. He beat him for twenty or thirty minutes. Then, at ten-thirty that night, he left him alone like that in that big old thirteen or fourteen-room, Dark Shadows-looking dungeon. He rolled in at seven-thirty the next morning while David Junior was fretting about getting to school--imagine what that was like for him. We can all picture where DR spent the night--it was a "house", alright, but not his.

The police took us to the Child Abuse Unit. I was panic-stricken because I didn't have an apartment to take him to, and was afraid I'd lose custody based on that. They had a place called D.J. Healey Home where David Junior was to stay until I found a place. I wouldn't let go of him until I was convinced that I would have no trouble getting him back. I was also relieved to learn that the facility also had a school, so I wouldn't have that to worry about as well as everything else. I began to feel a little less anxious. Plus, I was assured his whereabouts would be kept secret from his father. I finally agreed to leave him there. It was hard for both of us. But, we were in such a mess; I had no choice just then.

I got him back in only six days. But not before somebody who worked at Healey sent word to David of our hiding place. I can't remember any more how I found that out, maybe he phoned there. But I knew there wasn't a place far enough away to be safe from David at that time. I found a cheap townhouse (even with appliances included) in an outlying suburb and moved us in. We had all of one double mattress, a 5" black and white television, and a TV tray table. That's it. Believe it or not, we regrouped-- and regrouped well! It was a miracle.

We literally hid incommunicado for nearly two years. But there in Taylor, Michigan, David Junior went through a different kind of hell. The town turned out to be full of rednecks--and redneck kids. A few things that he suffered: Being shot at regularly with BB guns, being knocked unconscious while an entire busload of kids (and driver) stood by, being blamed for vandalism, and the piece de resistance--the time the redneck kids caught him and literally sliced his clothes to shreds, including his big, heavy leather insulated boots.

Ultimately, we could stand it no longer. The hiding, the waiting, the rednecks, and--especially missing David Senior. At last I admitted to DERj that I missed his father and wanted to call him. He was all for it; we concurred. I no longer had his phone number, but I had his brother's. It was around three in the morning when I called. Jimmie, of course, would not give me DR's number (I wasn't asking for it), but he finally agreed to call and "see if he wanted to speak to" me. Evidently, David did want to--he called me within five minutes. (Na-na-na-na-na, Jimmie!) How soon did he arrive? Don't remember, but it was very soon. He stayed three days, during which time we played, and talked, made mad, passionate love--and he promised me the world. He was sorry for beating David Junior; he didn't blame me for having him arrested (shock); he loved and missed us both.

Somewhere in there, prior to that visit, he'd been picked up on a warrant about six months after I had originally pressed the child abuse charges, and he had gone before a judge. Jimmie went with him to make sure he didn't have to do the right thing--like pay for what he did. Turned out the judge had asked DR what the hell he was doing beating someone else's kid, and he told him it was his kid--and he was just "punishing" him. The judge asked him why the hell the boy didn't have his name, if that was the case and issued him the ultimatum of doing token time, or acknowledging paternity--something he had successfully evaded thus far. Being the man that he was, he chose the latter, of course, and Jimmie could do nothing about it. So David Eric Sapia was adopted by his own father, and was finally bestowed, on August 3, 1979, his actual birthright name, Davis Eli Ruffin Junior. He and I still ponder that, on occasion.

DR had me drop him off around the corner when I took him home after those three days, and the light suddenly clicked on in my head. Duh! In all our plans and promises to me, he'd forgotten to mention the girl he was living with. Surprise, surprise! I was outta there!

We did still keep in touch, though, and it was at Druff Productions, that he and I often sat up all night, long after we'd permanently split in 1974. This specific evening I'd decided that, now that it was all over, I was going to go ahead and find out what made this man tick. After all, he had occasionally tried to criticize me and accuse me of not possibly being able to relate, since I didn't do coke. No doubt he was right. So this time, I decided to do it with him, in spite of the phenomenal fear and trepidation. It was a last ditch effort to possibly help him (Dr. Freud, I presume)--and perhaps even restore our gasping relationship. Incredulous, I know. I swallowed that big chunk of fear that one or, worse yet, both of us could lose our minds, and that he might beat me to death, and I declared my intentions--intentions to fry my brain or die, on his behalf. Why do you think they call it "dope?"

David had a big mountain of the sparkly white stuff in front of him. When I made my announcement, he looked at me real funny--as if he didn't know what I was saying. He was justly skeptical. You see, he knew it had been many years since I had re-embraced my tee-totaler ways, unable to handle the smallest drink or hit of weed, as graphically described in an earlier chapter. I didn't even like to take aspirin, and I couldn't handle caffeine on an empty stomach. He also knew I'd been physically addicted four different times to nose spray--actually to the result of it, which is breathing. Thanks to his breaking my nose twice, I sometimes had (still do have) trouble breathing. At times, I was louder than other times. Mister Paranoia swore that I was doing it on purpose, just "to f---k with" him! I was like, "Wow--I can't even breathe to your satisfaction--but thanks to you! Damn!"

Then, too, he could have been remembering my *psycho-delic* weed trip in Puerto Rico when that sudden look of consternation flashed across his face. Just as abruptly, the glaze left his eyes, and as he turned back to his sparkly mountain, he mumbled, "You don't need to do too much of a--air!" (No, that's not a typo).

I breathed a huge sigh of relief when he did not want me to do it, because I really did not want to have to anyway, and I kind of smiled to myself. So! I was special. How sweet --he cared. About me! I was touched. Years later, I realized that he probably just wanted to keep it all for himself. How do you vote--was he protecting me, or was he just greedy? Dial 1-900-DYSFUNCTION. Never mind, Jimmie; you're disqualified.

It was in that same so-called office where I saw him slap a pimp one night over a swig of Courvoisier--in front of a roomful of people. And the dude never even gave David a dirty look!

The two of them were passing the bottle back and forth between "lines," and when it came down to the last "corner," the pimp drank it himself. How dare he not know he was supposed to offer the last of it to DR? Well, David's speedy little hand flashed out there so fast and smacked him upside the head, that he didn't even have time to think. He just grabbed his face, tucked his tail between his legs, laid his ears back, and muttered, "You slapped me, man!" They were standing almost toe-to-toe, and DR never blinked. Plus, I thought I detected a faint smile on one side of David's mouth and in his eyes, afterward, though--as if to mess with the guy even more. We all finally exhaled.

Now, usually, I guess a man would've punched the pimp instead of slapping him, if anything. Not DR. That would have given the guy the chance to react. That was the closest I'd seen him come to fighting a man. Typically he just beat up on women, children and animals. I have heard a few vague references that he threw a punch or two at people his own gender over the years, but not his own height.

Knowing him, he threw more than a few. I never had the "consolation" of knowing it or seeing it. I was left to draw my own conclusions--which left me hard-pressed to conjure up even a shred of respect for that side of him. And, yes, he had a split persona. In fact, he had a personality of many facets. The weird part was that he knew it.

Once in 1970, I saw a black fluorescent poster that was David up and down to me. It was a Tazmanian Devil on a motorcycle coming directly at the viewer. The caption said, "Yea, though I walk through the valley of death, I will fear no evil--'cause I'm the meanest m----r f----r in the valley!" You gotta admit, although he had his sweet moments and his funny ones, the poster applied to him in far too many moments. You had to shake your head as it made you laugh in a bittersweet, sad kind of way. And he did seem to have no fear. He acted as if he had made some kind of Deal at the Crossroads to become invincible.

He lived dangerously. He rode his bikes like a maniac. He drove cars like a man possessed. He smoked cigarettes heavily--ever since I'd known him. He tried to see how much alcohol and drugs he could do.

(Marijuana, then cocaine. The so-called book put out about David, Eddie and Dennis says that he was a pill-popper, but I think that's a lie. I never in life saw him take a pill other than Excedrin P.M. and thank the Good Lord he was terrified of needles). He went from snorting cocaine "lines" to smoking it, then crack. If "someone"--whose name we dare not mention--hadn't beaten him to it, David would have been the man to discover it--strange behavior in a guy who was developing asthma, and who'd always had bronchial problems ever since he was a baby. He pursued married women--the crazier and more powerful the husband, the better. He messed with anybody and everybody. He threw motor oil all over the walls of the living room of a drug dealer he owed--anything for that dance with danger.

David used to joke and tell his friends that it must be a Libra thing that I left him every spring. I told him that if he'd stop beating my ass every winter, I wouldn't have to leave him every spring. I'd also known him to "jokingly" sing to me under his breath, "You Picked a Fine Time to Leave Me, Lucille." This time, even after five months, he hadn't changed the locks. In the hope, I guess--or perhaps expectation--that I'd return. I let myself in and went on upstairs to our bedroom. The house was quiet and empty except for him and the sound of the television. He was propped up at the foot of the bed on that humongous yellow and black leather hassock watching Jack Palance in "Jekyll and Hyde". He seemed very engrossed. Then he looked up at me as if five months hadn't just passed, and said somberly, "That's me, isn't it?" Yes, he knew it alright. It was both sad and hopeful. Yet as always, the new-found hope soon dissipated like so much dust in the wind, and Hell itself began to slither back into our lives. Little by little, it would suck away the very air I breathed. You see, every time I'd leave him, he'd promise to get help with the cocaine (therefore the violence), but that was the one area in which he seemed to be powerless. Even though he was always able to sing like hell, in spite of himself, he seemed to not be able to get out from under the drugs. I began to wonder just what the Deal was he'd made, and if it was worth all that. I felt utterly helpless. There's a heart-wrenching and on-going pain in watching someone you're that close to slip away through your fingers like so many grains of sand. It's a terminal illness like, yet unlike, any other--beyond the faintest shadow of a doubt.

Delivered From Temptation

They say He never gives you more than you can stand, and there'd have been no way I could've stood the pain of those years when DERj, with Debbie's help, tracked his father down in one crack house after another and dragged him out. I was far too terrified of him by then to have been able to coax him out of a cowering position in a closet and convince him that no one was lying in wait for him. I saw him pass out once when he was thirty from bad drugs-- that once was devastating enough for me. I'm grateful that I didn't have to see the time Debbie described when he had passed out, was clammy and sweaty and had evacuated his waste systems. As they are the first to go, he was, for all intents and purposes, dead then.

Also, he knew I was broken to the point that he no longer could count on me to save him from himself. My strength was depleted. My ability to continue to be his enabler was waning--slowly but surely. And so was my interest or inclination. I guess you might say that my love was dying. Or, I guess you might say that I was about to discover recovery. In either case, my fight was gone.

Genna Sapia-Ruffin

Debbie, on the other hand (according to Jimmie, it was with his guidance--if so, where was he when I needed him?), not to mention the constant nudging from Father Time, had David petrified of going to jail. Not that I hadn't tried. However, in the good old years, spouse abuse was brushed off by the police as "guy stuff." It didn't even have a name then--in fact, they acted as if they thought it was sort of cute. Not to mention the reaction that his celebrity brought. The Detroit (you-know-who-you-are, and f---k you very much) cops who came to our house more than once, became oblivious to me and/or my condition when it came to getting an autograph from their hero-- they'd practically push me aside. Not only that, there were not yet shelters for battered women and their children --a great-but-late concept.

In 1959 when I was sixteen, I had to briefly live with my so-called brother and his first wife. All I ever actually saw him do with my own eyes was to drag her up the alley by her hair and to pour hot tea all over her when he got her home. He was lazy, absurdly jealous, possessive, and generally treated her like chattel. Of course, he screwed every woman he could find, and continued to try to sleep with all her girlfriends. Not to mention with me--for the third time. This time, I woke up with him trying to crawl into my bed--he claimed he was sleepwalking. He tried the same trick with at least one of his wife's friends. He's also the guy who molested me when I was ten. He alone was enough for me to know that I never wanted to marry an Italian. I was horrified of it. So, what did I do? I fell in love with a "black Italian."

I swear to God if you closed your eyes, you'd have sworn David was an Italian with a Southern accent. His philosophy on life was completely "old world", utterly "macho." Without question, the man is the king, the boss, the dictator. One of his most common tirades was, "It's my (as he slammed the table for emphasis, causing everything on it to jump up and down) m-----r f---ing trip! If you don't like it, get the f---k away from around me!" And he'd always say, "I'm the king--there can't be two kings. There can be a king and a queen, but there can't be two kings!" And with him, there was no such thing as a difference of opinion--it was either his way or wrong. I'd gotten involved with a man whose opinion of women was as second-class citizens--objects; decorations. It was a job description with him. It was like: David's driver, David's valet--David's woman. And there were periodic openings for the position. I chided him when I left that he didn't even need to empty the closet of my size tens. I grumbled, "As fast as you change women, just leave the damned clothes! Leave the clothes and change the women!"

So, here he was being this Italian black macho man, and I think part of the way he validated his masculinity was to beat women and children (not to mention dogs and horses) into subserviency "whether they needed it or not." It just seemed to him to be the natural thing to do.

It's true, several months after I met him and had first arrived in Detroit, I had heard he used to beat Sandra, his daughters' mother (who was, unbeknownst to me, still his wife at that time). I never believed it because it hadn't happened to me, and I hadn't seen it. I did vaguely know about it happening twice, to the extent possible, since it happened just outside of my sight, and barely within my earshot. Once I had seen him lunge in a certain direction, and knowing that a situation had just taken place--I'd kinda known about it. Both times it involved her.

Delivered From Temptation

Once was when he and I were apartment-hunting. Apparently, she was following us around, and tried to confront him at some point. I think he dragged her around some corner or something--I know I didn't see it, but I guess he beat her up that day. And, I was just ignorant enough at that point that maybe on some level I figured she "deserved it--messin' with my man!" I don't know--maybe it was my way of justifying his actions so I could be in denial about him. (After about eighteen years, I began to get it that he actually sought out and preyed upon gullible women). It was always his manipulating that was behind him and every "woman." It was never really them doing the lying and manipulating. Except for Tammi Terrell and that other one in Philly about 1989--must be something in the Philadelphia water. So, if you did have to blame someone, for the most part you could rest assured that it had been the spider, not the fly.

The second time, she had come looking for him after we got our first apartment and tried to kick in our steel door. Angry words flew back and forth between the two of them, and he took off down three flights of stairs after her. I didn't care to know what happened when he caught her. This, of course, was wrong of me. But back then it seemed okay--like I was a winner. When I came home from work at the salon the next day, he met me at our door. He stepped out into the hall with me and closed the door behind himself. "Sandra's in there", he said. I was like, "That's nice." I must admit, I was afraid of her--it's true what they say about a woman scorned. And, in fact, there were incidents; once she poured a drink on me by "accident", once I felt I had to grab the butcher knife off the table at Jimmie and Shirley's place to keep her from getting it first. Of course, she was drunk--I guess she was too afraid of David to mess with me while she was in her right mind. Besides, this was a night that Brother Jimmie was responsible for choreographing--still don't know what he was trying to prove.

Even so, I had to go inside my apartment. He led me to our living room where she waited in a chair. I sat neutrally in the center of the sofa; David perched on the arm of the sofa to my right. He said to her, "So, you hate Ginni, right?" "Yeah", she grumbled, under her breath at first. "Why?" he prompted. "'Cuz she took *mah huhsbin*"-- there, she'd said it. Up until then, it seemed so rehearsed and/or guarded; then she let it out. It was weird.

Delivered From Temptation

Remember, I was only twenty back then--and very *naive*. I didn't see any reason to disbelieve him as he repeatedly swore to me that he was divorced. I still wonder sometimes why it was that important to him to "keep" me--I didn't have money or power, and I wasn't famous. I wasn't even pregnant yet. No, I was not his first involvement with a woman Other Than Black. Matter of fact, when I saw Otis on July Fourth '93, he said that even when I met DR in '64, they'd already been calling him "White David." That puzzled me, though, because at that same time, Mary Wells, Dee Dee Sharp, not to mention Sandra, were all three obviously black. And so were many women I suspected or knew he was involved with over the years. But I guess they were mostly light, and maybe that's what Otis meant. I guess. It was a strange thing to say.

Not only that, but as I said earlier, Jimmie often smugly informed me that in his opinion David never even loved me and that the only reason he was with me was that I badgered him into it. I can't tell you how badly that devastated me. Especially when he clubbed me with it just after David's funeral. I wondered what the purpose was at that point--other than cruelty.

By the same token, that's also when I was shown a way to bear that pain, because as everyone knows, DR never went anywhere or did anything he didn't want to do, which was the last thing he said to Sandra back at our apartment just before he showed her the exit ("I'm where I wanna be!") There was just no such thing as "badgering" David into something. So, if I did all that--I figure I must've been pretty helluva! Thanks, Jimmie! I needed that!

(*Author's note: Jimmie called me several years ago while in Los Angeles where David Junior and I resided with his two little sons, Eli [David III] and Drew. Jimmie and I went to dinner. At that time, he apologized for all that, saying the only reason he ever said anything like that to me, was because he was so mad at me for letting David hurt me so badly. And more to the point, he also said that, frankly, he had seen a violent end coming, and was trying to get me out of there before David or I got killed. He concluded by saying, as he leaned intently and purposefully over the table to within inches from my face, "He loved you, okay? He loved you." A few years later, I thanked him).

Delivered From Temptation

Back in 1965, I was unconcerned about, if not oblivious to, David's violence. It didn't apply to me, and surely it was particular to this one "loveless marriage." He had told me that his big brother Jimmie had made him do the "right" thing on February 7, 1961. David, having turned a ripe old age of twenty just three weeks before, married Sandra, the girl he told me he didn't love. She was pregnant. After that, maybe he figured that doing the "right" thing wasn't necessarily the best thing--at least not for him.

Surely, this anger and violence would not follow him past there. Nor was I the kind of person who'd intentionally invite abuse, certainly. Of course, he didn't see it that way, because anything that wasn't his truth or part of his reality was wrong, so there was a potential there for problems. Although at first, I utterly believed everything that David said. I mean, if I looked out the window and saw sunshine with my own eyes, but DR said it was raining? I took an umbrella. Shoot, if he said day was night, it was alright by me! Can I get a witness, a-man?!

Chapter Fourteen

"Tales From the Parkside"

When David first took me to Detroit, after that brief stint at Paul's girlfriend's house, we moved in with Jimmie and his common-law wife Shirley and their baby girl, Philicia. They lived in the lower half of a flat on Mackenzie--Uncle Lem (Lemiel, one of Eli's brothers) lived upstairs with his girlfriend, Sara. David and I slept on the sofa-bed. I don't remember how long we stayed there before we found our first apartment on Gladstone Street, but it was kinda like "family" being there. David had told Jimmie that he was going to marry me, and everyone treated me with due respect accordingly. Although, nowadays Jimmie says David never once in all those years said to him that he loved me, as incredible as that seems to me. He said that, to David, it would've meant showing weakness to his older brother, which he wouldn't have wanted to do. Wow.

Shirley and I were like sisters then, wearing the same sizes of everything from rings to shoes to dresses. We went everywhere together. Little Philicia loved to brush my hair and still talks about it when I see her. Uncle Lem was a gruff, funny old man who talked real crazy and fast. He looked like--well, he looked like David Senior would look when he got to be that old, trust me! Lem liked me, and when David Junior was born, he practically took him from us.

Shirley had known David down South. They were a lot alike, and they were fast friends. And, in those days, it seemed like Jimmie and I had a lot in common as well. DR was traveling a lot, and Jimmie was working at Ford Motor. Jimmie came home late at night, and lots of times he and I sat up talking or writing songs. He seemed like such a nice guy. We became fast friends too. Occasionally we all joked that maybe we were with the wrong partners. There was no hanky-panky, however; truly we were all just kin--maybe the first time I felt that way, now

Delivered From Temptation

that I think about it. I sometimes thought that secretly Jimmie had a little crush on me, but surely I just misinterpreted him.

Unknowingly, Shirley and I became pregnant at the same time, strangely enough. Must've been something in the water in that house! I had David Junior about six P.M. on July 1, 1966, and she had Jimmie Junior I on July 31! (Jimmie Junior II came later in a subsequent marriage).

At that time and over the years to come, it seemed to me that Jimmie was, indeed, very jealous of DR--of his career, of his women, his friends, his personality, his cars, of his money. You name it. It seemed that he saw David as "The Competition", and that David just wanted to be brothers. Jimmie, however, now claims it was the other way around. David seemed, and not only to me, to struggle in vain his whole life to win his big brother's approval; that was his father figure. And then, *de'ja vu*, I proceeded to painfully watch DERj fight that same sad battle with his father, which he never won.

David talked with pride to me and anyone else who'd listen about what Jimmie was doing professionally, but Jimmie's conversation was and is invariably focused on one subject: "I, Me, Mine." It became very off-putting and irritating to me, but it didn't seem to bother David as much. He took it all in his stride--that was his Big Brother.

You may have heard the legendary tale of how David supposedly stole Jimmie's gig as one of The Temptations. They were about to hire Jimmie, I guess, but during their regular gig at Chappie's Lounge in Detroit, DR jumped out of the audience and grabbed the microphone--he always was crazy like that. He did his turns and splits and he screamed and riffed and wailed and did His Thing. Needless to say, he stole the show, of course--quite literally. I don't think Jimmie ever forgave David for it. In fact, Jimmie completely denies it, saying it was he who got David into the group--gave him the gig that was offered to himself in order to keep his younger brother away from bad company and out of jail. Personally, of course, I wasn't there. Motown sax legend "Doc" Beans Bowles (among others) has said, however, that there was "nothing to forgive"--that Jimmie couldn't carry a tune in a bucket anyway, not to mention that he seemed inhibited and rigid on a stage.

I'm sorry to say, Jimmie and I grew quite apart over the years, and when he called me after David's funeral, it was

Delivered From Temptation

quite unexpected. Actually, I can't for the life of me imagine how he even found out where I was staying. This is one of the things he wanted so badly to share with me: Something about how everyone was so deluded about David being drug-free in London on his last tour. I must say, Jim, that in the video I watched of that last London performance, he was looking sober, clean and no vein bulged up in the middle of his forehead as it did when he was using. But JR went on to say that he knew for a fact that this couldn't be true. It seems that after Eddie and Dennis left the country, DR went to see his brother, who, of course, lives in London. During that visit, DR supposedly tried to make a crack pipe out of a soda can. So, it puzzled me when he told me later that David had "come to his senses" before he died, but that it was too late—and that his health was already shot, along with his will to go on. This aluminum can, lamented Jimmie, along with a purple comb and five hundred dollars cash in an envelope which David had given him that same day, was all he had left of his brother's.

Then I found out the real reason for Jimmie's phone call to me. He took the opportunity to warn me that he'd sue me if I wrote this book.

As I said, this is the fifth or sixth time I've started it--the first time was right after I left DR in 1974--and I've lost count of the rewrites. It was the same week that I went directly into therapy--Do Not Pass Go. Being paranoid at the time, I did use all fictitious names in that first draft--it was "Derrick David" and "The Fascinations" and "That Darned Christie Christal!" I was intimidated. Actually, I was petrified.

I tried again several years later, and then a few years after that. But I was always afraid to finish it for fear of being killed-- either by David himself or Motown and/or the forces behind it. I no longer hold any such fear of death--or much else, for that matter.

Frankly, back then I had even facetiously predicted that I'd have to wait until after David was dead to finish it. After all, I'd seen what had happened to the author and her book, Number One With a Bullet, which years ago attempted to expose the innermost workings of Motown. (Never heard of it, did you? My point exactly). Plus, I'd seen the havoc and experienced the pain which DR himself could inflict, as well. Frankly, I didn't know which to fear more-- David or Motown.

Delivered From Temptation

Some of David's cruelty stemmed from some odd heroes--he admired panderers and prostitutes for instance. Some of his best friends were pimps. It seems as if he wanted to be like one of them. I think the way he beat me was part of that mentality. Matter of fact, I think it was after the first bad beating, that I complained with shock and dismay to him that I'd seen whores on television looking like that. I tried to get through to him that, if he loved me as he claimed, this was no way to treat a lady. Of course, unless he wanted to perceive me that way, thereby transforming himself "by osmosis" into his own hero, the pimp. And, after all, I was a kept woman in a manner of speaking. Not even very well kept sometimes, at that. Eventually, I began to believe his hype, thus making it easier for him to perpetrate the fraud. He made me believe that I was incompetent as a woman, otherwise, I "would know what to do" to keep him from beating me. Besides which, he persuaded me that I was nothing and nobody without him and that no one would want me any more anyway. I was "ruined for any other man", he said. At the time, I couldn't fathom what he meant by that. I once told him that I knew he had been used to being with a woman who was a "beat-freak", but I wasn't her. He had me so confused--he'd say must like it or I wouldn't keep "making him do it." It was the one thing he and my sexist, racist "father" agreed on, even without comparing notes: It had to be my fault. That's a tough thing to swallow.

Because of David's brainwashing, in time I did, in fact, become so unsure of my ability to function in a relationship with a man, that I considered the chance that maybe I'd been dealing with the wrong gender, and that maybe I'd be more at ease with a woman.

I became so befuddled that I did touch on the initial stages of involvement with like-gender experiments--not while he and I were together, but twice over the years. I firmly concluded this was not for me--apparently it wasn't something I would've done on my own, had I not been brow-beaten. I don't feel ashamed, nor am I bragging. In fact, it feels more like just another effect of being abused. Still, I did it. It became clear that it would not necessarily have been any easier than a relationship with a man--no panacea. At least, not for me. You still had to, after all, deal with personality conflicts and egos. So I hastily retreated, as I wasn't sure that I wanted to deal with Pandora and her box of unknowns--no pun intended, although it is a good one. Besides, there was just something missing!

This brings us to the fourth question people never fail to ask: Why did I stay so long? I reply that by even making that inquiry implies that I was somehow at fault. And then it is I who asks; "Why do we always want to blame the abused?" It wasn't that I felt I deserved to be mistreated, I just didn't know how to stop it. We'd been together since '64. The beatings didn't start until six years later. I loved him; I thought I could help him. We had a baby, we had history, we were family. I didn't want to leave him, dammit. I wanted him to stop. I didn't grasp addiction.

It's a funny thing: the violence that I'd seen in my family before I met David had always seemed so shocking. It was nothing compared to "The Meanest M----r F----r in The Valley." He used to nonchalantly refer, say, the next day, to what took place as "fights", thereby reducing the impact, i.e., his guilt. Once I actually got the nerve to say to him "That wasn't a fight; it was a massacre."

Once, after a night out together, he was taking me to the basement to trip on me--probably something had happened

Genna Sapia-Ruffin

at the club which triggered his paranoia. This time he had a gun. At the top of the stairs, he kind of pushed me, and the heel of those beautiful tall, white vinyl platform boots he'd bought me caught on the metal threshold strip. I tumbled down, and my head hit the big old sewer pipe. As his panic set in, he frantically scrambled down right beside me. Relieved he wasn't going to be charged with murder, he pulled me up and dragged me into the bomb shelter. There was a raggedy old easy chair in there--he socked me down into it, hard. Truthfully, it was no more than garbage that had been forsaken there by the previous owners, but a few years later, Pinocchio told his next wife, Joy, that it was an antique of his.

He pulled up a chair at an angle beside me and pointed the gun at my stomach. I have no idea what nonsense he was spouting up to that point, but I remember him turning the gun around, practically putting it in my lap and saying in exasperation, "Well, you kill me then." I was like, "Right--I don't wanna kill you, David." For some reason, I guess because he didn't seem as maniacal as usual; I wasn't scared at all--just tired. It simply seemed as if he had started something, and then forgotten why he had wanted to do it. I could see that he didn't really want to kill me, or he'd have done it and not relinquished control like a scared little kid who needed scolding. He didn't know what the heck he was doing. The whole episode just sort of fizzled out, and we went up to sleep.

Once he ran home from the studio, all excited, and played for me the tape he'd just recorded. He asked my opinion. What he failed to mention was that he didn't want my honest opinion. Now, mind you, I'd become very good at couching, and I did word what I said very tactfully. I told him gingerly that his voice, as always, was amazing, but he needed new writers--someone fresh, with innovative ideas. But that was not good enough for him. Spontaneously, he combusted. Maybe he just didn't want to hear what he already knew, since he'd continually been thwarted in his efforts to do anything about the situation with Motown. I didn't know all that back then. Then, just like that, he beat my ass all the way from the upstairs music room, all through the house, even out into the backyard. *Botta-boom, botta-bing.* Then he jumped on a plane and flew to L.A. for three days!

He called after he calmed down, and came home bearing guilt-gifts (as always). He was full of remorse and new-found wisdom (as always). I told him that, since he knew I'd never been one of his yes-people, he shouldn't have asked me—of all people--if he wanted a lie, and that I was only trying to help. And that the next time, he shouldn't ask me unless he wanted the truth. He was all into it, and agreed wholeheartedly that I was entitled to my opinion and that he didn't want me to start being a yes-person now. Reggie had accompanied him, and apparently it was he who had made him see the error of his ways--for the moment.

When he came home, we talked it out, and I told him, "I'm not Berry Gordy. If you're pissed off at him, stop on the way home and punch a bag or something!"

Shortly after we moved in, DR (the frugal Capricorn) decided to have the old Doberman-stained carpet from Hazelwood installed in the new house to save money. The carpetmen had an daunting task before them. It was embarrassing. They had to cut and do piece-work all over--two big floors. There was a main guy and two helpers. The helpers spoke no English at all, and the boss's command was limited, at best. I don't know where DR scrounged up these accommodating guys, but I'm sure he paid them little or nothing.

Now, David was at a point of extreme jealousy and possessiveness at this time--extreme, irrational and paranoid. Way out-of-control--schizophrenic, I'd say--though I'm no doctor and don't even play one on TV. But he wouldn't let me give even his band members, who rehearsed there, a drink of water. I mean, he would threaten me with violence. They all thought that I was the world's biggest bitch--actually I was just petrified of David. Later I found out he told them that it was me who didn't want them in the kitchen--it was, of course, him.

Anyway, after the carpetmen were in the house in the morning and all set up, he sprung it on me that he suddenly had to go out of town overnight. "Oh." What could I say? "Okay, hon--call me when you get there", I sang merrily. I forget what car he had then, but it wasn't the 'Vette--it was a big car. He drove away, I waved him good-bye, and went upstairs. The laborers worked long and hard--way past lunchtime. I'm at least a normal human being, and I was feeling sorry for them, not to mention concerned. They hadn't eaten, not even had a drink of water--after all, David had warned me. Finally, I could no longer stand it, and when the boss implored me for some water, I bravely decided to sneak and give them a quick sandwich with the water. Instantaneously, out of nowhere, I heard a loud screeching in the drive-way. The doorbell rang repeatedly and incessantly; I looked through the one-way glass and saw David. He was in a rage. The car was in the drive, door open, motor running. I opened the door, he bolted in, took one fast glance around the wall into the dining room where the men were eating, and punched me dead in the mouth --all within a matter of seconds. Frantically, I objected, "It's only the carpetmen!" "I wouldn't give a f---k if it was Jesus Christ!" he proclaimed loudly. He proceeded to seriously brutalize me up the stairs, all through the house and ultimately into the shower stall. I don't remember how it wound down, but it turned out that he didn't have a gig at all (duh), but had parked out of sight and was somehow watching me. He must have been across the street with binoculars at his drug-buddy's house. Unless he just had that helluva timing. This jealous mode kicked in real bad once we moved into the house, and it escalated to the point of absurdity. Or was it to the point of paranoia?

Delivered From Temptation

This was a man who accused me of sleeping with everyone in every band he ever had--before, during, and after The Temptations. And with his brother, and the doctor, and the carpetmen, and the girl across the street, and, and, and, and. *Ad infinitum* and *nauseum*.

In typical misogynist behavior, he accused me of doing the things that he did; and had convinced himself of these truths. After all, since he was screwing around, to him, it stood to reason that it was common (no pun intended) practice! Moreover, this thinking (and I use the word loosely) was the only way he could justify his abusing me, and so he had no choice but to believe it. It was better to blame me than himself, after all!

How jealous was he? He was so jealous, he was even jealous of his own son. David Junior was an adorable child--perfect face and perfect hair for modeling. I had been *putzing* around with it for a while. As we moved into the house, I already had a deal in the works for him to represent Magnificent Hair Products, but when they called the house, the call was intercepted. David squelched the deal. He didn't want to share the spotlight with David Junior. Well, that was my analysis. Maybe I'm wrong--but there was to be no more modeling. At least while we were with Big David.

And paranoid? He'd grown increasingly so. He'd already reached the point of suspecting our bedroom of being bugged. And of my being "in cahoots" with Berry Gordy, of all things. I suggested to him that if anything was bugged, it was the telephone. After all, that's the instrument he used to confide in all his so-called friends. He'd try to make me believe that I was the only person he had told a particular thing to, and I was intimidated at first, not to mention confused. Then I realized he was telling others the same thing; I think he just liked to scare people. He'd set little traps around the house to see if a certain person was going in a certain room when he wasn't around. He'd place things in certain ways to see if they got touched. A mind is a terrible thing to waste.

I remember two especially alarming incidents when I became the target of his mind games. Once--it was our first or second Christmas there--he hid a gun from himself and swore I stole it. He chased me all over the house and out into the back yard while threatening and terrorizing me. I think the only reason he didn't start landing real blows was because he wasn't quite positive whether he had just hid it or what. Merry Christmas to you too, you bastard. Thanks for ruining everyone's holiday. His old buddy, Eddie Bush, was there, and he talked him down and off me. As far as I'm concerned, it's the singular good thing he ever did for David and/or me, and I was grateful.

The other time was the week before I permanently left him in 1974. He and I were driving to Orlando to buy some land (it turned out it was swamp land, but what part of Florida isn't?), and then on to Miami. His friend Reggie was going too. Before we left, David accused me of stealing his hundred dollars. Needless to say, it set a real bad vibe for the long trip ahead. And it's hell being trapped in a moving vehicle with an angry, paranoid Tazmanian devil! He made me paranoid too--big time!

Reggie slept in the back, and I fretted in the front. DR was giving me the cold-shoulder. That's a very heavy vibe--I sweated bullets the whole way. Finally I could stand it no more. I had to risk asking him (ever so calmly and carefully, but before I wet myself), if he'd found the money. He played it off nonchalantly. "Oh, yeah. I found that yesterday." I was thinking, "You m----r f-----!! You knew I was petrified. You could have told me." But, no-o-o. He had to mess with my head. And to make matters worse, he did confess to Debbie Rhone that he'd forgotten that he'd hidden the money under the rug, and that he knew he was wrong in how he treated me, but had done nothing about it. Nice.

We went from Miami to Freeport, and when we arrived, we rented a car and were driving around the island. And around and around. I was thinking he was lost, but I didn't dare say anything. Finally I carefully risked opening my mouth to make a peep--to which he denied that he was lost. I ventured, "But that's the same pack of wild dogs, I think." And then, a little braver, something to the effect of: "But how many dilapidated old school buses up on blocks do you think there could be on this island?" He stubbornly kept it up. That was his story and he was sticking to it. I looked heavenward. That was a mistake.

He slammed on the brakes which smashed my head into the dash. I looked at him like the crazy that he was, and he said, "Well, don't say [something, something,

Delivered From Temptation

something] then!" Like a little kid caught wrong with no defense--just say anything. He got out, came around and dragged me out of the car, and smacked me upside the head. I was shocked and horrified. Other than in Washington two years before, it was the only time he had ever hit me "Outside Parkside."

I remember the little red glass balls on a chain that had been my new earrings--he smashed the left one with that first blow. Not to mention my eardrum. He thrashed me around a bit more there on the road, and eventually we went back to the inn. I'm not sure if it was the same day or when, but at some point, we were parking the car. He told me to get out in front of the hotel while he found a space. He handed me a little brown gift-shop bag and said nothing, but nodded with his head. Silly me, I took that to mean, "Here." But, no, it turns out that was not what he meant at all. When he caught up with me, I was just opening the bag. Off he went! From the parking lot all the way up into the room he fumed--and then inside, he really got crazy. His story was that I had spoiled his surprise! Inside the paper bag were two little cheesy souvenir head scarves. One pink and one white, each depicting the local attractions. He didn't want me to see them until five minutes later. W-a-a-a-h! Of course, my conclusion ultimately was that they weren't for me at all--they were just too cheap.

Reggie did later confide in me that he and DR knew a couple of women down there, supposedly only friends; and in fact, he suspected that the whole trip was some kind of ruse to get me to co-sign a personal check from the joint account of David and I for this woman David knew. All the while, I was thinking it was for the real-estate. The alleged property never did come through--not in my time, but then, I left him for good a week later.

Here's the story of the straw that broke this camel's back: When we got inside the hotel room, he launched an attack. He ranted, he raved. He got over it. He called my mother to tell her we were getting married. Dorothy Kelly was not moved. She was like, "So, what else is new"? After the phone call, I broke the distressing news to him that I didn't want to marry him. He started again: "What? Whaddyou mean, you don't want to marry me?! I thought that's all you ever wanted!" I told him, "Not any more. I know you too well. Just look at how you treat me. And if I married you--uh uh.

Delivered From Temptation

You'd really go crazy, then. You'd probably kill me, for sure." He was nearly apoplectic. "Well, you're not the only one that's insecure in this relationship!", he yelled. I yelled back, "Well, if you think a piece of paper is going to keep me from leaving you, you've got another think coming!" His fists were flying again, and once again my hair covered my face to the point of obscuring his vision--he punched me in the nape of the neck. Consciousness started to drift away for the second time in four years. I began to hear scream after scream after scream. They were my own. My survival instinct was keeping my conscious self alive. "Security" heard the screams too, and the phone rang. As soon as he hung up, he frantically called Reggie and yelled to him something about going to jail. I couldn't even understand what he was saying--he was panicked. I ran and cowered behind the bathroom door in the little corner. He followed me, and leaned in with fist poised to punch me dead in the face. It was like looking down the barrel of a gun. I was begging him not to. Suddenly, he collapsed into tears, saying, "I don't know why I'm doing this." And I knew that he truly didn't. Suddenly, my heart broke for him. I guess Jimmie would say this, too, was just an act.

You see, David not embrace, share, understand or even relate to my belief (at the time) in the theory of *karma* and reincarnation. In fact, he was fiercely opposed. This self-imposed limitation of vision or perception prevented him from enjoying certain levels of peace of mind in certain circumstances. This was one of those cases. Knowing full well that I treated him nothing but the best in this lifetime, I'm afraid I must have been the one wielding the rod in some other. Thus, the true meaning of "an eye for an eye and a tooth for a tooth."

He had a gig in Saginaw or Flint once. I was going, Reggie was going, and my friend Marilyn from across the street was going. David hadn't slept properly beforehand (wonder why?) and needed to sleep on the way. He neatly folded a clean white tissue and placed it just so between his eyes and his black aviator frames to block the sun, and rested his head against the window in an attempt to do so. Reggie drove, and we ladies were in the back--I was behind DR. I happened to catch a glimpse of his face in the side mirror and it struck me funny. I've been known to have a wry sense of humor on occasion and said in a low voice, "Talk about a blank expression." (Well, picture it!)

Delivered From Temptation

Marilyn and I tried to stifle a giggle. Reggie didn't giggle, but he'd always appreciated my sense of humor, so I know he smiled. Fine. Then, hours later, after the gig was over and we had dropped everyone off and gone home, Mr. Hyde popped out! As soon as we walked into the foyer, he started throwing punches and continued all the way up into the shower-stall. He said that he had seen (in the rear-view mirror) Marilyn and I elbowing each other and mocking him "all the way to the gig"! (This is your brain on drugs).

You know, I never really quite figured out what caused the jealousy to get so bad just at that particular time. One theory is that it was all about belongings. It was his first house. He lined the walls with gold records and awards. He bought us matching mink coats. We had cars and motorcycles. We had diamonds and pearls. The baby and I were both well--dressed. He liked to buy me nice things from distant places--gifts, clothing, jewelry, and he did have superb taste. So, it seemed that in his warped little mind, I'd become a possession as well. He owned me. He owned David Junior. He owned the Dobermans (I never could figure out why he fancied the name Hondo Duke unless it was because John Wayne epitomized *machismo* to him), and he owned the *Bouvier*. He owned the horses. He owned the clothes and he owned the food. He owned the money--oil wasn't even ordered for his furnace in winter without his say-so--even if he was *incommunicado* for days. He owned me.

His one nemesis was the feline named " The Queen of Sheba", aka "Sheba". She would not allow David to own her. She'd even sleep in his chair and make him sit on the sofa. How I admired Sheba. DR never really liked cats, but he did make his little sacrifices for me. One of them was cats. He even named one kitten--Gerard. He was no bigger than a pack of cigarettes--a black and white fluff-ball. Unfortunately, I had an allergic reaction to something about this particular guy, and had to place him in an adoptive home.

While I'm on a roll, not to mention have a headache, I'll just relate one more incident: He had a new album out in February of '73. It was a good one--unceremoniously and forgettably entitled by Motown "David Ruffin", but artfully produced by Bobby Miller from Chicago. He had previously produced The Dells. The LP was the one with "Common Man", "A Little More Trust",

"Day in the Life of a Working Man", "Blood Donors Needed", and "Just a Mortal Man" on it--cutting edge for David. In the end, David being David, he caused poor Bobby to run back to Chicago pulling his hair and screaming all the way. That night, though, we had a handful of people over, and everyone was so geeked about the album. We were all having fun and laughing a lot. Meantime, I had a house to run: Lots of laundry to do, and David Junior and his (half) sister Nedra to get to bed, as she was living with us then. So, I was running up and down three flights of stairs from the music room to the basement--and up and down, and up and down. (Thank God some clever woman invented dryer sheets since then).

We had four bathrooms in the house, plus the commode in the basement, but the guests on that floor used the one just across the hall from the music room. I was on a run to the cellar to catch the rinse cycle, and evidently Reggie had stepped across the hall to the bathroom at that same time. All of a sudden, paranoia struck DR. It was like something snapped. Knowing him though, he might've been fostering this *vignette* in his warped little mind all night--and still been laughing and playing. schizo, I tell you--and frightening.

So, in justifying to me after he beat my ass later, he explained that he "knew" that Reg and I were in that bath having sex, because he'd gone to the laundry-room to see if I was there when I'd claimed that I was, and I was not there. O-o-o, that is scary. Of course, if I'd wanted to do it in a bathroom, it wouldn't have been that one. However, I'd always been true to David while we were together. I may have had a date or two in-between, when we were broken up, though that would've been rare--only for the obvious reason that I loved him and didn't want to. Plus, when it came to me, most men were scared of David--also for obvious reasons. I constantly tried to get through to him that I didn't want anyone else. Why would I want to do it with anyone else when I finally had what I wanted with him? I'd been trying to "get him" all these years--why would I do that? Besides, as any woman knows, if I'd really wanted to (and as I pointed out to him) I could've done it right under his nose without him even knowing, so "get off my case." (I think now that I do know why he always thought that I wanted someone else "after all this time." That was his very point. Now that I knew him so well, I probably wouldn't want him anymore. So he'd just see how much it would finally take to make me quit him, in order to see if he was actually safe and secure in the relationship. It's basically what a dysfunctional child--say in a foster home--does to find out if he'll be loved there no matter how badly he acts. Hindsight is invariably 20/20, but, hey, like I told David, "I'm not a professional. I love you and want to help you, but I cannot do any more. I don't know what else to do. All I can do is bleed, and that's not helping you. Nor me.")

As he tended my wounds and/or soaked me in a warm tub of Epsom Salts up to my nose, Dr. Jekyll would cry and swear to get help, but those promises became scoffs the moment Mr. Hyde lured me back. DR would say he could handle it, that he didn't need help--the classics. Maybe he even thought it was true--maybe he really didn't know. He did try to quit for a while every time, but he didn't change his so-called friends--so it was an exercise in futility, of course.

Society produced his problems, but it had not yet begun to offer the solutions that it does nowadays. Oh, baby, if, if, if...

Chapter Fifteen

"Don't Bring That Half-Breed!"

Soon after Joy left Los Angeles for London, I got word that my father had cancer back in Maryland. I labored over whether or not I should quit my newly-begun term at LACC--which had been just paid for with a one-time grant--and go back and wait for him to die. I was really torn. Finally someone advised me not to wait for the funeral--that I would never forgive myself. That made sense, so David Junior and I flew all the way back to the opposite coast--basically an alien environment. In fact, I had to keep DERj at my girlfriend's house--didn't want to piss off the Godfather just before he died. See, he had already issued the proclamation that "the half-breed" was not to be allowed at the funeral. Mom (an ally at the moment) and I didn't know exactly what that meant--was he going to sit up in the coffin if my son attended? Would he have henchmen positioned randomly throughout the funeral home to run us out? Or would he simply place in his will a Provision of Exclusion? I didn't dare test his word--I was not willing to take that chance. I couldn't let him have the satisfaction--not at that late date. I'd rather take his money and use it on "the half-breed." That would be my revenge. In February of 1982, he finally left his body. A particular hell was over for me.

David Junior and I moved back to Detroit a few weeks after the funeral. I rented an two-bedroom upper flat in a ritzy part of town for the two of us.

Elsewhere, David Senior was having problems of his own there in Detroit. He had been having trouble with those pesky police--they kept busting him in crack-houses for some reason. And that darned IRS wanted their money too--the nerve! He was sentenced to six months at a "country club" for evasion of taxes, but I was sure he welcomed the break in the struggle for daily room and board on the outside. He had lost our house to back taxes, and really didn't have a steady gig or a home. He just bounced from pillar to post. He'd really started living like a bum. He was definitely on the skids.

In October of '82, I was off to India as a guest of my "spiritual advisor" to converge with kindred spirits in a much-needed and welcomed retreat. My--actually David's-- cousin Bennie was having marital difficulties just then, and looked at my invitation to house/babysit as a Godsend.

I knew I'd only be gone three weeks, and David Senior was due out of prison by then, as he only had to serve four of his six months--what a surprise. I also knew he didn't have a place to live when he was released, so I told DERj and Bennie "Don't invite him, for God's sake, but if he needs a place, he can stay here." Sure enough, upon my return, he was sitting up there fat and happy--grinning like a Cheshire Cat. Of course, he had interrogated Bennie in regard to our sexual contact, of which there was none. Also of course, he felt the need to move on as soon as I came home--he wasn't about to do drugs and whore around in my face. Nor in my house! Thank you.

I had *naively* told him when we were living on Parkside that he had to choose between cocaine and me, and that I would be his cocaine. It just crushed me that he ultimately chose the drug over me, but an ex-addict whom I know then offered me the alternative explanation that maybe "choice" no longer existed for David. Retrospectively, I believe that this time when he felt compelled to leave my house was an example of just such a situation. Sadly, he laid yet another brick in the wall that drove us further and further apart--and brought him nearer and nearer to destruction.

It now turned out that my next-door neighbor was the cop brother of Kenny, the drug-dealer whose big diamond ring had broken my nose eight years prior that last fateful night on Parkside. Although David and the pusher had been thick as thieves for years, suddenly he conveniently also became very friendly with the whole family next door to the baby and me. This found him parking that big old blue Mercury Marquis in my driveway on a regular basis--whether I liked it or not. Secretly, I did--I thought it was cute that he felt that he had the right and that he was at home in my drive. I think it was also a way of marking his territory--after all, he could have parked in their driveway. In reality, it was just another way to keep my head messed up. Then, in the weeks and months ahead, he began bringing the Ms. Debbie Rhone along when he'd park in my drive--just to make me jealous, I'm sure. She was utterly oblivious, of course, but he forced me to get really ugly and start raising hell in order just to get him to stop it. Finally he did quit, but not before reducing me to screaming repeatedly out the window like some maniacal shrew. Damn!

Even at the "Fisher Theatre" in the '82 Temptation Reunion Tour, David was slumming. He'd met this Debbie person while she was bartending at a local after-hours joint, and that was just DR's style--a young white girl in a blind pig! At some point, he brought her down to the "Fisher" to flaunt her (and start sucking out her brain) even though his *femme-du-jour* was already there--wearing her tacky bedroom slippers.

I was sitting in a lounge with a roomful of people, when the door burst open and there stood DR with tall, blonde Debbie in tow--a cartoon-ish sight. They looked stunned at having seen my face first thing inside the door. He muttered as he slammed the door closed and dragged her off on a search for an empty room. Or, at least one that I wasn't in. A silence had held the room captive as if at gunpoint for the few seconds they had stood in the door-way--Debbie with her long hair and short little, cheap-looking, lavender polyester A-line mini-dress flipping around--but as soon as they left, a murmur took its place as everyone exhaled. I felt real stupid, and it seemed as if people felt sorry for me. I was embarrassed, true, but it was my hope that he had made more of an ass of himself than a fool of me. Let's face it, I no longer had a right to be offended, nor an obligation to be embarrassed for that matter. And although that was typically DR, he was starting to look a tad old for that kind of silly behavior--she looked to be fifteen or twenty years his junior. Not to mention that he was going both bald and gray, and losing weight, which he could ill-afford to do. *Tsk, tsk.*

In Los Angeles around 1980, Otis looked me up to ask my humble opinion as to whether or not I thought The Temptations should ask David back--that is, whether I thought it could work. I had to scoff. "Are you kidding!? That'd be like him and I trying to go back together! Wishful thinking!"

In spite of that, they did, in fact, attempt this ill-fated reunion that June of '82. I think it had an open end, but David (and others,

I guess) made it obvious that this dream would be shattered fairly quickly. It began in Detroit--"the home of rock 'n' roll, Ba-bay!" It was definitely a happening. Eddie had no voice, but for the most part, nobody cared. You got the feeling that he was happily, yet unobtrusively, carrying his pal Eddie.

Everyone--friends, family, fans, as well as The Tempts themselves--was elated just at the reunion alone. Hopes were high. On the other hand, a lot of time had passed, and personalities had become even less flexible during the separation of these grown men than they'd been when they were younger and more inclined to compromise.

I'm sure it looked great from out front, and we were all having a ball backstage, but I don't think the fellas were having much fun. Most of it was probably David's fault--he'd always wanted things his way, and now, he just didn't give a damn about kissing any ass or making any compromises. He knew it was too late for that. He did whatever he wanted. Showing up late or high, or both--with all his sleaze-bag parasitic pals in tow--he was being a general pain in the ass, I'm sure. After all, his main career objective had become to get enough money to score. He wasn't concerned about the group's future--with him or without him. I'm sure he probably knew they wouldn't put up with his old mess for long anyway (the old "alienate them before they reject me first" trick), and he probably planned to strike while the iron was hot--to get all he could, and crawl back into his hole. So damned sad. What a waste.

It seemed as if it were a struggle for the tour to stay together even for nine months. It must have been a certain kind of hell for Eddie, Otis, Melvin, Richard, Ollie and Ron. I'll bet they were glad when it was finally over. I know the feeling, fellas.

When the Reunion left Detroit to go on tour, David took David Junior along. Even though he'd done it off and on his whole life, David hadn't taken his son on tour with him in a while. All of a sudden, he got back into it. David was kinda grown, and he continued with his father as valet or assistant--or some such--even after that tour ended. David took his son along with him as he toured again later with Dennis and Eddie. And then to NY for the group's 1989 induction into the Rock 'n' Roll Hall of Fame--which, coincidentally, was on David Senior's birthday. In the true pattern of a kid from a dysfunctional family, David Junior loved being out there on the road with his father, even though David abused and humiliated him there as well as at home. For David Junior, it was better than nothing, I guess. Plus, it gave him more chances to try in vain to win his father's approval.

DERj, always having been very sensitive and loving, had a difficult time grasping the concept that his father, as a drug addict, could not love him. Before his father died, he told me more than once that he was going to make his father love him, if he had to die trying. Thank the Lord I didn't have to bear the unfathomable pain of losing him as well.

While the Reunion Tour was still in Detroit, June 21 rolled around. That, of course, was the anniversary of our meeting at Carr's Beach in 1964, not to mention Father's Day. I could no longer just arbitrarily buy him presents whenever I felt like it--we were not together, after all. So, I was glad for the chance to give David something--I guess it kept me feeling connected. In fact, it probably meant more to me than it did to him, although he did put on a good show for me.

For weeks, I'd wracked my brain to come up with something simple yet fraught with meaning. I'd long since learned to rely on my creativity and always get him something nobody else, even with all their money, could--for cheap yet. And, although this was not a holiday for which I had to compete with anyone, it still seemed like a plan--for I was, as usual, broke. Finally, I had the perfect idea.

Back in 1965 when we all were living together, Jimmie had a 78 rpm recording of DR singing "Statue of a Fool." It had immediately become my special favorite, and before I finally left him in '74, I asked him to re-release it, which he did when I'd gone.

It was an unspoken personal message, but what a bittersweet and empty victory it was for me. The lyrics say that a golden teardrop should be placed on the face of a statue of a fool who let love slip away--and that we should name the statue after David. As with all his releases, he didn't actually write it, but he could have.

I prowled the jewelry stores for that teardrop, prepared to have it made if necessary, but then I actually found it! I was elated. One night after a Reunion show in Detroit, while we sat on the cold stove top alone in the kitchen of one of his favorite sleazy, greasy ghetto bars, I presented it to

Delivered From Temptation

him, along with a very sweet and personal card I had made. One of his so-called best friends and main cocaine buddies owned that dump, but she was closed by that wee, small hour to the general public. Although there was a handful of loud old rummies hanging out with her and talking crap in the front 'til probably dawn, they ignored us, so we had lots of "quality" time to ourselves back there alone in the kitchen. Those times had become few and far between--it was very special, even in those unromantic surroundings. He took off the Capricorn pendant he always wore--it was a gold disc with diamonds around the circumference that some nameless "person" had given him years before--and very deliberately placed the teardrop on the same chain over the pendant. I never saw him without it again. In fact, the most touching thing on his whole four-page obituary program was the bottom inside photo of him wearing that chain with "our" teardrop on it. Of course, I didn't know the photo would be there and David didn't plan it that way (I don't think), but I'm smiling at fate for the personal nod and wink. After he died, I asked Debbie if she knew where the teardrop was, but she said she was afraid "all that stuff" had gone to my old enemy, cocaine--that demonic girl.

Genna Sapia-Ruffin

About a year after I came back from studying with my "spiritual advisor" in 1982, I got tired of fighting the woman in the downstairs flat for control of my own body temperature and decided to move. I decided that the next place I lived, I'd have my own darn thermostat, by Job. I had turned forty in September, 1983, and in October I bought a house for my son and me. I was so proud. Even though it took me until I was forty years old to do so, I still made it. And on my own. Well of course it was the grace of God--the very same thing which brought me through this battle called my life. But the point was, I had done it with no help from a man. In fact, I had done it in spite of a man. I was feeling pretty darned good.

With the change of address, David and Debbie had stopped hanging around, and I saw less and less of him. Debbie had horses, and that had captured his attention, as he had always liked being around horses. I would like to be able to say he liked horses, but I had seen him abuse them, so I really think they were just another exercise in control for him. Just like the Dobermans that he'd beat until he had them walking around all the time with their ears laid back, fear in their eyes, and their tails between their legs.

Delivered From Temptation

In July of '84, David Junior reached the age of so-called maturity, and couldn't wait to hightail it to Los Angeles for the summer. I don't want to say I was glad to get rid of him, but I was grateful for the chance for some space and peace of mind. It had been an extremely troubled and tension-filled year between us, what with both of us now battling for control, and I needed a reprieve. Luckily, he had relatives out there--Jimmie's former significant other" Clara (previously known as Shirley), and her two kids, Philicia and Jimmie Junior as well. I say "luckily" because it's a good thing they were, as I most likely would have helped him pack even if nobody were there. I probably say that facetiously, of course, but at the time, I was at my wit's end.

When he'd gone, I found myself alone in a four-bedroom house. I wasn't ready to sell it, but I was ready for a change of scenery. After what I thought was careful screening, I leased out my lovely home to a woman with several kids. I later found that all my screening did was prove what a sucker I was, and what a con artist and liar she was-- and she had her kids lying, as well. It turned out that they were, undeniably, THE Tenants from Hell. Of course, I didn't yet know that when I packed up and merrily moved to a one-bedroom apartment in the woods outside Atlanta.

Employment opportunities looked more promising there, and for sure, the attitude of the people there had to be an improvement over the one pervasive in Detroit. It was amazingly the first time I'd ever had the absolutely exquisite luxury of living alone in my entire life. I didn't even realize that until it had happened, and, boy, what a pleasant dawning! I was right about the people there--it was a pleasure to able to smile at folks on the street again without being considered an easy mark. It was nice to be able to be nice for once.

Although there wasn't a spiritual vibration *per se*, Atlanta is still one of my favorite places. My pet place--before I became more educated and delivered of the occult and New Age wrong and dangerous thinking--used to be Sedona and the area surrounding it.

I enjoyed it tremendously, so I'm sorry to say that life in my little Georgian paradise was a short one of only six months. I was informed that I'd better get back to see about my house, as the tenants' true color had come oozing to the surface and obviously was quite different than what they first presented to me. Just getting my own house back turned out to be beyond hellish.

She definitely had the advantage over me, as she was somehow connected at the courthouse, and knew how to work the system--to the max. Was it possible this wasn't her first meander down this lane? D-u-u-h. Ah, yes, life is an on-going learning process, is it not?

Learning process notwithstanding, I had to go to court thirteen, count 'em, thirteen harrowing times before I regained possession of what once had been my house. During the course of this time, both David Junior and I were berated, lied about and lied to. The tenant even sunk so low as to try to drag in the times that David Senior had been arrested and the time he'd tried to shoot at his son in a fit of paranoia out at Debbie's farm--all of which she'd seen on television, but was utterly unrelated to the circumstances at hand. So here she was attempting to put me in the position of not only having to defend myself, but DR as well. Both were despicable and ludicrous tactics which I did not dignify with a response. Still I was thinking, "What the hell does any of this have to do with me!? Just give me back my house!"

We were not only screwed by the tenant, but by the system as well--and we weren't even kissed first. I don't know what a witch hunt must have felt like, but these court proceedings unfortunately gave me a pretty good idea. Even though I was not only innocent of any wrong-doing, but the rightful owner of the house, it had become obvious that I was the minority there, and that bigotry had reared its ugly head at me from within the organization--not a pleasant experience, to be sure.

Of course, DR and I had run dead into other racial stuff, but that was almost always before he became a "star"--most just kept their big mouths shut after that, regardless of their feelings. This, however, was a whole different kind of thing--he was not by my side. I stood alone and suffered the pain and degradation and humiliation inflicted upon me by the tag team of this woman and the judge. There wasn't one damned thing left for me to do about it.

As a result, for the next six months-- three of which were Michigan-winter cold-- David Junior and I bounced around with no real place to live because of the damned system. All three of David's daughters (Nedra 'n' nem) had a flat together in

Delivered From Temptation

Detroit by now. DERj hung out there and with various friends. When two of the girls, Lynette and Kim, moved out around the same time, Nedra was thrilled to be able to have her pop stay there with her too. She'd always been mad about her daddy, and took after him in some of his ways.

He was doing a lot of drugs at that time, and he was real crazy. I should have known we were in trouble when "Oh, Sheila" by "Ready For The World" came out, and David thought it was Michael Jackson. I used to phone over there quite a bit--theoretically to check on the kids--and I called the police twice myself when I heard Senior in the background screaming threats at my son to kill him. Then I began spending quite a bit of my time there too, as David Senior had invited me to wait for my house there, if I wanted to. I guess it wasn't really his decision to make, but like I said before, we always did that--if one of us had a place, somehow so did the other. Of course Nedra didn't mind--I think she was happy to have me there--and I did want to watch out for them, if I could. DR crashed on a mattress in one of the bedrooms with the nineteen year old girlfriend he had picked up in San Francisco and then destroyed. I slept in the room where Nedra's little boy slept, or on a sofa or in a chair.

Another reason I was there was to make sure DR didn't actually kill David Junior. Like the time he had DERj drive almost to Chicago to find this girl he imported from San Francisco. DR had her driving her raggedy car all that way, and it broke down near Chicago in the middle of the night-- in the winter. She called DR, and instead of getting up off his mattress where he lay curled up in the comforting embrace of his real mistress--cocaine--he sent David Junior, who was a scant twenty years old, to do his dirty work. David Junior took his cousin with him, and when the boys got there, they couldn't find her--it seems she was not where she said she'd be, but with some trucker or something. They were hours late getting back, and Nedra and I were worried sick. When his only son finally returned though, David showed his concern by beating him with a broomstick and knocking him all the way down the cellar steps--bellowing all the while. David Junior literally crawled up the stairs, pleading to his father for mercy, but he wouldn't leave him alone. Finally, he tired of terrorizing him, but not before putting David Junior into hysterics for the rest of the night. He sobbed and wept and begged on his knees to his father--"What'd I do, Daddy? What'd I do? I love you, I only want you to love me." It was heartbreaking--still is. I tried to talk to DR when he calmed down, but it wasn't easy as I was scared shitless myself.

One night Nedra, having made dinner, tried to get her father to eat. She fixed a plate and took it to his door. She knocked, and whether or not she cracked the door I couldn't see. But she ran from the hall into the living room with him only inches behind screaming madly, in hot pursuit. She had tears in her eyes, and he was only wearing briefs--it was embarrassing. He knew there were people in the living room, but like I said before, he had reached a point where he seemed to not care about civility at all. Once again, no one dared say anything to the Emperor about his new outfit. He was raging about kicking Nedra's ass. For what, it never was really clear, but I think he was saying it was because she brought him food--or maybe because she opened the door. He probably didn't want anyone to think he might be doing drugs in there by himself--with no TV in there even. Hell-o! She was crying and protesting she'd only been trying to help.

I've never actually seen him hit one of his girls, but I don't think he was any better of a father to them than he was to David Junior. It's just that the baby and I spent more time with him and, therefore, were more often in his physical proximity--a questionable distinction, it turns out.

I finally regained possession of my house in January of '86, after six months in kangaroo court. DERj and I moved back in, and with us came Nedra and her little boy, Clifford. She'd had to let the flat go, and I had plenty of room. DR became scarce again--for the most part, I think he was back at Debbie's. As long as she could keep him isolated out in the country, he could actually have drug-free periods. But they were merely illusions built on air. And yet, perhaps it was better than nothing.

While I was at home, David Senior never came to my house, although Nedra and David Junior did keep in touch with him by phone quite regularly, as long as she was there. But before long, she moved away with her son's father, leaving most of her furniture and furnishings in my garage.

To put it mildly, the entire day had been war-like between my man-child and me on the day I forced him to go to his GED

Delivered From Temptation

graduation exercises, and when I screeched the car into the driveway, his friends were already parked there, waiting. Out of the blue he said to me, "Ma, I'm going to Boston." I exclaimed, "What!? When?" He said, "Now." Turns out one of his Detroit friends attended Boston College, and was going back after break. They had conspired a scheme that DERj should go along and try to get in on a football scholarship. The only little catch was, no one had felt any inclination to discuss this with me or to even inform me prior to that moment. Needless to say, I was rather taken aback, not to mention hurt. (To heck with it--I was beyond ticked! I was enraged). He and I were both participating in the struggle for his manhood, in our individual ways; so, once I dealt with the initial blow to my ego, I stopped objecting. I figured--what the hey, maybe it'd be good for him. I love my son dearly--always have. Still, there have been times! And I knew he needed something other than what he was getting in the house with me if there was any hope at all of him growing up with any emotional stability. Thus, off he went. He pretty much moved there--he took everything he could carry.

Suddenly, I was all alone in that too-big house--one I had purchased in a particular neighborhood specifically so he could continue at the same high school. It was not an area in which I would've lived if I'd had my druthers. But then he went and changed high schools--several times.

Now, I've had a bad back for many years, during the course of which I've had treatment from various chiropractors. And I'd never believed in anything metaphysical until my Northern Arizona experience began in 1987. So, as the chiropractor I was seeing for my sciatica pain tried to pinpoint the cause, this was the conversation:

He: "When did the pain in your *gluteus maximus* start?"

Me: "Well, let's see; must've been about 1974."

He: "And what happened that year?"

Me: (wryly) "Oh, what, like something metaphysical manifesting as something physical?"

He: "Well, yeah."

Me: "Well, that is the year I left David."

He: "Well, maybe it's just your *karma* to have a pain in the ass!" Ba-rum-bump!

He said he doesn't remember that now, but I thought it was notably clever. This particular time, though, I was about to find out just how bad my back really was.

While I was in Atlanta, David Junior had lent our power-mower to a friend of his. Conveniently, he had neglected to pick it up and bring it home before he jetted off to Boston, so it was left to me to do, as was most of the manual labor around there. My child was in a stage where all he would do was lounge, talk on the phone until four in the morning and eat--and, o-o-h, the boy could eat! (His father cursed when he once "joked" that I was going to have to pay him child support during DERj's visits with him). Yard work or house maintenance was not his thing--sorry. Let's face it--he was a brat! Or, as he put it a few years ago, "a terror." Thank you. And thank God for the mercies that the passing of time brings to us all!

So it turned out that I had to go get the mower, take it to the shop for repairs, and bring it home. When I got it home, the only way to get it out of the trunk of the car was to lift it myself. Bad mistake! I never disrespected my back like that again, by the way.

Genna Sapia-Ruffin

My bedroom was upstairs, but the bathroom was on the first floor. This had suddenly become a problem. I could not make that trip up and down. Yet, my waterbed, which would have been my best medicine, was upstairs. I somehow got a mattress into the smallest bedroom downstairs, the one with access to the back yard, and I camped in there. I had a five inch black and white television and a phone. The kitchen and bath were close by. I was all set. The only place I went, and even that gingerly, was to the nearest chiropractor-- three times a week. For three long weeks I was utterly and completely incapacitated. It was the worst my back had ever been, and I was really scared that I'd never recover. During that time, I began to wonder just how much space one person needed, anyway. I could actually see for myself that all I really needed was this 9'x 9' room. I got quite comfortable in there. I was also going through a lot of anger and resentment toward my son, as well as his father. I felt that the boy should have been helping me. He should've taken the mower to the shop and brought it home--in fact, if you really wanted to know, he had no business even lending it without my permission! He should have been the one clearing those cement blocks from behind the garage, and so on, and so on. I'd just had it with having no one to count on for anything my whole life. So when the money left to me by my "father" manifested five years after his death, I decided to sell the house and get the hell out of there. (I'm sorry son; I'm over it! [But my back's not, ha ha ha]).

I called Nedra, now at her mother's, and David Junior in Boston, and told them both that they had better come and get their stuff from the garage, because I had sold the house and would leave it if they did not. I called Angel, my girlfriend in Arizona who had already moved there from Michigan a year before. I told her I was selling the house. When she asked me where I was going, I said I guessed Atlanta. She asked why didn't I come to where she was, and I literally said, "What the heck--why not?" Up until then, I had found no place on the planet where I felt at home anyway, so one place was as good as another. At least I had a friend there. And she had friends there too.

I had a very successful moving sale--sold everything. I was ruthless. With that money, along with what Ralph had left me, I bought a motorhome, a 24' Winnebago "Brave"--

cash. It took some doing to condense my life from that size house into a 8'x 24' home on wheels, but I did it. It was quite a challenge to figure out what to keep and what to sell, but, hey, I've always liked challenges--she said, facetiously.

The two older gentlemen at the dealership who sold me the RV asked if I weren't afraid to go. My response was "Hmmph--aren't you afraid to stay?" And then, to them I quipped, "Why do you think they call it 'Brave'?" When neither Nedra nor David Junior returned to retrieve their belongings, I called DR and told him to come get his kids' stuff out of my garage and put it in the barn at Debbie's ranch in South Lyon, as I didn't want to leave it behind for the buyers of my house. He drove Debbie's truck in and we loaded up one big load, meant to be one in two or three. When we were transferring stuff, an old Christmas nativity scene showed up. It was the one he'd brought from Hazelwood--he and that darned Tammi evidently had it before we used it for three or four of our years. He did a double take and tears came to his eyes. He said he'd "wondered where that had gone." He put his arm around my waist, I put mine around his, and we just stood there staring at the past in those boxes in front of us.

Warm tears slid down my face as I said, "Did any of it ever happen? It seems so long ago it hardly seems real." He blinked back a tear as he turned and looked into my eyes and said, "Oh, it was real, alright." The moment quickly vanished, but not before becoming burned into my memory banks forever. The nagging thing is that even years later I realized that I just wasn't quite sure that we had both been thinking and/or crying about the same thing. Mine were tears of grief for the relationship and life we once shared--I wondered if his were shed in memory of his life in general, and more specifically Tammi Terrell. She was long dead, but obviously not forgotten--by either of us. It was ironic.

We spent the next two or three days together while he came back and forth helping me move into the RV. He'd had one before, so we spent a lot of time in there--with him giving me all kind of driving tips. I never knew what ever happened to his RV--probably repossession as with the limo or something scandalous. He seemed happy and excited about my RV and me all the while. It was almost as if he was glad to see me go out on my own. He presented me with a little space heater from his own RV--I still have and use it--it was a great housewarming gift. He also gave me advice and warnings and help as if he were sending a beloved baby bird from the nest to try out its very own wings. Maybe that's what's meant by "loving enough to let go." Or maybe, Jimmie, he was just glad to get rid of me, huh!? Anyway...

He clumsily hinted that he'd like us to go to bed together, but I knew he didn't have an inkling of a commitment, and that it was probably just melancholia talking--wishful thinking. I'd always fallen for that before and hated myself in the morning. Besides, he'd been gone much too long and much too far away for me to put myself in that position at that late date--emotionally or otherwise. I just couldn't afford the heartbreak. Not only that, I had my doubts about what was even left in it for me physically. I didn't know what state his sexuality was in as a result of using cocaine for so long. I did ask Debbie about that years later, though, and she seemed not have noticed anything amiss--but then, she could've never known how great, and special, our sexual life had been. Then too, obviously I was concerned about AIDS. So, I prayed for strength and fought away the fantasy. I went with the reality--I just said no. Well, I didn't have to actually say the word, I simply didn't respond to the mating call. I wasn't harboring any particular

Delivered From Temptation

desire to hurt him, merely to not encourage him. For a mega-second, he seemed like he was almost hurt, but then, naturally, he just blew it off with one of his (half-hearted) mutterings. And then it was over.

Oh, except for one other truly sad little thing. In all our life together, he had never, ever asked me for money. Not even a hint--loan or otherwise. But this day, it was as if his addiction had stripped him of even that small shred of pride as he asked to "borrow" a hundred dollars from me. And the worst part was it didn't even seem to bother him as he told the big, fat, pathological lie that his motorcycle needed brakes. Debbie, however, clued me in later. Never mind; I had the money, he needed it, I gave it. I gave a hundred and fifty, in fact. I'd believed him. Once again. I watched as he rumbled away in the truck. He was probably laughing as he rounded the corner. When I realized later what had happened, I had to shake my head. He--and therefore I--had hit a new low. At that moment, I felt real funky that I'd let him sucker me into, for all intents and purposes, buying him dope at that last second. It put a smudge on that special place in our relationship, but it was too late for that. The damage had already been done. He didn't even make it back for the rest of his kid's things. I guess that was expecting too much. I imagine he got distracted by a crack-house. Poor baby.

Chapter Sixteen

"Northern Arizona Times"

My RV undeniably needed a muffler, but I had to let the new owners have my old house in Detroit--including the drive-way where I'd been parking the Winnebago. DR invited me to hang out at the farm where he lived with Debbie as long as necessary. It was on the way to Arizona, anyway, I reasoned. I was kind of dragging my feet all of a sudden, oddly enough. Once I reached South Lyon, Michigan, my RV shuddered and shook over washboard dirt roads all the way to their long, jarring, bumpy lane, which was even worse. The RV lumbered in--me at the wheel--and I intended to make myself at home for a few days. No one was there when I arrived, but when they did pull in, DR just yelled to Deb that I was there in my RV, she and I waved, and that was the first time we'd ever really "met." I guess by now, we'd come to a silent understanding.

What I remember most about those few forgettable days was the *jillions* of horseflies, and their voracious appetites-- they ate me alive inside my RV. For those countless reasons alone, I was quickly inspired anew to continue on my way. (Hey! Whatever it takes!) So, as soon as I got the muffler done, I was outta there.

It was September 24, '87--four days before my birthday. Although I did speak to him a scant few more times by phone over the next four years, it was the last time I saw the Love of my Life alive.

A gorgeous New Mexican sunrise was presented the morning of my birthday, and I arrived in Arizona the next day. It was not an uneventful trip, but I'm sure you don't want to hear about my mechanical troubles. It's old hat for me anyway--I've always had "car *karma*." This time it had elevated to "RV *karma*!" I'm sure it was just part of such a long adventure. You do the best you can. And pray!

Delivered From Temptation

Against the odds, I got there. And I stayed there off and on for four years. I drove the RV back and forth four or five more times (alone), and had problems each and every time. Now I'm sure why they called it "Brave"!

Still it was worth it, because at last I'd found the spot on the planet where I felt at home. It didn't come easily, however. It took the four trips for me to put down my defenses long enough to let people love me and to realize that they were not trying to judge me. That was totally new for me, and it was hard to trust it, as I didn't think I was lovable and didn't yet love myself. What I failed to realize was that they'd each already been doing their work on themselves. After almost four years, my long initiation was through and it was my chance to be then able to help the newest pilgrims.

Being there really was major culture shock--the place is a cross between the TV shows "Twin Peaks" and "Northern Exposure". A spiritual, healing place where an exodus of the Children of Dysfunction continually converges in a magical setting of peace and harmony. A place where we were no longer outside of society, but society itself. Family--the first for most of us.

I lived in total anonymity in my little surrealistic town. That in itself relieved a lot of pressure and allowed the healing processes to begin for me. And, because of the remoteness, I virtually never heard David's music. As time went on, I got better, and I guess David Senior got worse. (All through life I've referred to the lesson in the story of when my twin half-brother and sister were entered into the first grade together. He was a little slow, so she nobly hung back to help him--they both flunked. As soon as they were separated, she took off like a shot. It only proves that I did what I had to do, after all, in leaving David. As I had told him, he was drowning, and he wanted to drown me right along with him--how romantic). Now, though, I was free to soar, but he was walking among the living dead. I couldn't bear to think of it.

Just while I was in Arizona, oddly enough, the dreams slowed down to almost nothing. It was really a welcome, if temporary, reprieve.

Meantime, David Junior was looking in vain for himself in Connecticut. He had migrated there from Boston that following spring and stayed there. I was enjoying my relative peace of mind in Arizona, but I was

Delivered From Temptation

nagged by this constant worry about my son. His communications with me had faded to few and far between. I could seldom contact him, as he was always on the move. He was catching hell in his brave pursuit of heart (and self) and found himself ill-equipped with the everyday basic coping skills needed for life in society--how to keep a job, how to keep an apartment, etc. Plus, he was still extremely child-like. I've--only half-kiddingly, but with love and concern--referred to him as emotionally arrested. I mean that clinically, not as a put-down to him or anyone else. I personally no longer even subscribe to the concepts of good/bad, right/wrong, as in fault/blame. It's more about generation curses and getting healed from them through the Word of God. But David Junior still sometimes has a need to hold onto them, and so I accept that blame--it's no skin off my spiritual nose. In the course of doing the best I could with what I had, it's possible that I somehow prevented him from acquiring those skills. I did not do it intentionally and have often apologized to him, as I do again here and now--in front of God and everybody. Love you, son.

I'm still not sure if he buys any of this, but because I loved him, I gave him very little help as possible in Connecticut--

only when all of his other avenues had been utterly exhausted. I watched from a distance, and I let him get hurt a lot, but I wasn't going to let him die. It killed me, true, but I had to help him find his legs. I often saw him straddling that very thin line between dark and light in an attempt to survive. Fortunately, although he may not see it, those of us who have watched him grow know that he is a protected child. In fact, I used to say that since God was said to watch out for fools and children, we'd both be safe. So, that was all in the line of Heavenly Duty.

In the case of no news not being good news, I didn't hear much from my son, and when I did, it was in the face of some disaster or another--word of which failed miserably to comfort me.

I spent the next year materially destitute but spiritually prosperous. I was in Arizona waiting for nothing in particular--something that takes quite a bit of getting used to. At least, for somebody with a life like mine. ("Chaos" is the middle name of dysfunctional people. They learn it at home as kids, and when that old familiar feeling is missing, they tend to subconsciously create it. That way they can have that comfort zone they're used to--just like back home with Mommy and Daddy Dearest. It's all they know, and they have neither the courage nor the self-esteem to chart any new territory, even if they do somehow feel the inclination. That's how it gets perpetuated through the generations. I was hooked on romancing that stone, so I really had to exert a lot of effort to kick it--I got a little better each time I tried to quit. That's the beauty. If you want to, you can get over all that stuff. You can simply change your middle name. You just have to read and then do. Once you recognize and identify it, you can categorize it. And then--and here's what they didn't tell you--you're allowed to annihilate and nullify it. Just ball it up and discard it as the useless trash it is. Invent your own visualization--dynamite, fire, white light, whatever works! Keep on trying--it's okay to get well. Now you've begun to love yourself-- let it grow. Hallelujah!

There was little or no employment in my little town anyway, and it's where I was when the recession began to insidiously grow like a cancerous cell--you could not see it, but you knew something was wrong. We thought it was only Arizona--the cost of the tuition for the critical lessons we were learning. Only upon my return to Michigan when David Senior left this particular plane of existence, did I find out the ugly truth that it was too late--the disease had spread throughout the body of the entire USA. I never had a day in Arizona when I didn't have to struggle financially--I just kept cutting back. And, we helped each other. It's amazing what one can do without if one is curious enough to find it out and courageous enough to conduct that experiment. As it turned out, things were just as bad financially back in the Michigan reality. But far, far worse spiritually--off the scale, in fact. What a crummy deal.

I hadn't heard from my prodigal son in four months. All the while, something kept gnawing harder and harder at my insides. I knew that he and Debbie had remained friends, so I called her, as I did occasionally, to see if he had been in touch with her. He still hadn't called her, but this time she had a telephone number on DR to give me. We figured maybe DERj had been in touch with his father. It was a Philadelphia number-- supposedly his "girlfriend's" house. Debbie told me to be prepared, however, because the girl was crazy. She had even gone off on Deb, who was the sweetest person in the world. With confidence, I told her not to worry, that mothers had certain rights.

HA! Little did I know what was about to take place--in fact, it all happened so fast and furious that I'm still trying to figure it out!

And so I called. Everybody but David answered the telephone. Near as I can remember, what seemed like a teenaged gangster-type boy answered first. There must've been at least three extensions in the house, and evidently no phone rules or common courtesy. Seems like as soon as I asked the boy for DR, some other rude teenager, a girl, picked up an extension. I repeated myself, and maybe by then, the first guy had signaled to DR's fan-turned-girlfriend Diane (those close to him all knew it was just another one of his many crash-pads--he had virtually been homeless since he lost the Parkside house several years before). Now, this was the first time I had ever called there, and I don't think I'd even had the chance to identify myself at this point, but the boy cursed me out, told me not to call there anymore, and slammed down the phone! When I called back, the girl did the same thing! It was almost as if they were attack dogs trained to pounce at the sound of my voice, and that they had waited years for this opportunity to protect DR from me. They acted like they were all high, but maybe they all were just normally that ignorant. Whatever their problem, I was stunned. By now, several people were on the phones and I was totally barraged by insults. I mean, Diane was screaming "@#*+" and "+@*!#" and I don't know what all! That girl had never even spoken to me before, let alone had the honor of meeting me, but I know she knew who I was. It wasn't like I had ever bothered her or invaded her home previously with phone calls--or in any way, for that matter. I just could not comprehend the reason behind the rudeness and the unwarranted attacks--other than just plain ignorance. Finally I got a word in edgeways but in order to accomplish that, I had to yell even louder than she did: "I don't want anything you got--just let me talk to David so I can get my son's phone number!" Somehow, DR eventually got on the phone. He seemed quite coherent, if not even glad to hear from me. As always, he spoke to me as if our last communication was yesterday--although it was more like three or four years before. Even though our conversation was brief, he had an obvious little lift in his voice at first. It was barely perceptible, but I did recognize it--what a pleasant surprise. Even though I could only speculate as to what depths he had allowed himself to sink, I didn't get the idea that he was very happy.

Delivered From Temptation

As I was not trying to get into his business (not to mention there was a very strong probability that he was not the only one on the line), I simply greeted him and asked if he had a phone number for our son. (I had planned ahead of time to say "our son" in case he was too muddled to know who I was--to me a very real possibility).

He asked me to hold on while he got his phone book. I could hear rustling noises, and he first said (to Diane, I assume), "Give me my phone book." And then, with disbelief, "This is not my phone book." He didn't yell it; he spoke that line as if he were almost afraid--or very ill. Then there was more shuffling and rustling, and the phone just went dead. I never spoke to him again. Ever.

Obviously, Diane refused to allow him to speak with at least me, and I don't know who else. It seemed to me as if she were keeping him isolated, and perhaps under some kind of control. It was too late for him to be whipped and that wasn't his style, still it may have been just the right time for him to be manipulated. Just what she had over him, we'll never know. I just know that there was more to that whole scene than what came out in the investigation of David's death.

I was still living in Northern Arizona in my Winnebago on the first of June, 1991. I'd been waiting two weeks for an RV space with a phone hook-up. A mere two hours after I got my new telephone in, Debbie Rhone called and left a solitary message on my machine. When I got home from work that evening, of course I returned her call immediately. She had left no indication that something was wrong, just that I should call, but I had a feeling, nonetheless. Over the years, we had on occasion spoken about what to do when David someday succeeded in killing himself--it wasn't an "if", it was a "when." I think everyone felt the same. Yet, who can ever truly be prepared? I wasn't. To our credit, I guess, neither one of us ever thought of taking out life insurance on him--I guess we were both still thinking with our hearts, not our heads.

Mind you, I still hadn't been able to contact David Junior, nor had I heard from him in months. So when I returned Debbie's call, and she asked me if I'd heard about David, I could only ask, "Was it Junior or Senior?" I was trying to be calm, but I was right on the verge of hysteria. Then, she

Delivered From Temptation

told me the pathetic news. What she told me was the first in a series of versions of how it happened.

Once I sat down by the phone, I didn't move from that spot. I never even got out of my work clothes. There were so many calls I had to make--and they were all long and difficult. I stayed up until six in the morning. I later realized that I hadn't wanted to go to sleep so that I would not have to face the dawn. But then, by six, I was drained and exhausted. Everyone I talked with already knew, everyone had seen it on television, heard it on the radio, and read it in the newspapers. Everyone but me and David Junior. And every one had a different--and inaccurate--version.

It was shortly after six that morning, a full twelve hours later, when Sandra (Nedra 'n' nem's mother) called me. As far as I can recall, it was the first and only time in life she'd ever done that, and I wasn't real sure what to make of it. She had called to make sure I'd "heard about" David's demise. It was in that same conversation that Sandra shared with me how she intended to have David's fancy tux shoes removed from his feet at the funeral. "For the Smithsonian", she offered. I was dumbfounded--I guess I never did get the thinking behind that whole shoe-switching thing. I never did see it happen, but I was told that it did take place. In fact, I couldn't help but notice--first he wore the silver and black slippers, next time I looked, plain black! It was just too weird to me.

After a few strange minutes, Nedra picked up an extension at her mother's house, and she and I talked a while. Some of the time, I couldn't understand what she was saying--her words were slurred and sentences faded to black near the ends. It had been a long and difficult night--she probably had not slept, since she kept nodding out on the telephone. She must have been very highly upset.

I had numerous conversations with an extremely nice gentleman named Gene Supple'. He was the medical examiner on the case, and kindly shared with me a wealth of information--both officially and otherwise. He was one of the people I first spoke with most immediately and most often after David's death. He even offered to be a liaison in case my son called there, as I still had not heard from him, nor had I been successful in any of my attempts to track him down. I had even sent the police

Delivered From Temptation

to both his last known addresses, as well as his last known job. All had changed, without any forwarding information. Ultimately, he found out by someone walking up to him on the street and telling him--and not very kindly, I'm afraid. It was a tough way for him to find out his father was dead. Odd how David Junior was born July 1, and his father died June--twenty five years later.

Mr. Supple' informed me that an autopsy had been performed (on the legendary David Ruffin? My David? It boggled my mind). The results wouldn't be final for a couple of days, but tentatively it was being recorded that cause of death was "drug overdose." The official account of what had actually happened was that the limo driver did, in fact, go inside the hospital with David, not dropping him off and speeding away as earlier reported, and said something like "This guy's in bad shape." That was 2:55 A.M on June 1, 1991--University of Pennsylvania Hospital. The staff attempted life resuscitation processes for the "required amount of time", and then pronounced him dead an hour later--3:55 in the morning.

Somehow the image of the autopsy and what must've happened during that last hour, really got ahold of me--I was starting to collapse. I mean, I have seen him in the hospital before. I've seen him comatose-like in an embryonic position before. I've seen him lose consciousness from bad drugs before. I thought I'd seen it all. Still, I couldn't help but be upset by the pictures in my mind during that final hour. They probably had tubes up what was left of his nose, tubes in his little skinny arms, an oxygen mask on his face, and were probably blasting powerful currents of electricity to his lifeless heart with the paddles, repeatedly contorting his body into a quaking arc. His clothes had been cut or ripped off him, he was probably wearing no more than a sheet, if that, and his glasses were gone--which he couldn't stand to be without.

Suddenly I remembered a time in the fall of '64, when I played a little trick on him about his glasses. I've worn them myself probably over thirty years, so I can appreciate one's dependency on them! While David and I looked for our first apartment, I was staying at Paul's girlfriend's house. David and I slept in the back bedroom whenever he was there. The ironing board was set up alongside the wall on "his side of the bed". He put his specs on the board before getting into bed. Now my

Delivered From Temptation

prescription was obviously way weaker than David's. He had fallen asleep while I was in the bathroom, and on my way back, I replaced his glasses with my own. When he woke up in the morning, naturally he put on what he thought were his glasses. Even the frames were just like his--in fact, sometimes I used to try to dress like him. You should have seen the look on his face! He laughed and said he thought he'd gone blind. Doesn't sound like such a big deal now-- guess you had to be there. It was funny at the time, but my smile faded as I came back to the reality of the moment.

Three days after David died, on June 4th, 1991, I called Mr. Supple' again from Arizona to find out the results of the autopsy tests. In our first conversation, in regard to the issue of whether or not David had been murdered or had simply overdosed, it was my contention that only if they found a needle hole in his body or heroine in his blood, was he murdered. First of all, he was deathly terrified of needles (not to mention spiders), and secondly, he would never have used heroine to my knowledge. So, I told Gene to go back and look for those two things. He looked closely; he found neither--so no one "speed-balled" him like they did John Belushi. With that I was personally satisfied that he had simply asked for, and was given, cocaine more pure than his body could handle at that particular time. And/or, maybe too much of it. To those who say that he was an experienced drug user and wouldn't have made that mistake--yes, but anybody's system does wear down inevitably. He had no way of knowing that his body, on that particular day, wasn't going to be able to take the usual abuse he so regularly subjected it to with such reckless abandon. Or as he would have put it, his body just said "f---k it!" After all, he'd been pushing his luck for at least thirteen hard years that I know of. Some people say longer--or even much longer. Funny, though, how you reap what you sow. If David was murdered, that too has been swept right there under The Rug alongside his ghosts of Tammi Terrell. And I just can't believe the sardonic irony of his dying in Philly, since that's where she died as well.

I had a girlfriend in Arizona named Toni who is an incredibly accurate and insightful astrologer, among other things. Since there was so much confusion as to whether or not DR was murdered, she did me the favor of casting what is known as a Death Chart, as opposed to a Birth Chart, on him. Her research included the positions of the planets at the moment of his death; it was indicated that David would've had to have died on that particular day at that particular time, and that, in fact, there had been no foul play. There was just no more getting away with it. The cause of death was no longer the issue.

He could have as easily been hit by a truck, but instead, all his systems simply shut down --after his heart, for all intents and purposes, just blew up from the cocaine. I called it "the point of no return."

When the autopsy reports came back, Gene Supple' also said that the official cause of death was now listed as "adverse reaction to cocaine." No kidding! Here's how it happened: David was in the crack house with his limo driver friend, Donald Brown, who drove for Butch Morrell. It was rumored that David was a silent partner with him in a small limo company; probably for no other reason than to have a limo at his beck and call at any given moment and a place to do cocaine--a rolling crack-house. Whatever the case was, the police had interrogated Donald Brown, and he told them that he and David had been there smoking crack for about three hours when David said he wasn't feeling well.

The guys told him to lie down on the sofa, which he did. Supposedly, after about ten or fifteen minutes (but, I'm sure it was only whenever their crack was all smoked up), they went to check on him again and found him unconscious. Donald Brown then took him to the hospital, which, sadly, the police department thought was real special. Gene said they usually just find such over-dosed bodies decaying anonymously somewhere in a ditch. Donald Brown first took David to the "day door" of the hospital and found it locked. He then dragged him around to the Emergency Room entrance, where he left David on the cement outside and went in to get some staff members. The rumor was absolutely false that he was conscious when they carried him in and that he whispered his name with his last breath. Appropriately dramatic, considering his legendary lifestyle, but false. He was comatose when they rushed him in, and he never regained consciousness. He had not been beaten up. The men and women in the emergency room frantically tried for an hour to revive the man upon whose voice they had built the memories of their youths--must have been very strange for them.

On June 3rd, two days later, the cops finally raided the empty crack house. They'd

Delivered From Temptation

gotten names "of the parties involved" (from Butch or Donald, I imagine), and were looking for them. Of course, they never did.

Now, this asthma that everyone talks about must have been a relatively recent development. He hadn't yet succeeded in manifesting it when I left him, although he was working on it. Nevertheless, I imagine he did have scar tissue on his lungs from his struggle with rheumatic fever as a toddler, and he'd always been predisposed to respiratory ailments. Cigarettes notwithstanding, that crack pipe was literally death on his poor lungs, but he knew that. Either he thought he was immortal and could "dance with the devil in the pale moonlight," or he just didn't give a flyin' fig. In my humble opinion, he was a tortured soul. But, he had as much fun as a tortured soul was allowed to have! And, just maybe (knowing him), even more. If anybody could beat that system, DR would be the man to handle that task.

Talking to Gene the second time, I asked him what DR had been wearing. He said it was a bathing suit. Well, as soon as he said that, I pictured him in Hawaiian printed drawstring short-type trunks--with an inside pocket. When I asked Gene if that was true, he said with amazement that it was.

How did I know? I told you before, son--logic. It's not "E.M.P.", as your father referred to Extra-Sensory Perception. I mean, I'd seen the man in a Speedo, even at twenty-five pounds heavier--he had died weighing only one hundred and twenty five pounds--I didn't think that even David was mad enough to do that again! God, I even remember when he wouldn't ever wear shorts--or sandals. He was too insecure about his little bitty legs and big bony feet! In fact, crazy me, I have the honorable distinction of being the one who convinced him in 1964 or '65 that it was cool for him to wear them and to hell with what people thought. I even bought him his first pair of sandals. He carted those things around on the road for years and years. I must point out here that, although he did have huge red and blue hairy monster-feet houseshoes, I can't take credit for that, thank you very much!

Then Gene told me that DR was wearing a lime green pullover shirt--something between a tee-shirt and an Izod. Lime green? Okay, David. Sure, why not! Then it really got weird. I asked Gene what David had on his feet. He did not remember at first, and went to look at the file to refresh his memory. "Sneakers", he said when he came back to the phone. "Slip-ins?", I asked. "White, with no socks?" Gene was buggin'. "Yeah! How'd you know that!?" "I just know him", I said. "It's what he had on when I met him! And he'd always liked them." (See, son? Logic again). It was kinda sweet, and I got kinda tickled.

At some point, Gene told me that although he'd never had the pleasure of meeting David, he "must have been a great gentleman" judging by the response of the people. I don't remember in which conversation it was, there were too many, but again, Gene, thanks for that--and everything else. And, yes, he was--in his own strange and inimitable way.

When I asked Gene what happened to the briefcase David had with him, he said that it had been returned to Diane. (Ms. Multiple Television Interviews--my words, not his). A player by the name of Omar returned it to her. Conveniently, it had been relieved of some thirty or forty thousand dollars in British travelers *cheques*. (I must interject here that one of the more interesting things revealed to me by the police investigation was that, although virtually no one except Diane knew that they were British, that info had somehow spread around her neighborhood. When the police questioned the neighbors, they knew it by then also. It was almost as if someone had been bragging. Allow me also to say that I never was one of those who believed that David was murdered, *per se*. I believe some of those physically close to him would have liked to have seen him dead, and maybe even planned--or at least fantasized about-- his "accidental" demise. I also believe it was those same two or three no-class people who committed this incredibly tacky, not to mention cold-blooded, crime of opportunity I believe they took the briefcase from the crack house, having known where it was and what was in it, and split the monetary contents. It was as if the murder plot never actually had to be implemented--but that they got what they wanted anyway. David was out of the way, and they got paid.

By the way, Toni's Death Chart also indicated that there'd been some kind of conflict with a woman who was within close proximity earlier that night. If you wondered, as I did, what would cause a man to rush out of the house at midnight clad only in shorts and a tee-shirt, could it

Delivered From Temptation

have been an argument? An intentional one? (Things that make you go h-m-m-m).

He had on him some keys and fifty-three dollars when they took him into the hospital. Supposedly nothing was leftover in the briefcase except some pictures, some papers, and a Bible. And, as far as a Bible is concerned, if it was even true, all this pseudo-religion must have been a relatively newly acquired trait as well, because I never saw one in his hands (or even in the house) all the years I knew him. The only vague vestige of a belief in God that I ever saw was manifested in a print of a sketch of an African Jesus that he had hung without a word in our dining room. In fact, he resented my faith, and actually told me he wanted me to worship him. He was even jealous of my "spiritual advisor". One bloody night he beat my ass for four hours whilst he raved and ranted such things as, "Go to India and live with that m----r f----r!" "Forgive him, Lord, he doesn't know what he's saying." It's what I prayed that night, and it's what I pray always. I must admit, though, that David did surprise me sometimes. Ultimately, he gave me his blessing on the subject: "Everybody's gotta believe in somethin'." I just wish he'd shared then with me what he knew of Jesus. But he didn't.

Then or ever. Obviously, he wasn't ready to abandon his back-slidden lifestyle yet. And I guess I was part of that lifestyle.

According to what I was told, Ms. Diane had a connection in TV from when she used to work there. Apparently, she called in marker(s) owed her, and found her way onto several interviews. She claimed to have been his fiancee for the last three years of his life, and they owned this big house in West Philadelphia. (Other sources have refuted this, claiming that it was something she had bought from the life insurance settlement of her most recent late husband who also died under mysterious circumstances--not to be confused with her first husband, who passed on under the same cloud. In fact, if it had indeed been in David's name, it would've been long since seized by the IRS and/or the last rehab center he left owing nineteen thousand dollars to, *et al.* That didn't happen. Same 'Vine has it that Diane, for mysterious reasons, had power over men in high places in the police department there. Seems like she and DR had certain traits in common).

I was also told by my inside source, that the reason for the delay in shipping David's body home to Detroit was because

Delivered From Temptation

Ms. TV was so busy with interviews, that it took her three days to find time to take his clothes to the morgue. Unnecessarily, my baby lay in there cut up and naked--but not unidentified, Otis--on that cold marble slab for those three days, without his glasses, because "no one" brought his clothes--one of contemporary times' most well-dressed men (when he felt like it), with just a sheet over his face. A dirty rotten shame.

Elsewhere at the salon in Northern Arizona where I worked, a radio consistently played soft rock music in the background. No news was cast, or if it was, evidently no word about DR had yet been received on the wire in my remote Arizona valley. So I was in the dark--virtually clueless. I wasn't watching much television in those days--I think my TV was in a closet--so maybe you can imagine what kind of shock-wave hit me when I arrived back in the Detroit Reality! It was, of all the places on the planet, the city most turned absolutely upside down by the incredible news of the tragic death of its reluctant hero.

As many entertainers happily know, Detroit loves its music and musicians anyway, but here, David was "The Mayor." More so than the other Temptations even, because he still lived here. He walked among the people. He shopped, he pumped his gasoline, he did laundry, he went to clubs--he lived life similar to most Detroiters. And, for the most part, they had him on a pedestal. It was a shaky one, at times, but nonetheless, Homeboy could do no wrong--even when he was caught right on the videotape of news cameras.

So it was that this place was in an absolute state of pandemonium when I arrived there. My head began to spin instantaneously upon touchdown. In fact, it even started in the air. I was dumbfounded to see that people knew and were talking about it on the plane. It was amazing. There were folks on that plane coming in from California just for David's funeral! Frankly, the memorial service was more like a sideshow--I'd said that this was the best show that he'd ever done.

From just knowing him like I did, I could almost always spot his favorite kind of woman a mile away--not all of them though, as he did associate with several women over the years who were ugly and/or sleazebags. As soon as I got on the plane, however, I saw a woman who stuck out like a sore thumb. I said to my new friend in the seat

Delivered From Temptation

next to me, "That's one of David's women over there." I'd never seen her before, but, sure enough, I did see her again--at the grave-site. I kind of shocked my own self!

The night before David's funeral, there was one in a series of tributes held for him. There was a girl there in a short, white, low-cut, tight-fitting, cocktail dress with a flounce around the hip, and one a few inches lower, and then another. I went up on the mezzanine to say hello to Martha Reeves, and that is when she introduced me to this flouncy girl. She said both proudly and protectively, "This is Diane, the woman who kept David alive for the last three years. Diane, this is Genna (no, she probably said "Ginni.") Well, Diane and I both knew how she and her kids had treated me on the phone. She stared daggers at me; I just stared in disbelief. Being a courteous and civilized woman, I then automatically muttered, "Thank you" as I walked quickly away, bidding Martha a farewell over my shoulder. So stupid; I couldn't believe I said that--she didn't deserve the civility.

You know, I never knew until I read it a few months later that Martha had once been institutionalized, but even so, that night, I knew that somehow she just couldn't be in touch with reality. First of all the obvious: David had not been living in Philly for three years. Then the subtle: What in the world had this girl told Martha to have deluded her into thinking that she was some kind of heroine? Not the truth, that was for sure! Wow!

I was devoured by grief and chaos at the funeral, so somehow I forgot to look for this Diane there, but I was told that there she wore a "pretty off-white suit." David's daughter Lynette had people at the house before the service, and his old pal CeCe had the wake at her house afterward. I was told that in both cases, this Diane person wore cut-off jeans and a red tee-shirt! Go figure; I'm still at a loss.

Chapter Seventeen

"My So-Called Life--The Movie"

Naturally, I left Arizona as soon as possible and returned to Detroit after DR died on June 1, 1991. I had endless conversations there with Debbie. In one of these exchanges, she said that he'd just been on this tour with Eddie Kendrick and Dennis Edwards which included London, and that he'd called her around the middle of May, just two weeks before he died, and told her that he was bringing his thirty-forty thousand dollar share of the booty home, but that first he was going to stop in Philly to "finish up some old business." We took this to mean the business of this involvement with Diane, the fan who apparently played him--to the max. From what I understood, their thing had been over with long ago, but of course, you couldn't really believe everything David said. She, of course, told the media that they were still together, but then, I don't believe a thing she said either. The truth was somewhere in-between probably. Knowing his past patterns, he simply still had the proverbial Stuff at Her House--hers and likely others as well.

What Debbie said was that he was planning to move back to the Detroit area as soon as he was through in Philly. In fact, I do believe he'd told her that he was going to "come back and marry" her. She laughed it off nervously, but I wouldn't have been surprised. She had taken care of him for some of the hardest years of his life--starting in 1982 when he was already real far gone. In fact, I always say that God spared me and brought in Debbie for the hardcore stuff. Not that she was so strong, but because she wasn't yet jaded and ruined. She didn't yet know him well enough to know what a Tazmanian Devil he could be--and I don't mean like the cute one in the cartoons nowadays. I remember the beauty of that state of innocence myself. It was when a girl was still allowed to be in love without fear.

Delivered From Temptation

I haven't had that feeling of terror since David died. In fact, what I did experience while standing with his body in the funeral home changed everything.

I had stood there by myself behind the velvet rope with what has once been David. I was utterly alone in that crowded building. I had no idea what I was supposed to feel, and for a second there, I was afraid I wasn't going to feel anything. Then the emotions started flowing and they didn't stop. At first, I was just angry. I felt like I wanted to smack him and say, "You did not have to go this far (to get our attention, *i.e.* help), dammit." I just wanted to slap him. Then things began to get clearer. I have no idea how long I was up there, but I felt that, to the funeral home, any of us who were so close to David as to get so grandly and dramatically escorted behind that rope, automatically and unwittingly became part of their sideshow.

I heard that something like thirty thousand people traipsed past the display that was his body--while the funeral home distastefully piped in "My Girl" continuously and incessantly from some Mickey Mouse, make-do sound system. I could just hear him grumbling. That country Capricorn would have put me "on the door" as he'd often done in the past--this time with a donation basket. That is, where were all these "friends" (although David's language would've been brutally honest), when he was alive and really needed them? Still they streamed by for a free look--with nothing to offer? Nu-uh!

And I'd have been right there with the collection plate, too. Then maybe the family wouldn't have had to go scrounging around and begging for money to bury him and to get a proper marker.

(If it's not too late, I like to say thanks again to every single one who helped, even though I don't even know who you all were. Special thanks go to Michael Jackson who donated seven thousand dollars toward the funeral expenses, Robert Townsend who raised several thousand for David's kids, Aretha Franklin who paid for a couple thousand dollars worth of printing, and my personal thanks to Suzan Jenkins and everyone at the Rhythm and Blues Foundation for the kind donation of twenty-five hundred dollars for a stone. That meant everything to me. It bought a magnificent ledger of South Dakotan granite, 6' long x 30" wide x 7.5" thick, which befits the grave of the legend that DR was. The epitaph

Delivered From Temptation

was co-designed by all four of his children, Cheryl Lynette, Nedra, Kim and David Junior. Both it and the portrait it bears were artfully etched by David Goldsworthy, one of the co-owners of The Simpson Granite Company. His partner, David Blake, who was so gracious and helpful to me throughout that whole ordeal, told me that it's one of the first pieces they did using the Europa style lettering. Also, not only is it the only one quite like it in all of Woodlawn Cemetery, but Elvis has one similar to it at Graceland. They chose it because it was unique-- apropos to the uniqueness of David. Thanks again, Misters Blake and Goldsworthy).

As I stood there by the casket, I asked the director through my sobs if I could touch David's hands. He exclaimed with glee, "Yay-as!", as he literally grabbed my hand and tried to pull it over onto David's. In disbelief, I struggled to retrieve my hand from him, exclaiming I would do it myself when I was ready.(Pu-leeze!) I finally got up the nerve to touch him--but with just my forefinger. After a moment, I was drawn to trace the 3/4" diagonal incision I spied in the middle of his forehead right where his infamous Big Vein used to bulge and throb with a certain life. My heart melted. I remember feeling that now I had lost him twice. Nowadays, I just feel as though he's basically out-of-town. I then ran my hand across his shoulder, and then down his thin arms onto his hands. It felt like home to feel the fabric of his expensive suit under my fingers again--it was a pleasant shock to find that it was, in fact, erotic. Another shock was that he was down to a hundred and twenty-five pounds! His long, beautiful, expressive hands, the very ones which had wreaked so much havoc for me, lay still. And cold. And bony. They were so placed. Just so. Right over left. To me, they looked like wax. His hair was thinner than last time I saw him, and they had combed it straight back--too close to his head for my taste. And like I'd always told him he would, he did look like his late old Uncle Lem, God love him. Also, his lips were puffy in some places and flat in others. It was not good. Hopefully, most people didn't notice.

So here he was--my partner-in-time, my buddy. My daddy, mama, child, brother and sister--my best friend and my worst enemy. He was the father of our only son--a struggling soul, a beloved child of God--my same God. And I loved him. We had roots. We had history. We were family. I knew that he had loved me too--as well as he could. Not the way I wanted, but the best he could.

Delivered From Temptation

All my fear flew away and a sense of pride and unity replaced it. I "got" that I would now be able to love him freely in death as fear had kept me from doing in life. And he could not stop me! So there! Nah-nah! I had no more fear that he could ever hurt me again--emotionally or physically, so now I could love him as much as I wanted, whether he liked it or not! Weird, huh? Selfish? Well, I wasn't hurting anyone. No one would even know I was loving him-- until now! I felt closer to him than I had in many a year. I felt that he knew that he could leave me in charge of David Junior and all that that encompasses, knowing I was strong and had always handled it in the past whenever he couldn't or wouldn't. I felt like the "designated hitter." I wouldn't fail my self-appointed mission.

I also realized that my need to write a book filled with revenge, anger and bitterness fueled by years of frustration, humiliation and resentment, was gone. It no longer had a point. All it could possibly do would be to hurt David Junior, and my own precious grandsons. None of which I had a desire to do. In fact, it was my job to prevent that. Still, I needed to write the book--just for my own completion, if nothing else. I finally saw why my first attempts were prevented from Beyond--I wasn't supposed to write a "trasher" book. It wasn't part of "My Assignment."

You see, I've had continuing dreams of David, ever since I left him in '74. Every night at first. Sometimes good, sometimes indifferent, sometimes absolutely horrendous. In the beginning, I used to wake up ducking and dodging and twitching. The sounds that would awaken me were my own sobs. Those dreams were exactly like the real events in every way, except I didn't have to bleed--otherwise, just as painful.

I even dreamed that DR was satan one traumatic night and he was on my back--I can't put this any other way--f---king me from behind. I could even feel the weight and the movement of his body as I began to awaken from my sleep. The horrifying and appalling part was that I liked it. I had quickly counsel with my "spiritual advisor" on that one! It took me a long time to deal with it. In spite of that, I continued to dream. Sometimes we were happily in love, sometimes he was playing his head games, sometimes I wouldn't even see him, but I'd know he was there. I was always left sort of dazed. It would take me twenty--thirty minutes just to get out from under the fog. Gradually, over twenty-five years, they diminished to maybe once a week, maybe less--unless something kicked it off during that day. If someone spoke of him, I heard a song, saw a blurb on TV, wrote a book, showed our grandson a video--any little thing. Maybe they dwindled to a few times a month; maybe only occasionally in the years just before his death. That's why I loved living in my little valley in Northern Arizona until DR died. There I was able to live anonymously and wasn't reminded of David daily--I had the most peaceful and relatively dream-free years of my live there.

The dreams, however, began again when David died, and when I got that clearing at his casket, they started back up full speed. I was coming back around strongly to the realization that I had to write a book in order to finish my therapy. I'd tried to write it for maybe the fourth time immediately after he died, but it wasn't yet the right time--or (head)space. I was still in a negative zone then--a rather sarcastic one, I'm afraid. I guess we all react differently to grief.

I'm a strong believer in what some may call "*syncronicity*". Although people had been telling me for ten or twelve years that

We were again holding each other so tightly in that oh-so-familiar oneness. We were kissing through tears as if we were trying to devour each others very souls. It felt so familiar and so right. I tried to speak, but he wouldn't release me, so I wound up saying into his open mouth, "I hate it so much--because I know it means we'll never be together again and we'll never have another baby." (Fade to black).

The next sound I heard was my hyperventilation along with little sobs wanting to turn into big ones. The noises literally woke me up--my heart was pounding. The shrinks will love that, I know. It is a doozy--fraught with symbolism. To me, there were two outstanding aspects. First of all, if I had to tell him that he was dead because he didn't know it, and we were both in the same form and communicated as if we were both the same, does that mean that there's no difference between being dead and being alive? Or, are we all dead? Or, are we all alive? Or, is it that he's still alive on some level? H-m-m-m. That's deep. Or as DERj might say, "That's past deep--that's steep!"

The second part was about "invalidating our thing." Seemed to me that my buddy was coming to me in a dream to tell me that if I didn't write the damned book, it would eventually be as if "we" never were--and I wouldn't have anyone to blame but myself because I didn't write it down. So, like I said, I crawled across the floor, got a pen and paper and began scribbling.

At the funeral, the reason I never saw the infamous shoe-switch was because I was out of the room with David Junior at the time. When the staff began to close his father's casket, he freaked out. He's a big boy of 6'4", and about 235 pounds. And when he let out that big moan, people moved quickly to aid him. It was almost as if they wanted to get to him before he hit the ground.

Throughout the whole chaotic affair, the ushers had been doing an unbelievable amount of the shifting about of mourners. I'd asked Debbie to go to the funeral with me, and she and David Junior and I had been shuffled several times as well as everyone else. It was all rather surrealistic. David Junior now sat in the front row slightly to my right. I'd gone to sit with Eddie Kendrick and Dennis Edwards for a while, but they were gone by then. I sat alone, a row behind my son to his left, lost in my own private world--one of both memories and grief. David's cop friend Mike Bowie had to call my name twice to get my attention. He motioned to me saying only, "It's David Junior", and once I snapped out of it, I rushed with him to follow my son who was being carried out of the room. Only a few seconds had passed.

Several guys--I think it was Mike and his pusher-man brother, and the two Jimmie Ruffin Juniors--were carrying a semi-conscious David to some side room of the church. I think it was the kitchen. A small crowd was picked up along the way. They put three wobbly tables together and deposited him there. When I rushed in seconds later, he was lying uncovered on those hard, shaky tables, sweating, trembling and with his eyes rolled back in his head. What was supposedly Emergency Medical Staff was standing around the tables just like all the other gawkers doing nothing but looking. Something snapped in me. I started barking orders. "He's in shock! Cover him up! Gimme that shawl! Nurse, put out that cigarette!" It was like a "B" movie.

I was hoping someone was getting some oxygen or an ambulance while all I could do was shout at him to come back--I didn't dare leave his side. "David! Come back! I don't want to lose you. You can't die on me too.

Delivered From Temptation

I'm not going to have this up in here today! Not today! Come on, son! Think about your son! He needs you! Come back for Baby Eli! Say something, Son--even if it's only 'Shut-up, Mom--you're making a fool of yourself'!" At that point a little smile crept across his lips and although his eyes were now closed, we all exhaled. "He's coming around", I told Mike. I don't know what would have happened if he had not by then, be cause no medical help ever did arrive.

After a while, the men helped him to a hall chair between the kitchen and the church. He could still see the service from there. It was then he asked for Melvin Franklin, who still called us family 'til he died a few years later. Melvin came and calmed my son--I never knew what they said, but it must've been very deep.

I do know that David Junior was panicking because the casket had been closed while he was passed out, and he felt he didn't get to say goodbye properly to his father. I knew that he had done that when he placed his Father's Day card in the casket, but I told him that if he needed it to be reopened, it would be done--no question. Yet somehow after Melvin talked to him, he was able to deal with it. Knowing Melvin, it probably had something to do with God, making Daddy proud, and maybe even something about being strong for Mommie.

I had placed nine roses and a love letter across David Senior's abdomen by his hands. I'd originally purchased a dozen, but had given one to each of the girls. David would have liked that.

Following the sadness and the madness they called a funeral, I stayed on in Detroit to take care of an insufferable amount of Stuff. DERj had decided to move back to Detroit even on the day he first arrived from Connecticut. He needed me now, certainly, but I also spent an incredible amount of time with my ear stuck to the phone. So many things needed handling. I found out it is the most selfish thing a parent can do to a child--to die without a will.

It became clear to me at once that I was spending more time on the phone trying to identify and justify myself to countless people than anything else. So, out of simple exhaustion, when they called me "Mrs. Ruffin", I eventually stopped explaining. Things became a lot simpler that way, and I began to feel like I'd come across a favorite old shirt that I'd been looking for. It felt so good, I never wanted to take it off. I found

Delivered From Temptation

myself pondering a legal name change. I asked my son's permission, and having been given it, I looked into the matter. I searched inside myself for insight on the subject, and looked for a sign from David Senior. My feelings were that he was behind it a hundred percent, and that I could have done it years ago with his blessing while he was alive. I didn't feel so much as if it would be a marriage--more like an adoption. Sort of as if I were being welcomed back into my own family after a long absence.

I charted it out with my numerology; I wanted to cover all the bases I could. It was right. I found no legal objections from anyone when for thirty days I announced my intentions in the newspaper.

And, just to put the cosmic icing on the metaphysical cake, the change became final a year to the day of David's funeral! That was my nod from him.

By the time those three very arduous weeks immediately following the funeral were through, I was too. Fortunately, as fate would have it, my Teacher was in Chicago at a retreat, and I found myself being driven there by some very kind and understanding sisters and brothers who took the weight off me. God knows, I direly needed some peace and quiet--and centering.

I had originally planned to connect with my "advisor" in San Francisco, closer to Arizona where I'd been living, but things changed so quickly. (That is why I always say that "plan" is a four-letter word and I try not to use it). Subsequently and "co-incidentally", I was able to change my previously "non-changeable" tickets due to special funeral dispensation. This would be only the second time I'd have seen this new Professor. The previous one, who I loved deeply and studied with for nineteen years, had left his body on June 1, 1990. But wait, here's the unbelievable irony: David died on June 1, 1991! Coincidence? Only God knows.

After a week of blissful peace in retreat, I went back to Arizona to tie up my loose ends. It was obvious that life as I had known it for the last four years no longer applied. I was back in Michigan in two and a half weeks. I was where I had to be. I was where I was needed. I did what I went there to do-- this book, for one thing.

Also I was--for the first two years after it's inception, which was just after David died--one half of the management team of the "David Ruffin Junior Music Project." I'm

Delivered From Temptation

not saying this just because I'm his mama, but that boy can really blow! He was singing a little before his dad died, but his voice has improved 1000% since then. Could it be a psychological release, as a friend suggested, or something more cosmic? H-m-m-m.

His voice is deeper than his father's, but there are times you'd swear it was him, if you closed your eyes. His style is completely different, of course--he's young. His material (most, he writes) is fresh and new.

People often say that things do run in cycles, and sometimes, it makes you wonder--where did the heart of "David Ruffin--Superstar" really go?

Here's a scenario: One dark and cold night in December, as my cat Rusty slept at the foot of my bed and I sat there deep in meditation in my little trailer in a field in Northern Arizona, a sound I'd never heard before broke my reverie. Looking back, I guess you could say it was a sputter or a sizzle. But it stopped as fast as it started, and I never had a chance to process what was happening until after the sound had ended. So, I sort of heard it after it had already happened. I normally used earplugs when I sat, but just this time I didn't have them in, for some reason. Instinctively

I opened my eyes. First I looked at the digital clock; it was one-something in the morning--1:43, I believe. Then I realized that my electric space heater--the same old one that David had given me so many years ago--was doing something. It had had a small, contained, spontaneous combustion--a very polite one.

Almost within reach was the little fire extinguisher which I'd had the same length of time. In fact, it came with the RV. I'd been lucky in that I'd never had to use it, but on the other hand, I had no clue whether it worked or not. I swung my legs over Rusty and jumped out of bed onto the floor. As I reached for the red cylinder, I came up another level--I woke up.

All the previous stuff had been done without my full awareness and/or participation. It must have all been in *slo-mo*, because it seemed like a really long time. It probably was only a few seconds. As I realized what was going on, I started to talk out loud, as I do frequently. (I used to think I was getting senile--talking to myself--so now I call it talking to my cat). I said something like, "Boy, I wonder if this thing works..." I picked it up, looked for a seemingly long time at the little blue flame

Delivered From Temptation

sitting calmly in the bottom of the heater. Still the flame did nothing--it didn't grow, it didn't sputter or smoke or threaten. It just sat there looking at me--sort of harmless-like. It was my move, so I sprayed it. The extinguisher worked; that was nice. I put the heater in the front end of the trailer, and went to sleep. Next day I cleaned up the powdery mess and told several people about it. It was odd, but I hadn't really found out yet just how odd.

Next night I had one of my David Ruffin dream sequences. They say the average dream lasts twenty minutes, but since neither my dreams or I are average, I'd venture to say it lasted a lot longer, as they ordinarily do.

Earlier in the dream, somewhere/sometime, David had told me he might do a certain gig that night, which was being held at some sort of theater. Mind you I never saw David, but I knew he was there, and he had told me this. I seemed this happened early in the day. I had laundry to do, so I went on about the business of doing it at the local laundromat. Evidently, I decided to just damp-dry it, and when I finished the wash, I headed for the theater where the gig was to be that night. I wore the five damp dresses in layers, and carried the rest in a bag or basket. It was still early afternoon. The theater was empty except for a few people who were setting up, and the Master of Ceremonies who was setting up, and a few of the perpetual hangers-around.

There was a nameless, faceless friend of mine there, sitting in one of the seats, just hanging out, so I went and sat one row behind her and one seat over. We greeted each other and spent some time just observing and talking about folks. Someone recognized me as David's woman, and sent me--by way of the emcee--a bag of "salty snack" mix. (Hey, it's a dream!) As the emcee started away after making a big production of bringing it to me, I called him back and returned it to him, saying that I didn't want it. Then, evidently, my friend and I were talking about how the headline act for the show was supposedly some relative of Marvin Gaye. This was his talent! He came in, probably for some sound check or rehearsal or something, and walked up the left aisle. My friend and I were elbowing each other and talking about him. He obviously was no kin to Marvin, and couldn't sing, which is precisely why he was promoting himself in the way he was. It was the best he could do.

Delivered From Temptation

At this point, some guy went up the other aisle to the front of the stage where the emcee sat at some kind of dais/table covered in white material, and whispered something in his ear. He walked right past us, but I never noticed until I heard some groupie-girl sitting in a row near the emcee. Apparently she had heard what the messenger told him, and she yelle out loudly: "Well, make sure you announce him as "DER.", he doesn't like "David Ruffin!" This, of course, caught my ear and focused my attention to a pinpoint. I froze like a deer in headlights.

Even though I don't drink the stuff, I had a medium-sized red paper cup of COKE in this case. I'd set it down on the (movie) seat next to me, while I ate my salty snack, which I had changed my mind about. When I put it all together, and figured out that David was on his way, I jumped straight up, spilling the COKE on the light blue, painted floor--under the seat. I exclaimed to my friend, "David's coming!" As quickly as I had jumped up, I sat back down, because what was I planning to do about it anyway. I still had to go and take my laundry home and get dressed. My friend turned around and started to pick up one of my still unmelted ice cubes. I yelled, "Don't put that back in there! I'm taking this

Genna Sapia-Ruffin

cup with me!" She said she wasn't--that she was going to eat it. Anyway, I was trying to figure out what to wear later on, and I saw my face as I stood and turned around to go. I had shoulder-length brunette hair, but my hair has actually been in a blonde semi-buzzcut for years in real life. (Whatever "real life" is).

In the dream though, when I started to mentally go through my wardrobe to figure out something great to wear that night, my hair was in the now! And so were my clothes. I was planning to wear a certain gray dressy pantsuit with satin trim that I actually have, and "those gray and gold earrings with the big stone in the center", and "those black quilted suede pumps with the silver trim"--both of which I also actually have. I was excited; so much so that I woke up with my heart just racing. Again, I swung my legs over my cat and onto the floor. I started pacing and mumbling: "No, I think the black patent-leather oxfords with the 3" block heel would look better in the 90's." And as I woke up a little more: "OMIGOD! You'd go in a New York heartbeat! You're still attached! But, go where? To see David? Can't do that--David's dead. But attached to 'The Life'--getting dressed up and going someplace special? Oh yeah, you're there!" I strode to my trailer door, threw it open, and said to my cat, "Yeah, we're still in Arizona, alright!" My heart was still racing.

I had to talk to somebody quick-- somebody who would understand. I immediately called my kid; he wasn't home. I called my *confidante.* Thank God he was home. We've been friends for years. In fact, I met him the same day I met David. He knows everything about me (almost--wait until he reads this book). He knows that I put "the project" away in storage in a box entitled, "My So-Called Life--The Movie" years ago, and thought that I was through with it. Now, I asked him, after relating the dream, if he ever missed just getting dressed up. We talked for half an hour, but suffice it to say that the conversation moved me to go and unpack my box, call an old editor friend for some re-start guidance--yet again--on how to start the dreaded rewrites and get it done!

Once again, one of my David Ruffin Dreams had motivated me back to the drawing board and on to do the work I was assigned to do.

And, as if that weren't enough, on November first of 1998, David Junior and Eli (who turned eight the next day when the second half was shown) watched Otis's movie together. It, as with his earlier book, was the white bread version as far as I'm concerned. And to make matters worse, it had some inaccuracies--particularly concerning David's death. Otis wasn't there when David died, so he would not know the details. In fact, in my humble opinion, he would have been the last person in a position to know anything about David at that point. I was then just that much more driven to tell my story. As the saying goes, "It ain't over 'til the fat lady sings." And I had, after all, had all those intimate conversations with the medical examiner on the case.

Chapter Eighteen

"And in The End, The Love You Take is Equal to The Love You Make"

Around the year 2000, a young biracial woman in her early thirties, put up for adoption by her mother as a baby, was searching Cyberspace for her birth father. Her birth mother had told her a tale of how it so happened one rainy night in Detroit that David Ruffin had become her father. She didn't know whether to believe it or not, but decided to search online for clues. Some twenty-five years later, in the year 2001, her efforts paid off. Kelly found David Ruffin Junior's website.

During that first year, she and her brother talked and visited--unbeknownst to me--and then Ms. Kelly (tired of waiting for her brother to introduce us) decided to email me the first week of February, 2002.

I imagine that the reason he was procrastinating was that he suspected that I would be very upset, heartbroken even. He didn't to be the bearer of this news. His girlfriend was finally the one who told me. As soon as I'd heard about Kelly, I knew that sooner or later I'd have to face this destiny--this child--and I guess I had needed that year to see that she hadn't gone away and wasn't yet another wannabe.

In spite of myself, thanks to a little three-way trick by my son, I wound up talking with her briefly on the cell phone while he and I were grocery shopping! Both she and I were caught off-guard, so it was uncomfortable for each of us. But that's how he decided to introduce us. He and I'd been arguing, so it was a huge effort to then put on a happy face and meet this child for the first time. But I did rise to the occasion. And the wheels were set in motion.

At first, I didn't want to believe it. But I had, in fact, always been facetiously amazed that more children hadn't emerged, as opposed to this one who did. Though I played it off at first, finally I admitted to myself that I was, indeed, very upset--not at her, but I was jealous. I felt I had been betrayed one more time by David. We had an agreement, dammit!! My initial response to David Junior's question to me was that it was his decision whether to believe her and accept her, not mine, and so I left it up to him. His heart and his head said she was his sister, so I replied to her email. She quickly became like a daughter to me. In a way, she is--or at least could've been. As I told her, she had to come through somehow!

I did give her quite a few hoops to jump through, and she met every challenge. Nowadays, Kelly and I email and telephone constantly. In my prerequisite investigation, I found that the time when Kelly was conceived, David actually was going with either Tammi Terrell or Tonya. It happened at the time he lived off Woodward. It was an apartment he lived in with both of them (one at a time, that is!)

Strangely enough, I didn't feel jealous anymore! It wasn't me he was cheating on! Anyway, it was Detroit in the sixties--we all did some crazy things--me included!

I think it was in 2000 when I suggested to the Mississippi Musicians Hall of Fame that they induct David. Due to their prior commitments, 2002 would have to be the year. When the organizer asked me sometime in 2001 if David Junior would be there to receive the award, I told him not to fret, that I would attend in his stead were he unable to. Then DERj moved a few months before the induction back to Los Angeles in response to that Call experienced by all Artists Driven, so I doubted he'd make it to Mississippi after all.

I asked Ms. Kelly to meet me there for several purposes: I'd have company, I could meet her and her husband and boys, and she could possibly meet her older sisters if all went well.

Kelly had loving, Christian, adoptive parents, and is now married to the wonderful Luis Diaz. They have three great sons, who are now grandsons to me. She was raised in a home with a functional family and with a spiritual center--something foreign to me or anyone I know. She says "I want people to know Jesus loves them no matter where they are or what they have done. When I see my brother David, my sisterly love for him is so overwhelming, something that has been held inside for a long time, I think it is so overwhelming because I am giving him love also that would've gone to my father". I hope she

Delivered From Temptation

doesn't mind me sharing her feelings with the public here. If so, welcome to your Dad's world, Kelly!

We're back now--each to our respective homes--from the induction ceremony, more of her father's world. Kelly spent a few tentative minutes with her sisters and their mother--the wheels have been set in motion there, I'm sure they'll be fine--and Kelly and Luis and the boys got to experience a taste of "the life". We had just a magnificent time all around.

But most importantly, Kelly and I have bonded as mother and daughter!! She looks just like my mom (Kelly) did when she was young! I keep forgetting that there's no way she could be my birth child, or even the spirit of the child I lost in 1972, since she was born in 1969. Luis is such a sweetheart and the kids are dolls. I just love them. Now I have another tall, dark and handsome son. Both my sons are loving and have great hearts; this one just has hair!! The kids call me Gramma, Gramma Genna, or GG. Kelly phones me every night (and sometimes day too), and Luis and the kids always sends me hugs and kisses. They care so much about me--in a way I've never known before!! As Luis says, I've been alone my whole life--

until now. And I know I will never be alone again! I don't have to wonder any more who will keep me out of a nursing home when I'm old and decrepit. Of course, nowadays, I do know that I will never be alone, for Jesus is with me always.

Still, Kelly worries about me living alone--especially with her brother now in California--and has had me give her name and address to the manager of my apartment complex as emergency contact! Now, that kind of thing is new to me! To paraphrase David Senior on June 21, 1964, "It's so good to have someone to care about and someone that cares about you". I miss them already--especially the kids. David's boys live far from me, so I get to hug them rarely.

Good, bad or indifferent, it's true enough that I have spent my live giving--but not getting--love. But I happen to believe that eventually you do reap what you sow, and so I give myself permission to accept it now! Good for me!!

Kelly has told me that she is meant to bring healing to the family. At first, that surprised me, but as time passed, I realized that if anyone can, it will be her. And that is because--based on God's master plan--she was born outside the "traditional".

Delivered From Temptation

Outside the box, so to speak. Thus she was raised in a different culture and a different environment than his other children. It was one without abuse and without chaos. It has allowed her to become a loving, sweet person without rage and drama. This is the type of person God has prepared, and then sent, to come into our lives and close the circle.

Speaking of which, some of the titles I entertained in search of the title of this chapter were: "Full Circle", "It's a Girl", "Genna's Big Payoff", "More David Ruffin Grandchildren", "The Jackpot", "It's Growing" and "The Happy Ending". Then, in a flash, "And in the end, the love you take is equal to the love you make" suddenly had a brand new meaning to me after all these years. Divine timing; *syncronicity* strikes yet again!!

Thank you, Kelly; thank you, David my dear, I love the gift you left me. But mostly, thank you God!! Nedra has also thanked me for bringing Kelly into her life and she told me she also thanks God. All is well.

Chapter Nineteen

"The Long Road to my Salvation"

"So", you probably wonder, "how did you make the transition? How did you get saved"? Well, that story is indeed, one of a long and winding road--which is why I'm writing it down here.

I guess I'd have to say that even as a child I had a longing--a spiritual void. As a kid, I went to Catholic church sometimes with my father's people. I never "got" all the empty rites and rituals and "costumes". Plus, the mass being in Latin was utterly useless and entirely impractical, to say the least. Not only that, the Catholic kids were biased against me because I was only half Italian and because I didn't know about their rule of "not eating meat on Fridays" (a rule which, of course, the Catholic church changed when the pressure came, much like their birth control pill rule, amongst others). But nope, "it" wasn't there for me. In later years, I discovered that people like me were known as "seekers". And I sought--here, there and everywhere.

At about fifteen, for a while I went to a Methodist church (with a friend or neighbor, I guess--certainly not my mother). But selling hard candy and hayrides didn't do it for me, either. I did have a few Sunday School classes there. That must be where I picked up the psalms and verses that were still vaguely familiar to me. Or perhaps I learned them in school; I think back then it was "acceptable" for teachers to say things like "God", in the olden days.

Years (and life) went by, with me struggling all the way--no God in my life. I met David, we had the baby, we broke up. He and The Temptations were hot and touring the country and overseas a lot. This was when he was with first Tammi and then Tonya, but we still saw each other too, off and on.

Then when David Junior was a a little older, but still a baby, I finally got "involved" with someone else, as I mentioned earlier. An ex-friend of David's, he had so conveniently become my "shoulder to cry on" over him. But he turned out to be yet another misogynist and manipulator; of course he did. This man was scary. And I was dangerously *naive.* He had a good one in me. He intimidated me and controlled me both physically and emotionally. He was into pills and would hold me down and literally shove them down my throat when he wanted to. He didn't have a key to my apartment, but felt free to break out my window and unlock the door whenever the mood hit him. I found it very difficult to extricate myself from that situation.

And, yes, he beat me too. I vaguely remember running down the street (high) in my nightgown at dawn one morning in an attempt to escape. Of course, he easily caught me. I had lost control of my life.

In my desperate need for something spiritual, when he wanted to build an "altar" in the room, I didn't--or couldn't--object. I never really understood what exactly was going on with all that, but I did ultimately begin to believe that he was actually into satanism and the altar was there to worship satan.

I believe he called satan in there at least three different times that I can think of. Once, "something" touched my fingertips as we both lay on our backs on the bed with arms stretched toward the ceiling. True, it may have been intensified by the pill high, but something did happen. And once I saw a black ball of energy dash around the living room baseboard and disappear. That time, I wasn't high.

Also, in the name of my quest, I used to read a lot of so-called self-help books. I read some weird books too--I think today they'd be classified as "New Age". One of them ("The Supernatural", of all things) had a black dust cover with a close-up of just a pair of piercing eyes staring out. This man tried to burn it on my snow-covered porch in order to--he said--close the door for satan to come through. The cover burned; all except for the eyes. They didn't burn. They just stared back at him from the snow. As I watched from inside, I was dumbfounded. And frightened. So, nope, the thing I sought wasn't there at that altar either!

I took David Junior and left with my agent for Los Angeles supposedly for some dancing gig which never manifested. The agent left--and me with no job and very little money. I had to find a cheap motel for my son and I.

I was basically walking around, not sure of where to go or what to do. I'm sure I looked just like what I was--somebody in a daze who just fell off the turnip truck from the Midwest. Someone on a street somewhere in Hollywood came up and started talking to me and led me by the hand into some nearby basement. I wasn't high, but it was so strange that it is all just a surrealistic blur. There was no furniture, just a room full of what looked like hippies (well, a lot of people looked like hippies--whatever that means--back then, even "normal" people, so who knows), but they were packed in the basement rooms shoulder-to-shoulder kneeling on the floor. With hands raised, they were all talking loudly in what sounded like some strange *gobble-de-gook* chant to me. I thought it was some kind of druggie cult and hightailed it back out of there as fast as I could. I didn't know what weirdness I had gotten into! As I scrambled out, I squinted against the sun, but it was good to see it's bright light again!

In retrospect, lo these thirty-seven years later, I realize that they were probably nothing scarier than a bunch of tongue-talking Pentecostals. (I guessed that that was what was meant by the phrase "holy rollers"). But "it" wasn't there for me either--at least not on Hollywood and Vine! (*Author's note: Recent information would indicate that they were actually not Pentecostals, but the now infamous "Children of God" cult).

Not very long after after escaping him (by moving while he was out of town. David helped me), I ran across something called s*atmat* (aka *radha soami* aka The Science of the Soul aka The Path of the Masters aka The Path of Light and Sound, *ad infinitum*). "But why did *satmat* have so many aliases?" you ask. Why indeed. As I mentioned earlier, it was "not a religion", *per se*; it was "a PATH--a lifestyle, an Eastern philosophy." Some would say it is the largest "secret cult" in the world. Well, actually, it's not secret; it's hidden in plain sight. But it is most certainly and intentionally not publicized. It was based on reincarnation and *karma*--that overused and misunderstood woo-woo word. Back then, no one even used the word, not to mention overused it! It was a strange and unfamiliar idea. And the followers of the *guru* who was at the center of this path were strange too. We were all lacto-vegetarians when it was hardly known, let alone trendy. We ate dairy products but no animals, seafood, poultry or even eggs, or anything containing "the essence thereof". The idea with dairy was that you didn't have to kill the cow to get the milk. We never ate anything that would one day-- upon having experienced the entire "eighty four hundred thousand" species of life on the "wheel of transmigration"--magically become human! (Of course, now I know that there is no such thing as cross-specie migration. But back then I believed it; I believed in everything--except Jesus! In fact, it was a time when, unfortunately, a lot of people believed in everything! Peace and love, man)!

Guru. Yes--that's another strange word. What does that really mean? I think now that it is no more than another word for "false prophet". But hey, I was lost and seeking some peace--or something.

Anything to fill the void I felt deep inside. *Satmat* taught us (*santsangis*), that that lonesome feeling "all humans have" was the "longing of the soul to merge with 'The Source'." We were to accomplish this by two and a half hours of chanting a *mantra* (in this case, the repetition of "the seven different names of the rulers of the seven heavens") in so-called meditation per day--ideally at three in the morning! Yeouch! Not to mention at all other possible times: between thoughts, simultaneous with thoughts, while falling asleep. I became so inculcated with that last one, that until recently, I sometimes found myself attacked by that when I'm falling asleep. I quickly start saying the "Lord's Prayer" to replace it. It's a matter of essentially saying "Get thee behind me, satan" and replacing satan's words with Jesus's words as He taught his disciples how to pray. And I never did like "meditation". At first, I thought it was just because I was new and didn't know how to do it correctly. But after about thirty-four years of trying unsuccessfully to do it, I had grown to detest, loathe and despise it. It had become the biggest, hardest chore on my daily "to do" list and I even resented it. It was nothing more than a major source of the very stress I was trying to rise above! Ironically, it was what was became my dread (God's built-in escape route) of the meditation that started my gradual pulling away and, finally my departure from s*atmat.* I began to skip the "satsangs" (meetings where we gathered to read the teachings of the *guru* to each other). I just wanted less and less to attend. The *satsangis* began to get on my nerves. I couldn't stand them! I started to want to have some protein (besides beans and tofu) in my diet. (I had developed bad knees and I decided to believe that my knees were saying "Ok, time enough on the veggie thing; we've been patient. Now we want some protein!" And I wanted to give it to them. I felt poultry and fish would be fine. (I do eat them once in a blue moon at this point, but I still don't do quadrapeds!) Ha, ha, ha.

I hadn't cooked meat in twenty years or so, and didn't really know how. A couple of my co-workers walked me through these first months of my gradual return to carnivorism. At first, I couldn't bear the idea of seeing any bones or insides. So, one of the girls educated me about 'boneless, skinless chicken breasts"--a foreign concept to me. Also, I had never heard of "Chicken Nuggets'! Oh my stars!! I loved those!! I binged on them for a few weeks. And I still have some now and then! Yum!

But you know, eating all that soy for about thirty-years did do me some good, I think. I sailed right through menopause without so much as a flash--didn't even know it had come and gone. I believe it was all the soy--which is, after all, rich in isoflavones. That's a plant hormone with an estrogen-like effect. So, I had done my own "hormone replacement therapy"! Unknowingly, of course! So, all things do work together for good!

In the so-called meditation, the idea was that if you chanted long enough, you would "see the light" that was the *guru* inside the third eye and you would "hear the universe"--the sound which pervades the entire creation (whatever that was)--and it would lead you to The Source via the *guru*, of course.

Oh no, you could not get to The Source (did they ever even use the word "God"?) without the *guru* leading you there. After all, he had made the trip daily and knew the way. They even taught us that the ringing in the ears that one sometimes gets (tinnitus) was actually a beginning stage of hearing this sound! Don't get me wrong though, I was no better than my mom OR my son's father in that I was no saint either. As I say, all addictions and experiments with addictions basically stem from a longing to fill that God-shaped hole in your soul. Prior to my initiation into *satmat*, I was fully immersed in the world and many of its temptations while I sought that Something.

Delivered From Temptation

It was the sixties. Like many, I looked for love in all the wrong places and chose some poor ways to express it. True, I didn't use cocaine or heroine or hallucinogens (at least not intentionally, but you never knew what would be in the weed you smoked in those days). And I did smoke marijuana off and on for a few years after my son was born--after his father abandoned us, that is. I was no kid the first time I smoked it. I was twenty-three and I was finding it hard to cope. And I had swallowed the sporadic upper and the occasional downer in recent years, but I knew better. The angel on my right shoulder finally won out over the devil on my left shoulder when the baby was about three. I did not have my mother's propensity or capacity for alcohol. I seldom drank--I was pathetic when I drank. I was never mean or cruel, but I would get loud, cry, vomit and pass out--in that order. And that would happen after only a couple drinks. Yuk! Thanks, but no thanks!

In fact, I had a very low tolerance for the "loco weed" too--a few "hits" and I was "trippin'"; (and then I was sleepin')! I had the reputation of being someone you didn't want to waste your drugs on! And, let's be honest, that's why they call it dope--because you act like a dope after you smoke it! (By the way, didn't you ever wonder why they call alcohol "spirits"? Didn't you ever hear someone say the day after doing something stupid while drunk "That wasn't me; I wasn't myself." Of course, that's because disembodied evil spirits take advantage of the weakened state of a drunk and quickly take that body in which to reside--and do demonic things! Once the drunk comes "back to himself", the demon has to move on in search of some other vehicle to use! So, dope and spirits. Yeah. I got that. I don't think the fact that the baby was biracial added to my problems more than simply being poor did. Being poor, without a college education, essentially unskilled and blinded by "love" is what did me in and sentenced me to the welfare system. In my pain and ignorance, I was a messed-up mother, looking back. My son is still punishing me for that. (Go ahead and judge me if you feel you must, but only if you are sin-free yourself: *"He who is without sin among you, let him be the first to throw a stone at her."* Deuteronomy 17:7).

Anyway, this was also the time I ran across the '*guru*'--the late sixties. Part of being a '*satsangi*' was that we didn't drink, do drugs, ingest animal products or have illicit sex. So in that way, it was good. (It

Delivered From Temptation

could even be seen by some as a stepping stone to righteousness, as God does work all things together for the good of the righteous, as I have since learned). My son's father and I were separated at the time I became a *satsangi*, so when we went back together, it never occurred to me that I was living in sin with him. The sex that we had was the same sex we had been having, and it would never have crossed my mind to make a distinction. I felt married to him--I had no reference point, so I don't know what I based that on! But I know now that this was a wrong doctrine. We had no God in our life, in our house or in our pretend marriage. I didn't know any better--I didn't know Jesus. He knew, but chose not to share that with me. We never spoke of God or Jesus. No wonder we were doomed. Nine years after we split for the last time, as I turned forty years old, I bought my own house for my son and me. That was quite an accomplishment, considering all the previous circumstances. I felt that was a turning point for me. A few years later, once my son went out on his own adventures, that's when I sold the house and moved to Sedona, Arizona. It turned out that there were a lot of *satsangis* there. We were taught, and also believed, that John the

Baptist was Jesus's master--not the one who heralded His coming, but His master. (Throughout their teachings were ran the underlying concept that there was "a perfect living master" at all times ["Buddah, Jesus, John the Baptist, Krishna, Moses, David, Mira Bai, Mohammed, *et al*"]--from the "beginning of time" through the present. In that scenario then, the *guru* equates himself to both John the Baptist and Jesus). I'm sorry, but what a crock! All I can do is pray for the four million plus *santsangis* in the world and fall on my face in gratitude to God that I have been plucked out from their multitudes and rescued! Not to mention praying for the multitudes of others who are being deceived into following other false prophets!

I lived there in Northern Arizona in that RV off and on around six years. It was so beautiful! This was a place that had once been the bottom of an ocean thousands of years ago and the red rocks blazing and glinting with rust jutted out at all kinds of angles no matter which way you looked. You could walk up and touch them. You could look at the petroglyphs--symbols carved there in the rocks by ancient civilizations. The Native American culture was so thick you could have cut it with a knife. And that was what appeared at first glance to be

Delivered From Temptation

a beautiful thing--something I was totally unfamiliar with. Of course, God as Christians know Him is not--for the most part--the center of their culture. Still, I loved the place and talked about it so much that folks often told me that I should work at the Chamber of Commerce.

Even the weather there was awesome--snow thunderstorms, rainbow balls, torrential flooding rains, billows of fog hanging around tops of the low mountains and rock formations,you name it. When the fog rolled in, as it often did, you halfway expected to see a dinosaur appear on the horizon. Sedona has all four seasons, and flora and fauna of both the desert and mountains, as it is about three-quarters of the way up a mountain between Phoenix and Flagstaff. So you had oak trees and Saguaro cacti all in the same yard. Fruit orchards co-existed with coyotes and rattlesnakes. Yes, it was and is magical. But all magic ain't good magic!

Once I left the Sedona area for good and got some distance and perspective, I saw that it was, in fact,

THE center for "New Age", *i.e.* a hotbed of occultism. I went there a hard-core skeptic (in spite of the fact that I had had my times of playing with a *Oiuja* board even some fifteen years earlier--and as I found out many years later, that was nothing but a venue for the evil 'familiar spirits'. And it did lie to my friends and me, even back then). But I quickly became a believer and was sucked into the occult lifestyle myself. One after the other, my first seven crystals found their way into my hands in a hurry. In fact, I collected a large bag of all kinds of gems--for their "healing properties". I was into "pyramid power", I was using a pendulum to get what I believed to be information from my "spirit guides", and I became a practicing numerologist into which I incorporated my gemology. So, not only could I find the "holes in your aura" for you, I could prescribe which gemstones you should wear, carry or keep by your bed to "fix" you or improve your meditation, love life, business, health or whatever. I went to "drum circles" and "medicine wheels", I was regressed into previous incarnations even to Egypt, I got readings from channelers, psychics, astrologers, learned of "soul-mates"--you name it. Everyone there was a reader and/or a healer of some kind or another. There are "vortexes" all over the area with six "primary vortexes". It's said that there are more there than anywhere

Delivered From Temptation

else on earth. One of the theories is that these are flows of energy on which beings from other planets could travel both up and down.

And indeed, at night in the pitch-black sky with no light pollution for two hundred miles, you could often see various lights moving around--it was fascinating. I myself had seen what I believed to be four spaceships almost two decades before in 1968 about forty miles West of Phoenix. I find now that according to some, these vortexes (although the plural form of vórtex" is generally "*vortices,*" in Sedona, "vortexes" is used) actually are gateways to hell. Sedona absolutely attracted weirdos of every age and ilk--of which I was one. A couple decades went by and the interesting thing is that the closer I got to the time of my upcoming salvation, the more nervous satan got about losing me and the more clever about trapping me. He was hanging onto my leg for dear life! I had been one of his best disciples and he didn't want to be deprived of that. As recently as about two years before I was born again, I was going fairly regularly to group sessions of a channeler. Along with others, I communicated with my late loved ones there. At least, that's what I believed at the time. I was told that many on the "Otherside" knew of me, I was given the names of my spirit guides, and many similar things. I was reading a lot of the books written by psychics, even "famous" ones who you still see on TV talk shows. The lies and misinformation from these people almost did me in. I see now how satan uses them to trick people to be sucked deeper and deeper into the occult. During that same time, I was on the computer a lot, and that being the place where I spent most of my time and where I was most comfortable, it was the field on which satan chose to attack me. He started in my comfort zone: Instant Messaging. I was never interested in "chat rooms"; I chatted with my two good friends only. Satan (or his demons) started talking to me right there through the Instant Messaging! He would disguise himself first as one of my friends and then, later, the other one. He was there once through the first friend and several times through the second friend. In neither case did the friend know or remember what had happened. It was just as if I were having conversations with my late "husband". It was very nice to visit with him--very tempting, very alluring, and very seductive! He answered some questions I had and we talked about the old days. He gave me some instructions of

Delivered From Temptation

things he wanted done, we talked about our son and grandkids on which he gave me advice, he told me that our daughter and both our moms were with him--so many, many things. And, he asked my forgiveness. The talks were a definite comfort, and I waited for those sessions. I saved all that on disk; I printed it all out. So then, I ,myself was channeling--fluently and in great detail. I thought I was channeling my late "husband", but I was channeling demons. It was the best trap satan could have set for me, with the best possible baits. But, praise God, Jesus caught my attention in the nick of time!

Greater is He that is in me than he who is in the world! 1 John 4:4.

In my ignorance, what I thought was so beautiful about "New Age" was that there were no boundaries, no judgments on what one believed. And that is exactly the trap. All beliefs were accepted and embraced. At the end of my studies of and participation in the occult, I realized that that was, in fact, the precise problem! Jesus had no place in all of this! To the very large concentration of *satsangis* who had been drawn to live there, as well as all the other bleeding heart liberals, Jesus was just a nice man and a great teacher of his day (and only of his day); one in that on-going, never-ending series of "masters".

Yeouch! (Forgive us, Lord, we know not what we do).

There were also some Christian churches, but having not been saved at the time, I never visited one. I wonder if the Christians there are like Christians elsewhere. Or if they, too, have become steeped in the local New Age culture in some ways. I pray not!

In the beginning so long ago, I thought of calling this book "From Victim to Victorious". Someone has beaten me to that title, I've since discovered, but the gist is the same: I was lost, but now I'm found. I was a prisoner of my own ignorance and now I'm free. Jesus is The Truth and He has set me free with a river of His blood flowing through the streets so long ago. That blood is as fresh now as it was then. I was a victim (or was I a volunteer?), then with His grace and mercy, I became a survivor. In fact, I'm more than a survivor and I'm more than a conqueror. I am a believer. I am an overcomer. And this thing called my life is the very special coat that My Father has tailor made and given me to wear! It's very colorful and different. And it fits only me!

Delivered From Temptation

(As yours fits only you). It may seem like I'm overstating the case here, but I want to emphasize the difference between before and after Jesus came into my heart.

I guess one of the first and most interesting things that happened was at the beginning of December 2003. I was still a "*satsangi*", but barely. I was working at my computer with the television turned on across the room. From the corner of my eye, I could see that a show came on featuring singing groups from the "doo-wop" generation. Like many of that genre', The Flamingoes had split up and one of the more prominent lead singers started his own group. Terry Johnson & The Flamingoes were performing.

I had known Terry back in the seventies in Detroit where we all lived, but hadn't seen him in years.

Naturally I was tickled to see him on television in 2003. I had come to know him for two reasons.

Come to find out, he was writing music for the record label that my son's father recorded for and secondly, I discovered that he was a "*satsangi*" too!! I was at a recording session with my son's father watching him record when Terry walked up behind me, bent down and whispered "Do you know what the phrase "*radha soami*" means"? That was the "*satsangi*" greeting--supposedly meaning "I salute the Lord in you". When I turned with a start to see who was speaking, I was so shocked that I almost fell out of that chair. I guess he had seen me at "*satsang*", but I didn't remember him. That was how we met. From then on, I often saw him at "*satsangs*", and the group of us frequently had lunch afterward. So we were pretty close. When he later became engaged, I met his (non-*satsangi*) fiancee, who also sang in the group he had at the time. And I then introduced them to my son's father one night at one of their shows, as a few of his most popular songs were part of their repertoire. After that Terry season, I didn't see or hear from him any more, as we went our separate ways. I guess you could say (and I might agree, in retrospect) that I was quickly led by the Holy Spirit at the time I saw him on television to do an internet search of his name immediately. I found him fast and I found him close. He was living just a few miles from my apartment in Florida. I called the number listed and he answered the phone! That in itself was a miracle, looking back.

Delivered From Temptation

Shortly into the conversation, I asked him if he still went to "satsang". He replied that no, he had found Jesus! I might think that that would have taken some nerve to say to a "*satsangi*", considering the polar differences in the teachings and what I might think, but he said it right out. And although his next words are a blur at this time, it was along the lines that I should check out Jesus myself!

To make a long story short, we talked for hours. We shared many things, including my experiences of Instant Messaging with the "familiar spirits". Within the next few days, I bought my very first Bible—the WWJD version. That was pivotal and that was because God put Terry in my way. As my walk with Jesus has progressed and I have gained perspective as I get further from those early days, I can see the amazing absolutely supernatural way in which God planned and facilitated the bringing together of Terry and I. Who else on the face of the planet could have served that purpose and filled that description? He sang in a group, so he knew that life, he was from Detroit--or at least living there—so he knew that life too. He was with the same record label and recorded at the same studio as my son's father did. He knew David--or at least his reputation, so he knew what I was going through, he was in the same age group as we were, and for the absolute *piece de resistance*, he was a "*satsangi*"! How likely is that!?

And the best part? He was a "*satsangi*" who had given his life to Jesus Christ! I am in awe of God!

Every so often throughout the years, I would attend the occasional church service, at the end of which I'd almost always go to the altar for the "altar call"--once I knew what that was, that is! This was the time at the end of a service when one could ask Jesus into their hearts and to be the Lord of their lives. I'd do this in desperation, even though I never believed that it really worked. I'd tried it a half-dozen times or so, and after all, it had never worked for me before. Every time, I'd walk away shaking my head and muttering under my breath, because I never felt any different. Nothing ever changed in my heart.

I have always been more or less a "channel hopper" when it comes to television--unless I run across something interesting--and in my hopping, I would often come across "religious programs". It was unavoidable, in fact! And I couldn't change the channel fast enough. I hated "those preachers". Bunch of thieves and liars and phonies. Garbage. No more "real" than wrestling!

Yet, somehow here a few months later--and also during the two or so years prior to me being saved-- this repulsion toward "religious programs" began to somehow shift. I found myself watching something here and there for a little longer than the usual few fleeting seconds it usually took to change a channel. This was happening at the same time that my impatience with the *satsangis* was accelerating and my attraction to eating seafood and poultry was increasing. Also during that same period of time that I used to spend hours on the phone with an old friend of mine--someone I had a hot and heavy affair with in the eighties and hadn't talked to in two decades. We had reconnected through a mutual friend via the internet and he had long since become a preacher. Go figure!

He and I spent many hours on the phone talking spirituality during this same two years, give or take.

Very interesting in retrospect how this time period was so obviously being choreographed in the finest detail by the

Genna Sapia-Ruffin

Lord! I'd say that man of God was pivotal in my salvation.

And I still thank and bless him for that, wherever he has disappeared to now! Yes, he came back into my life for a season. He taught me so much and shared so much and was then gone again. God, in His infinite wisdom, matched me up with exactly the one person on the planet to whom I could relate both in a worldly way because of our past, but then in a Godly way as well. Awesome!

In March of 2004, I was doing laundry at the communal laundromat in my apartment complex and of course, was running in and out of the apartment. Back and forth, back and forth. I had left the television on for some reason, and on TBN at that! And on one of my trips back through, a familiar voice caught my ear as I passed the television. I looked back over my shoulder and there was Tiny Lister testifying. I was like "Hey! I know him". He is, of course, an actor. As a makeup artist, I had worked on a movie set he was in. I found out later (not being that wrestling fan) that he was also known as Zeus in the World Wrestling Federation. A giant of a man with eyes of two different colors and directions, he most often played a bully, criminal or worse in these many movies.

Although now I know that he often testifies on TBN, and also just played a major role in the movie "One Night With The King" (the bible story of Esther), I had never seen him on TV before. It was first his familiar voice, then his familiar face, which caught my attention that day, but it was his inimitable style which captured me and caused me to sit down on the sofa and listen to him. I was fascinated!

Unbeknownst to me, God was doing His thing in my heart! I can't really tell you what Tiny said that day, I know it was him and his style which was meant to catch me.

The second step in the plan that day materialized on my next trip back from the laundromat: Dion Sanders (again, not into sports, but vaguely knew the name and the face), was now testifying.

Actually, there were three men sitting side by side, I found out as the camera panned left. Dion was on my right. I didn't recognize the other two men, who were apparently pastors. One of them asked Dion about his spiritual father, and he spoke about Bishop T. D. Jakes--a name unfamiliar to me at the time. He mentioned Bishop Jakes' church, The Potter's House in Dallas, Texas. My first thought was "Hey, there's a Potter's House up there on the main drag; I pass it almost everyday." (God was doing His thing)! Then the pastor on the far left got his face right up in the camera and (among other things which I didn't remember) he emphatically told me to find a good home church! Again, I was like: "Hey! Lemme get the phone number of that Potter's House up the road there"!) The computer was on across the room, as usual, and before that pastor had finished, I was looking up the phone number! I called the first number listed and it was disconnected. I called the second number listed and couldn't get through there either. I knew I was going past it the next day, so planned on just going there then to ask when the services were.

Oh, by the way, having so many and very deep talks with my old (now pastor) friend had inspired and slowly driven me to want to finally know Jesus. I had mistakenly assumed that I was a child of God-- that we all were--not knowing that until you are born again, you are NOT! You are a creation of God, but not a child of God! What a shocker!

Delivered From Temptation

Satan had lulled me with that false sense of security.

I had always believed in God (and found no contradiction in the New Age lifestyle, duh)! But for some reason (satan!), whenever people talked about Jesus, I just never felt that Jesus applied to me. I never believed in the Bible and had nothing but negative to say about it. But what was I quoting? I had never even read the Bible! I never owned one; I'd tried to crack one a few times over the years, but something was between It and me! I just couldn't stand it! Hard to read--like it was in another language! Plus, it was only written by men anyway. I was sure they had translated it to fit their own agendas, or even just accidentally translated it incorrectly. King James just used it to control his subjects! (Huh?) See, I had no idea what I was saying. That was purely satan--knowing he surely didn't want to lose me, one of his most staunch supporters!! Anyway, in one of the last conversations we had before my salvation, I remember yelling to my friend: "What is wrong with me? Why don't I believe the Bible?" It was at that moment that I knew I could believe the Bible if I wanted to. I gave in then and let him teach me. I mean, he was already--to the degree that I would allow--but then I just

Genna Sapia-Ruffin

wanted to know. I wanted to learn. I wanted to be included. I wanted to follow Jesus. "But", I thought, "I asked Jesus into my heart before and nothing happened. How can this time be different"? Something in me--knowing that the overly analytical type of mind I'd had was the roadblock--spoke out and this time said "Jesus, please BYPASS MY MIND and come into my heart!

Be the Lord of my life. I've been Lord of my own life for sixty years, Jesus, and trying to choreograph all this stuff myself. And not doing a very good job of it, I might add"!

The next day, I drove up to the Potter's House. It was locked up tight as a drum; not even a vehicle in the lot. Confident that I was supposed to go to service at the Potter's House (and that Jesus was going to meet me there and that I would truly be saved), I just sat there and waited. In a few minutes, a white pickup truck drove up and parked. Inside it were a white man and what looked to be his small son.

They got out of the vehicle and I asked him when the services were. He told me about how this temporary building (it looked like a huge, gray igloo to me), was no longer being used for services and that they were being held at 10:00 A.M. the next day at another recently acquired building at an intersection somewhere nearby. I thanked them and went home.

My car found the way that next morning to the Potter's House straightaway. I knew Jesus was sitting on my hood, making the way clear. I went in and, as expected, Jesus met me there as I knew He would and I gave my life to Him! It was as if we both understood that I'd had this appointment on this certain day and at this certain time my whole life. This was both the end and the beginning! Since then, God has done so many wonderful things in my life, that they can't all be told. I'm not as good as I want to be, that's for sure, but I'm better than I was! That's for sure too! And the glory of it all is that all that Jesus has miraculously done in my life, He can do and wants to do in yours! And more! And why would you want to give your life to Jesus? Because--to put it simply-- everything of self (self-rule) is death. Death is emptiness, misery and pain. To live a victorious life, we must die to the lie that sin satisfies. And all sin falls under the umbrella of self-rule. How would you go about giving your life to Jesus? Here's an answer from allaboutgod.com:

Salvation Prayer - The Cornerstone is Christ?

What is the so-called Salvation Prayer? What do I do to get "saved?" At one point or another we all ask ourselves this question.

"That if you confess with your mouth the Lord Jesus and believe in your heart that God has raised Him from the dead, you will be saved." (Romans 10:9)

"Jesus answered and said to him, 'Most assuredly, I say to you, unless one is born again, he cannot see the kingdom of God.'" (John 3:3)

Salvation Prayer - Back to Basics

The Salvation Prayer is merely a road to rebirth in Jesus Christ. To be born again you must confess Jesus as Lord and believe that He is. When you ask Him into your heart, you are allowing Him to be the Lord of your life.

A. Salvation is the "permission slip" to enter heaven when you leave this world.

B. Salvation takes place when a person listens to the salvation message, believes it, and makes a decision to receive Jesus into his or her heart.

Salvation Prayer - The Simple Steps:

1. Acknowledge in your heart that Jesus is Lord.
2. Confess with your mouth that Jesus is Lord.
3. Believe that Jesus died for your sins and was raised three days later.
4. Repent of your sins and get baptized in the name of Jesus.

Salvation Prayer - Merely a Tool to Communicate Our Faith

The Salvation Prayer is not a ritual based on specific words. This is not the power of a prayer, but the power of truly committing our lives to Christ as Savior and Lord. The following is merely a guideline for our sincere step of faith: "God, I recognize that I have not lived my life for You up until now. I have been living for myself and that is wrong. I need You in my life; I want You in my life. I acknowledge the completed work of Your Son Jesus Christ in giving His life for me on the cross at Calvary, and I long to receive the forgiveness you have made freely available to me through this sacrifice. Come into my life now, Lord. Take up residence in my heart and be my king, my Lord, and my Savior. From this day forward,

I will no longer be controlled by sin, or the desire to please myself, but I will follow You all the days of my life. Those days are in Your hands. I ask this in Jesus' precious and holy name. Amen." If you decided to repent of your sins and receive Christ today, welcome to God's family. Now, as a way to grow closer to Him, the Bible tells us to follow up on our commitment.

1. *Get water-baptized as commanded by Christ.*

2. *Tell someone else about your new faith in Christ.*

3. *Spend time with God each day. It does not have to be a long period of time. Just develop the daily habit of praying to Him and reading His Word. Ask God to increase your faith and your understanding of the Bible.*

4. *Seek fellowship with other followers of Jesus. Develop a group of believing friends to answer your questions and support you.*

5. *Find a local Bible-based church where you can sense the Presence of and where you can worship God.*

Again, welcome! Your life will never be the same!

(*Author's Note: Only with this printing is my story finally told and the book complete. But the work has just begun. Here I am, Lord. Choose me)...

Discography Of David Ruffin 1958-2009

PRE-TEMPTATION SOLO SINGLES

12/58---Vega----------"Believe Me"/"You & I" (Recorded by Eddie Bush, as David Ruffin, under the name "Little David Bush").

??/58---Unknown----"Statue of a Fool"/"?" (Originally a 78rpm. Undocumented, but I saw and heard it. Jimmie had it in 1964).

06/61---Anna----------"I'm in Love"/"One of These Days"(Lead ; "The Voicemasters" w/ Marvin Gaye on drums).

07/61---Checkmate---"Action Speaks Louder Than Words"/"You Can Get What I Got"

03/62---Checkmate---"Mr. Bus Driver (Hurry)"/"Knock You Out (With Love)"

TEMPTATION SINGLES

01/64---Gordy---"The Way You Do the Things You Do"/"Just Let Me Know"

04/64---Gordy---"The Girl's alright With Me"/"I'll Be in Trouble"

07/64---Gordy---"Girl, Why You Wanna Make Me Blue?"/"Baby, Baby, I Need You"

12/64---Gordy---"My Girl"/"Nobody But My Baby"

03/65---Gordy---"It's Growing"/"What Love Has Joined Together"

06/65---Gordy---"Since I Lost My Baby"/"You've Got to Earn It"

09/65---Gordy---"Don't Look Back"/"My Baby"

02/65---Gordy---"Get Ready"/"Fading Away"

05/66---Gordy---"Ain't Too Proud to Beg"/"You'll Lose a Precious Love"

07/66---Gordy---"Beauty's Only Skin Deep"/"You're Not an Ordinary Girl"

11/66---Gordy---"(I Know) I'm Losing You"/"I Couldn't Cry If I Wanted To"

04/67---Gordy---"All I Need"/"Sorry Is a Sorry Word"

06/67---Gordy---"You're My Everything"/"I've Been Good to You"

09/67---Gordy---"(Loneliness Made Me Realize) It's You That I Need"/"Don't Send Me Away"

12/67---Gordy---"I Wish It Would Rain"/"I Truly, Truly Believe"

04/68---Gordy---"I Could Never Love Another (After Loving You)"/"Gonna Give Her All the Love I've Got"

07/68---Gordy---"Please Return Your Love to Me"/"How Can I Forget?"

04/82---Gordy---"Standing On The Top" Pt 1/Pt 2 07/87--Gordy--"More On the Inside"/"Money Is Hard to Get"

POST-TEMPTATION SINGLES

02/69---Motown---"My Whole World Ended"/"Got to Find Myself a Brand New Baby"

Genna Sapia-Ruffin

07/69---Motown---"I Lost Everything I Ever Had (Now I'm Losing You)"/"We'll Have a Good Thing Going On"

12/69---Motown---"I'm So Glad I Fell For You"/"I Pray Everyday) You Won't Regret Loving Me)"

10/70---Soul--------"Stand by Me"/"Your Love Was Worth Waiting For" (w/Jimmie Ruffin)

02/71---Motown---"Don't Stop Loving Me"/"Each Day Is a Lifetime"

03/71---Soul-------"When My Love Hand Comes Down"/"Steppin' Out On a Dream" (w/J. Ruffin)

07/71---Motown---"You Can Come Right Back to Me"/"Dinah"

06/72---Motown---"A Little More Trust"/"A Day in the Life of a Working Man"

04/73---Motown---"Blood Donors Needed (Give All You Can)"/"Go On With Your Bad Self"

07/73---Motown---"Common Man"/"Just a Mortal Man"

11/74---Motown---"Me & Rock 'n' Roll Are Here to Stay"/"Smiling Faces"

Delivered From Temptation

03/75---Motown---"Superstar (Remember How You Got Where You Are"/"No Matter Where"

10/75---Motown---"Walk Away From Love"/"Love Can Be Hazardous To Your Health"

02/76---Motown---"Heavy Love"/"Love Can Be Hazardous To Your Health"

05/76---Motown---"Everything's Coming Up Love"/"No Matter Where"

10/76---Motown---"Statue of a Fool" (re-release)/"On & Off"

07/77---Motown---"Just Let Me Hold You For a Night"/"Just Rode By the Place (Where We Used to Stay)"

1979---Warner-----"Break My Heart & Set Me Free"/"Sexy Dancer"

1980---Warner-----"I Get Excited"/"Chain on The Brain"

1980---Warner-----"Slow Dance"/"?"

1980---Warner------"Still in Love With You"/"I Wanna Be With You"

1985---RCA--------"My Girl"/"The Way You Do The Things You Do"--Live at The Apollo w/E. Kendrick and Hall & Oates

Genna Sapia-Ruffin

10/87---RCA--------"I Couldn't Believe It"/"?" (w/E. Kendrick)

01/88---RCA--------"One More For The Lonely Hearts Club"/"?" (w/E. Kendrick)

1990---Motorcity----"Hurt The One You Love"/"instrumental (12")

TEMPTATION ALBUMS

03/64---Gordy---"Meet The Temptations"(DR sings only on "The Way You Do The Things You Do" recorded 01/09/64)

02/65---Gordy---"The Temptations Sing Smokey"

11/65---Gordy---"Temptin' Temptations"

06/66---Gordy---"Gettin' Ready"

11/66---Gordy---"Temptations' Greatest Hits"

03/67---Gordy---"Temptations Live"

07/67---Gordy---"With a Whole Lot O' Soul"

08/67---Gordy---"In a Mellow Mood"

04/68---Gordy---"The Temptations Wish It Would Rain"

04/82---Gordy---"Reunion"

POST TEMPTATIONS ALBUMS

05/69---Gordy----"My Whole World Ended"

11/69---Gordy-----"Feelin' Good"

10/70---Soul-------"I Am My Brother's Keeper" (w/J. Ruffin)

05/71---Motown---"David" (never released)

02/73---Motown---"David Ruffin"

12/74---Motown---"Me & Rock 'n' Roll Are Here to Stay"

10/75---Motown---"Who I Am"

10/76---Motown---"Everything's Coming Up Love"

06/77---Motown---"In My Stride"

01/78---Motown---"At His Best"

1979---Warner----"So Soon We Change"

1980---Warner----"Gentleman Ruffin"

1985---RCA-------"Live at The Apollo" (w/E. Kendrick and Hall & Oates)

1987---RCA-------"Ruffin & Kendrick"

Genna Sapia-Ruffin

POST-MORTEM RELEASES & COMPILATIONS

07/91---Motown---"At His Best"

03/93---RTM--------"Sun City--Artists United Against Apartheid"

04/95---Motown---"Motown Legends"

03/96---Motown---"One by One" (w/E. Kendrick & D. Edwards)

--------Polygram---"The Ultimate Collection"

--------RCA--------"Family" (w/E. Kendrick)

--------Motown----"Baddest Love Jams Volume 1"

--------Hot Pro----"Best of Motor City"

--------RCA--------"High Octane--Hard Drivin' Hits"

--------Motown---"Hitsville USA: The Motown Singles Collection"

--------Motown---"Hitsville USA: The Motown Singles Collection Volume 2"

--------Motown---"Motown Year by Year: "The Sound of Young America"

--------Motown---"Motown Year by Year: "The Sound Of Young America 1975"

--------Motown---"Motown Year by Year: "The Sound of Young America 1976"

--------"David Ruffin-Compilation Listing"

--------"David Ruffin/Eddie Kendrick-Compilation Listing"

09/99---Motown---"Lost & Found (You've Got to Earn It)"

2000----Motown---"The Best of David Ruffin--The Millennium Collection"

2001----Universal--"Motown Legends: Walk Away From Love"

2002----Universal/Spectrum---- "Essential Collection"

2004----Hip-O Select-----"David--The Unreleased"

Epilogue For David

"Temper"
(Author Unknown)

When I have lost my temper, I have lost my reason too.

I'm never proud of anything which angrily I do.

When I have talked in anger and my cheeks were ruby red,

I have always uttered something which I wish I hadn't said.

In anger I have never done a kindly deed or wise,

But many things for which I felt I should apologize.

In looking back across my life, and all I've lost or made,

I can't recall a single time when fury ever paid.

So I struggle to be patient, for I've reached a wiser age;

I do not want to do a thing or speak a word in rage.

I have learned by sad experience that when my temper flies,

I never do a worthy thing, a decent deed or wise.

About The Author

Genna Sapia-Ruffin is a baby boomer who was born and educated in Baltimore.

In 1964, she met David Ruffin of The Temptations in nearby Annapolis. That was the day that she came face-to-face with her destiny. In a few months and at his urging, she moved to his town of Detroit to be with him. A couple of years later, they became the parents of David's only son. Thus, although it was in Maryland that she was born and educated, it was in Detroit that she was raised and schooled. Her abusive and confusing childhood had been far from idyllic, but was a mere glimmer of what lay ahead in Michigan.

Having kept a diary for years--and no longer able to resist the drive to do so--she began the painstaking job of gathering, organizing and chronicling the scribbled notes of her chaotic life. In 2002, her book entitled "A Memoir: David Ruffin--My Temptation" was ultimately published. Now with the discovery of important information about David's childhood--and with the salvation of her soul through Christ--she is inspired to complete that story here in "Delivered From Temptation".

She now aspires to a career in speaking with the hope of inspiring and encouraging people who find themselves dealing with some situations she too has faced--and survived to tell. This is where her passion lies and her attention is focused. Even as a new Christian, she believes that this is what she was born to do. She'd like to speak in prisons, churches and schools in hopes of saving someone from the destruction that ignorance in parenting and in drug use inevitably brings.

In 1992, a year after David's death, she once more moved away from Detroit and now enjoys a warmer and more peaceful environment.